Privatizing Education and Educational Choice

Privatizing Education and Educational Choice

Concepts, Plans, and Experiences

Edited by

Simon Hakim
Paul Seidenstat
Gary W. Bowman

PRAEGER

Westport, Connecticut
London

Library of Congress Cataloging-in-Publication Data

Privatizing education and educational choice : concepts, plans, and experiences /
  edited by Simon Hakim, Paul Seidenstat, and Gary W. Bowman.
      p.   cm.
   Includes bibliographical references and index.
   ISBN 0–275–94751–3 (alk. paper)
   ISBN 0–275–95081–6 (pbk. : alk. paper)
   1. School choice—United States. 2. School Choice—United States—
Case studies. 3. School management and organization—United
States. 4. Educational change—United States. I. Hakim, Simon.
II. Seidenstat, Paul. III. Bowman, Gary W.
LB 1027.9.P75   1994
371′.01—dc20   94–16456

British Library Cataloguing in Publication Data is available.

Library of Congress Catalog Card Number: 94–16456
ISBN: 0–275–94751–3
ISBN: 0–275–95081–6 (pbk.)

First published in 1994

Praeger Publishers, 88 Post Road West, Westport, CT 06881
An imprint of Greenwood Publishing Group, Inc.

Printed in the United States of America

∞™

The paper used in this book complies with the
Permanent Paper Standard issued by the National
Information Standards Organization (Z39.48–1984).

10 9 8 7 6 5 4 3 2 1

Contents

Privatizing Education and Educational Choice

1

Introduction

Simon Hakim, Paul Seidenstat, and Gary W. Bowman

The National Commission on Excellence in Education stated in its 1983 report *A Nation at Risk:* "For the first time in the history of our country, the educational skills of our generation will not surpass, will not equal, will not even approach, those of their parents." A more recent study conducted by the Educational Testing Service (*The New York Times* 1993) revealed that half the adults in the United States are not proficient enough in English to write a letter concerning a billing error or calculate the length of a bus trip from a published schedule. Almost 10 percent of the adults have severe reading and writing difficulties. Between 40 and 44 million Americans perform at the lowest level—unable to calculate the total of a purchase, determine the price difference between two items, enter basic personal information on a form, or locate a street intersection on a road map.

The most revealing symptom of the poor quality of education is performance in the workplace. Inadequate education is considered a major factor in the decline of productivity that is reflected in a decline of the U.S. competitiveness with Eastern Asian and Western European nations. Executives of major Japanese companies have indicated that their lack of interest in building production facilities in the United States is based upon the low educational level of American workers. Further, businesses estimate that they lose between $25 and $30 billion a year in reduced productivity, errors, and accidents attributable to poor literacy. Only 25 percent of the worker population is highly literate.

It is evident that the level and quality of education in the United States is found lacking. Accumulated human capital is crucial for improving the standard of living and maintaining the quality of life in the community and the nation.

The question is the extent to which governments are able to improve the level and quality of education.

GOVERNMENT INTERVENTION

In order to determine the effectiveness of government intervention it is necessary to analyze the reasons that lead to poor education. Once the reasons are identified, the relative importance of each reason can be addressed. When the reasons and their relative importance are known, solutions can be developed to address the problem. On the surface, it seems obvious that implementation of a single solution is insufficient to solve the problem. If there is no single solution, a combination of policies may be necessary to improve students' educational attainments.

Any one solution that can offer improvement for some students even though it does not help all students is efficient. For example, educational choice may not yield improvement in educational attainment for all students. However, if it improves the level and quality of education for some without significantly worsening that of the rest, it is an efficient policy.

Should we let parents and/or students make the choice of school without collective intervention? Should government accredit schools that participate in a choice program or should we allow market forces to operate freely? Economic theory and, in particular, the field of public finance provide an answer. Government involvement in education is desired because of the externality feature of education. If others in our society are well-educated, then we all benefit from a well-informed electorate. Further, education may create more pleasant social interactions, may lead to less social unrest and crime, and may help ensure that society's values are preserved. Hence individuals or families in a context of no government involvement in education would underinvest in education since they do not capture all the benefits that result from their own education. Government subsidy of education increases education expenditure and can reduce or eliminate this underinvestment. Of course, such government expenditures should increase the learning of useful skills that would be in the interest of parents and children. However, the learning of society's values, ethics in human interaction, and good citizenship are in the interest of society at large in the provision of education.

Society may benefit the most from education that focuses upon developing general reading, mathematical, and reasoning skills since these skills may be essential for making better citizens. Indeed one might argue that emphasizing these skills is most likely to benefit the student's long-term development. However, parents and students may be more interested in developing vocational skills that are useful for the student's first job.

Generally the more parents care about and are involved in their child's education the better. However, in some respects what well-informed parents want for their children or what a student wants is not good for education. A school typically performs at least two functions. One is to help the student learn. The other is to evaluate what he or she has learned. The latter may be in the form of grades in courses, advancement to the next grade, or a diploma. However much the student has learned, it is clearly in the parents' and student's interest to pressure for inflated evaluations for just this student or just this student's class. Hence there is continuing pressure on every school "temporarily" to lower standards. Such rational behavior of individual parents and students is clearly not in the interest of general education achievement. In a context in which parents could choose the school for their child one might expect that schools that have, over time, maintained consistently high standards would tend to be selected.

Another (indirect) purchaser of education is business. Business certainly needs literate workers and has consistently supported educational improvement. Basic education may be needed to get any job, and better education means better jobs. However, businesses' interests might, in part, diverge from students' interests in the nature of education. General education can generally be expected to increase the value of the student's work in the marketplace and his or her wage. Education specific to a particular job may do more to reduce the costs of job training for the company and do less to increase the student's market value.

If the voucher system is put in place, then many new schools will be established. Some schools may be ineffective and/or have an orientation that is not consistent with society's values, which are explicitly expressed in the Constitution and its interpretations by the Supreme Court. Accreditation of private schools may be necessary but must not be simply a device to stifle competition and choice.

Education experts claim that the deterioration in educational quality is caused by several factors including the subpar performance of schools, urban blight, drugs, the prevalence of television, the abject failure of national leadership, and the erosion of the family (e.g., *Newsweek* 1991). Poor performance in literacy tests and the grim prediction about the future educational state of the nation are also partially attributed to the rising share of the adult population whose first language is not English.

What we do not understand is the relative contribution of each factor to the low educational state of the nation. It is reasonable to say, however, that an improvement in school performance or in any other single factor may not be sufficient to bring the United States to an educational state comparable with Eastern Asian and Western European nations. The budget is not a major reason for success or failure of schools. Japan spends about 50 percent less per student than the United States, and Japanese students consistently rank higher. In another measure of spending, the percentage of gross national product devoted to education, the United States is about average. Experts believe that what matters is the way the budget is allocated and not its magnitude. In the United

States more is spent on buildings and administration, and we have relatively low teacher salaries. Other countries, especially Japan and Germany, spend more on teacher salaries, and have modest buildings, and employ fewer administrators.

PUBLIC AND PRIVATE SCHOOLS: STRUCTURE AND PERFORMANCE

The public school system nationwide includes 16,000 school districts, 40 million students, and three million teachers. Eighty-nine percent of the nation's children attend public schools. The number of private schools, however, has increased by 30 percent through the 1980s, reaching 26,800, while the number of public schools has declined 3 percent to 83,800. In 1991, 5.3 million students or 11 percent of the total number of students in the nation were attending at least twenty-two different types of private schools ranging from arts-oriented Waldorf schools to conservative Christian academies.

Per capita expenditures have jumped in the public school system in constant 1991–1992 dollars from $2,035 in 1960 to $5,247 in 1990. School districts spend up to 75 percent of their budgets on teachers' pay. Private schools' cost per student is 50 to 75 percent of the per student cost of public schools. For example, Catholic schools spend one half the public school rate per student; average tuition is $1,000 for elementary schools and $2,500 at the secondary level.

The main reasons for the lower cost in the private system are the fulfillment of administrative duties by the teachers, leaner administration, and lower salaries of teachers. For example, the archdiocese of Washington, D.C., runs the schools serving its 50,000 students with seventeen people. The District of Columbia public school system supports its 81,000 students with 1,500 administrative workers. Introduction of computers in the management of schools might have reduced the reliance on manpower. However, the lack of incentives to improve efficiency in administrating schools that have monopolistic power and powerful unions may have prevented efficient substitution of computers for manpower.

In spite of being outspent, private schools appear to outperform public schools. Among fourth and eighth graders, private schools place 10 to 15 percent more of their students at appropriate grade level for their age than do public schools. The sophomore-to-senior dropout rate in the public system is 24 percent compared to 12 percent in the private system. In 1990, approximately 33 percent of all public school students took the SAT exam and had an average score of 896. In the same year, 67 percent of the private school group took the exam, and the average score was 932. Fewer than 30 percent of public high school students go to four year colleges and six years later only 13 percent of them graduate. Half of all private school seniors go to four year colleges and 31 percent of them graduate. Student performance of the nation's public school system has continually declined from 1961 to 1991. Median SAT scores have fallen almost 80 points over the 30-year period (Chubb and Moe 1990 1991).

Some choice exists already in the public school system. The types of such schools within the public system are as follows (e.g., Young and Clinchy 1992, 4–8):

1. Alternative and magnet schools. These are concepts that were conceived in the early 1960s by people who were unsatisfied with the conventional schools. One of the major reasons for their spread in the 1970s and early 1980s was to encourage desegregation. These individual schools offer special curricula for specific areas like the performing arts, math/science, foreign languages, and comprehensive academics. Some schools are oriented toward a specific student body like the gifted, at risk, or students of multicultural background. They are not restricted to a particular neighborhood but rather enroll students countywide. Magnet schools are found in every metropolitan school district. They include also free and open schools and schools without walls. In the 1980s and early 1990s another form of magnet schools started to flourish. These are magnet schools established by school districts that stress continuing education and learning centers aimed at serving students at risk.

2. "Second Chance" schools. These schools aim at students who have academic or discipline difficulties in the regular schools. The state funds enrollment in these statewide schools whether they are public or nonsectarian private. By 1992 this option existed in the states of California, Colorado, Minnesota, Oregon, and Washington.

3. Postsecondary options. The state or the school district pays high school senior and juniors to enroll in vocational schools and/or colleges and receive academic credit.

4. Intradistrict plans. Students are allowed to enroll in any of their own district schools. In the open enrollment plan, students are initially assigned to their neighborhood school but are allowed to switch if space permits. In the "controlled" choice option, parents make a list of their school preferences within the district, and the board takes them into consideration in making the school assignment. The usual criteria for the assignment is space availability and racial and ethnic balance within each school.

5. Interdistrict plans. Parents are allowed to choose a school outside their own district. The costs are borne by the district, the state, or partially by the parents. Transportation costs are usually paid by the parents. Districts are required to accept such transfers if space permits and if racial imbalance does not result.

6. Charter schools. These are self-governing units outside the control of the local school districts. The state legislature allows funding of such efforts. A charter school can be organized by teachers and parents who can choose the curriculum and design an academic program free of the regulations imposed by local school districts.

The types of existing and planned private schools are:

1. Parochial schools. There are 8,600 Catholic elementary schools. These schools have a 95 percent graduation rate compared to an 85 percent graduation rate in the public system. Eighty-three percent of graduates attend college versus 52 percent in the public system. It is the largest non-public education system in the nation. Nationwide, the number of students in the Catholic system has declined from 5.7 million in 1964 to 2.5 million in 1991. From 1970 to 1991 their minority enrollment increased from 11 to 23 percent.

One important reason for the success of this system is that the schools emphasize the basic courses: mathematics, advanced English, and foreign languages. The schools do not own much equipment and offer few elective courses or extracurricular activities.

2. Prep schools. There are 1,500 non-religious private schools educating 400,000 students. These schools are characterized by rigorous academic standards, and they usually emphasize liberal arts courses. Almost 100 percent of their graduates attend four year colleges and universities. Teachers unions are rare and teachers perform administrative duties with little bureaucracy. In 1991 the average salary of a teacher with fifteen years experience was $29,000 compared with $34,000 in the public school system. The average prep school tuition was $7,200 in 1991, and in boarding schools it was $13,700. Tuition has been rising 10 percent per year.

3. Home schooling. This type of schooling is usually practiced by conservative Christians who stress the Bible and believe in the integration of family life and education. In 1970 there were nationwide a total of 10,000 such students. Since 1982, thirty-four states have passed measures to make it easier to practice home schooling. As a result, in 1991 there was a total of 300,000 home students. Fifty percent of these students attend four year colleges. They lack, however, knowledge in science, calculus, and foreign languages. The annual average spending per student is $400 to $500.

4. Afrocentric schools. These schools stress African and African-American culture. There are 300 such academies nationwide educating 50,000 students. They promote tribal separation, emphasize racial pride, and support segregation.

5. For-profit/not-for-profit schools. Corporate America has turned to education and has begun to run schools more effectively than the public sector does. In Baltimore, Education Alternatives, Inc., has contracted to manage nine schools for five years and spends $5,400 on each student in the form of teachers' salaries and school supplies of the $5,918 per student total available from the Baltimore system. The school district spent only $4,300 for classroom purposes while the rest was spent on administration functions. Contracting out of maintenance and administrative duties is responsible for some of the savings. Other savings result from lower salaries for custodians, teachers aides, and other paraprofessionals.

Education Alternatives, Inc., has also created a partnership with Dade County's Florida school board and taken control of South Pointe corporate/community elementary school. It runs year-round and is open from 7:00 A.M. to 7:00 P.M. It includes children from the age of two since it believes that it is important to reach disadvantaged children from an early age.

Whittle Communication plans to invest in schools through its Edison Project. It plans to build and open 200 schools by the year 1996 and 2,000 schools nationwide by the year 2012. It will provide schools from kindergarten through twelfth grade. These schools will use the latest technologies, have longer school days and a longer school year, and will incorporate teaching innovations to produce high performing education systems. Students will do much of their own learning through links both at school and at home with electronic libraries, databases, and teaching programs. Each student will be equipped with a computer, a telephone, a fax, a VCR, an electronic graphics tablet, and an audio system.

The teacher will define the parameters of study and refine the learning which is based upon students' performance and initiatives. The teacher's role becomes similar to a coach where the athlete is expected to follow the regimen in using the special equipment to build physical strength and endurance. The idea is to put the teachers on top by transferring decisions regarding students' educational needs from the school boards to them. This notion of the Edison Project is derived from the currently popular method of *Total Quality Management* in which the number of the bureaucracy levels is reduced and decision-making powers are transferred to the production workers (Deming 1982 1986). Teachers will be paid higher than the prevailing public or private school wages. All others at the school will provide support services to the teachers and the students. The number of teachers per student will go down. Currently, the expected cost is less than $5,500 per year per student, which is cheap in comparison with both the public and private systems.

Some corporations have created not-for-profit schools for dropouts and other students who struggle in traditional schools. Examples include Rich's Department Store in Atlanta and Burger King academies in ten cities. In Chicago a group of more than fifty major corporations (e.g., Sears, UAL, McDonald's, and Baxter International) opened a tuition free elementary school. The YMCA operates similar schools for homeless children from preschool through eighth grade in Portland, Oregon, and Spokane and Tacoma, Washington.

The main objective of for-profit schools is to improve the academic achievement of the student. These schools do not aim at affecting other dimensions of students' lives. These institutions will serve middle and low income populations. The not-for-profit schools are aimed at improving the welfare of students by providing them with the skills to compete in the job market and enhance their earning power.

EDUCATIONAL CHOICE AND VOUCHER SYSTEMS: STRUCTURE AND EVALUATION

Educational choice programs open statewide public school options to students. Neighborhood schools are expected to lose their geographical monopolistic power and will need to compete in quality of service and curriculum offered by other public schools in the state. By 1991, thirty-seven states had considered public choice bills and eleven had passed laws allowing some form of choice within the state. In fact, there is little resistance even by unions to educational choice within the public school system. The 1980s saw the spread of public choice programs. In 1991 President Bush suggested the private choice option in which state (and possibly local) vouchers can be used by students to buy private education. Proposals have been brought to the voters in various states to provide half of the state's per capita school contribution in the form of a voucher eligible for use for private schools. For example, Proposition 174 in California, which failed in the 1993 elections, offered vouchers worth $2,600 for each of the state's 5.7 million elementary and high school students for use at any school. This amount represents only half of the state's cost per student.

School choice is a catalyst for school improvement, not an end in itself. Successful schools have a clear vision of where they are and the goal that they wish to achieve. These schools are expected to offer autonomy for teachers and encourage parents to be actively involved in the administration and the programs of the school. The basic idea behind school choice is to transfer responsibilities from school boards that are detached from teachers and parents to the latter two groups.

We should view public school choice and the voucher system from a wide scope. Some private companies and governments are in the process of re-organizing their structure—shifting more responsibilities to the lower level of workers and managers, eliminating middle management, and providing workers with incentives to both increase their efficiency and introduce innovations. Customer satisfaction and explicit consideration of their preferences are at the core of these changes. Methods like Total Quality Management, Statistical Process Control, Employee Involvement, Process Re-engineering, and Just-in-Time Production have been used in both the private and public sectors. Along these lines, teachers might be given more autonomy in the classroom and take upon themselves more administrative obligations. Parents, who should be viewed in part as customers, might be involved in the designing and monitoring of the curriculum and the administration of the school.

Implementation of the above public school operational methods can change schools' basic features. Schools may need to differentiate their "product" in order to become attractive to parents and students. Under competitive school systems, each school will develop in the long run a comparative advantage in a specific discipline or for a particular student population. Schools will need to offer a particular concentration in order to attract students from a large geographical area. Concentration could be in the natural sciences, liberal arts, fine arts, or vocational training. Alternatively, schools could concentrate upon a particular population like special education, new immigrant, or gifted students.

In order to improve educational achievement it appears that effective choice for parents and students and related incentives for schools and teachers are necessary. Although this must be in some respect market-like, it might function within a largely public system. In the context of a mostly public system, the following seven conditions are important since the elimination of any one would substantially restrict meaningful choice and the resulting incentives for schools to excel.

1. Principals, teachers, and other key people at the school must realize personal gains for their successful efforts. These benefits could take the form of merit awards, promotion, and professional recognition. Parents must realize that their efforts do affect the way the school runs and that programs will change to accommodate their wishes. The principal and the teachers should have an incentive to attract students to the school and persuade existing students not to transfer to other schools. If salaries and other awards are related to the number of students in the school and in individual classes, then teachers will exert more effort. Other measures of success could be evaluation by students and parents of the teachers, dropout rates, number of the high school graduates who attend four years of college or university, or number of graduates who do well in national tests.

2. The geographical monopoly of schools should be eliminated. Even the new types of schools like the magnet or the charter schools enjoy monopolistic power. They differ in that their territory is enlarged to the entire district. As long as there is a significant difference in tuition between the public and the private schools, the former enjoy market power. Monopolies can afford inefficiency in service production and supply. A key element for success requires introduction of competition in schooling. When competition is introduced, efficiency rises.

3. The centralized system, where most administrative decisions are made by the school district, prohibits innovations and efforts by the service providers— the principal and the teachers. Decentralization of schools and the provision of individual schools with power to make all administrative, recruiting, programmatic, and personnel decisions is necessary.

4. Monopoly of schools is not the only obstacle to achieving workable competition and the efficient allocation of resources. Teachers' unions are resource monopolies that have strong influence over the price of labor and the production function of the school. Most teachers in public schools are members of the union. The union's first obligation is to protect jobs. The second obligation is to maximize the income of its members in an equitable fashion.

In labor negotiations, unions generally attempt to negotiate an across-the-board equitable salary increase rather than salaries based upon output/quality factors. Such salary raises are seldom related to the output level of individual teachers. Salaries grow according to input rather than output variables. Of course keeping teacher salaries higher tends to attract and retain more and better people to teaching.

If teacher compensation were based on output, more incentives to improve performance could spur innovation and higher quality education. Even though measuring output and evaluating performance make this approach difficult to implement fully, nevertheless some movement in this direction would be better than the present compensation system. At the same time, paying teachers more to carry administrative obligations as is done in some private schools might be a way to reduce overhead costs.

Teachers' unions often successfully bargain for resource allocation provisions in the labor contract. Such provisions include limits on class size, restrictions on course load, and limits on administrative tasks. This may tend to improve the quality of education immediately and (like higher salaries) make teaching a more attractive profession but may interfere with the principal's efficient use of resources.

Introduction of competition into the system in which schools depend upon attracting and retaining students for their livelihood may weaken the centralized power of unions. If the responsibility to hire, raise salaries, and make teacher assignments is transferred from the district to the individual schools, then the union loses its influence. If unions insist on retaining influence over these issues rather than decentralizing them to an in-school union, the ability of individual schools to compete may be weakened.

5. Most budgetary decisions are made centrally at the district level. A key element required in successfully decentralizing is shifting the internal resource allocation to the individual schools. Schools should be receiving a lump sum amount based upon the number of students attending the school and the total school district's tax collection. The principal, teachers, and parents should share the decision on the internal allocation of both the operating and capital budget. Thus, if the school loses or gains students, it will be reflected in the budget. It is important that short-term gains in student numbers are not achieved by lowering academic standards in a way that weakens the long-term reputation and quality of the school.

An implication of the above budgetary principle is that if a school loses so many students that it is unable to operate, then it will be forced to close. A viable threat of school closing due to lack of students will force the school to initiate programs and recruiting activities to increase enrollment.

6. Competition in both the provision of education and the acquisition of inputs (i.e., the supply of teachers) is key to the successful implementation of educational choice. Thus, if a particular district introduces a choice program,

then it requires a sufficient number of schools in the same category (e.g., elementary schools) in order to avoid, by default, local monopoly. A choice program should be implemented for a large geographical area which encompasses several schools of the same kind. In fact, a reasonable choice program territory would be an entire state with even possible spillover of students to neighboring states.

7. Transportation costs to remote schools pose a severe difficulty to poor families. Most parents in Minnesota, the first state that has created voucher payments to private schools, chose schools by proximity to home or work. Clearly, parents who do not own cars cannot take advantage of school choice if school buses are not available. Transportation costs have been so far borne by the states where choice and voucher programs exist. Low income parents are reimbursed for most of the car costs of commuting to distant schools. It is important that transportation costs are considered a part of reimbursed costs by state and local governments in order to make choice and voucher program widely available.

It is evident that increasing competition and providing penalties in case of failure force schools to respond to customers' (parents and students) needs and desires. Budget allocation which depends upon performance will force efficient use of all resources. The currently almost monopolistic stance of public schools allows for inefficient use of resources.

One immediate consequence of budgets which depend upon performance is exposing school workers to competition. It is likely that more services will be contracted out in order to reduce costs. Responding to customers rather than deciding for them makes education similar to any other good or service in the marketplace. In order to succeed in implementing optimal educational choice, all of the above seven conditions must be met.

The question is whether under the existing political system it is possible to make such significant changes. It is unlikely that legislative proposals allowing choice within districts or even within states will be successful without all the conditions being fulfilled. The major political obstacles are the potential resistance of existing school systems to the disruption that can flow from *effective* competition and the weakening of the power of centralized teachers' unions.

Private school competition would certainly increase the benefits of a public school choice system. The voucher system allows students to draw on the state and sometimes even on local school financial resources to share the costs of the student's tuition in a public or private school of his/her choice. The private option provides additional viable competition to the local schools in quality, diversity of programs, and price. Indeed over many years a voucher system could develop a substantial number of meaningful choices for parents and students. These would create incentives for public schools even if the public system did not offer any choice within itself.

Of course, a voucher system would need from one-half to the whole amount spent on public school students. Clearly, instituting the voucher system will entail costs higher than those associated with the transferring students. Students who already attend private schools are allowed to draw on the support thus causing additional burden on state resources.

Private schools' success is reflected in strong relationships with families, focus on academics, provision of professional environment for teachers, and concern with achieving tangible results, especially on national tests. The public schools will need to compete on these grounds and offer special programs that do not exist in the region in order to enjoy a part of the students' market.

CONCLUSIONS

It is evident that the educational attainment in the United States is below par and is lagging in comparison with other Western and Far Eastern nations. In order to assure technological development and improvement in quality of life, it is essential for a nation to provide good education to its future generation. It is also evident that efforts can not be restricted to merely schooling quality improvements. The erosion of the family, the decline in family values, urban blight, and drugs are some of the other factors contributing to poor educational achievements that may need to be addressed.

Human nature requires personal incentives to make changes. Increased competition to break the local monopoly of schools provides direct and indirect incentives for teachers and administrators to excel for either fear of losing territory or hope of gaining in income. Increased competition with private and other districts' public schools will force public schools to offer special programs in order to attract students from the district and from other districts. In the long run we may witness specialization of schools in particular fields or with special groups of students.

Nationwide recognition of the importance of competition and increasing educational options to students is evidenced by the spread of educational choice programs within or across districts. Participation in educational choice options has been, however, of limited degree in places where choice was adopted. No more than 2 percent of students in these states took advantage of such programs. Interestingly, the prevailing reason for participation in choice programs by parents was proximity to home or work and not the academic superiority of the chosen school.

It seems that the public school system offers limited choice programs for students. Local schools still enjoy a monopolistic position in the community. Opening competition with private schools will enrich the spectrum of choices for students. It is most unlikely that we are going to witness a mass transfer of students from public to private schools. Only motivated students or well-informed and educated parents will take advantage of choice programs. The inner-city and rural poor students' condition will not significantly change in the short run. However, what is likely to occur in the longer run is that the existing private options will force the public schools to become more efficient, offer richer programs, make more efforts to satisfy their customers—parents and students—and enable parents to become more effectively involved in the way the school is run.

Simple implementation of the voucher system may, however, lead to undesired outcomes. Should we let market forces solely determine the parents' or students' choice of school? A related question is whether government should accredit schools that can participate in a choice program or allow market forces to operate freely.

Government involvement in education is required because of the externality feature of education. If others in our society are well-educated, then we may all benefit from more well-informed voters, more scientific improvements, more pleasant social interaction, and less social unrest and crime. However, government may wish to assure that society's values as reflected in the Constitution are preserved in the education provided to its future generation. If the voucher system is allowed, then some consideration will have to be given to the type, program, and focus of schools receiving public funds. Thus, accreditation of private schools by governments may be required to avoid using public money to educate children in ways that may contribute to adverse social effects.

An important element for the success of the voucher system is dissemination of information about the available schools. Unfortunately, markets may not be efficient in providing such information. In fact, the lower the income and the education level of parents, the less familiar they may be with the available options. In order to assist parents, information might be provided on school programs, the quality of the school, the rate of placement in four year colleges and universities, the quality of the physical facilities and other measures by a public agency or private information service.

It is true that the positive externalities associated with education may require some government involvement. However, the basic values of the voucher system still hold true. The exposure to competition has proved to be effective in other industries. Even government-dominated Eastern European economic systems are moving to market economies.

The public school system has not been performing effectively. Increasing the financial support of an inefficient system never leads to significant improvement. It is time to try something new. The voucher system with adequate quality control by state governments could be the answer.

Part I of this volume discusses the merits of school choice, guidelines for implementation, and types of contracting methods. David Beers of Wichita Collegiate School and Jerry Ellig of George Mason University show in chapter 2 that U.S. educational history casts doubt upon three economic rationales for government-run school systems: external benefits, imperfect consumer information, and wealth redistribution.

In chapter 3, Florida State Representative Tom Feeney offers guidelines for drafting school choice legislation or referenda and discusses practical political difficulties in garnering support for educational choice in the legislative and public area. Suggestions are made on ways to generate support and take on the entrenched educational establishment.

Albert Shanker and Bella Rosenberg of the American Federation of Teachers examine in chapter 4 the evidence on public-private school achievement and conclude that the claim of voucher supporters is unsubstantiated; that private school "choice" would yield little or nothing in terms of improving student achievement.

An alternative to privatization is presented by Paul T. Hill of the RAND Corporation and the University of Washington in chapter 5. He suggests that schools be operated by private organizations under contract with public authorities.

Part II presents particular plans for implementation. In chapter 6, Thomas H. Kean, president of Drew University and former governor of New Jersey, focuses on three private sector efforts that have the potential to improve both public and private schools: Education Alternatives, Inc., The Edison Project, and The New American Schools Development Corporation which is chaired by the author.

In chapter 7, Peter W. Cookson, Jr. of Adelphi University advocates an alternative method of financing public and private education based on what is called a "just voucher." The three elements of the proposal include an "educational trust fund" for every child, a voucher system that financially favors the poor, and the creation of "model" schools.

Pierre S. duPont IV, former governor of Delaware, argues in chapter 8 that choice gives all students the access to a good education. It is a proven concept: 18 million men and women used a choice system—the "GI Bill"—to get a college education. What is needed is a "GI Bill" for children.

Chapter 9 presents a plea by Ernest L. Boyer, president of the Carnegie Foundation, that it's time to move beyond the ideological confrontations and develop a larger, more inclusive strategy for school reform—one that focuses not on school location but on learning, not just on choice but on children.

In chapter 10, Kevin C. Sontheimer of the University of Pittsburgh considers the case of public versus private provision of higher education services. The chapter accepts public funding as an embedded social fact. It addresses the problems of converting from a system of public domination of the supply of higher education services to a system with only privately supplied services supported by a mix of public and private funding. A six-point proposal for a privatization process is made.

Part III exhibits experiences and evaluations of implementation plans. It starts in chapter 11 with the evaluation of an early voucher plan in New

Hampshire by John Menge of Dartmouth College. He found that parental demand for significant educational change at the local school district level was weak, or non-existent, and the supply of educational alternatives was sparse, at best. In addition, says Menge, bureaucratic administration and ideological advocacy have further imperiled the chances for successfully implementing or testing a "free market" voucher.

Thomas Hetland, formerly of the Heartland Institute, offers in chapter 12 a brief background on the Milwaukee choice program and its provisions, including an examination of the David and Goliath players in the lawsuit it precipitated.

In chapter 13, Thomas H. Peeler of the University of California at Los Angeles and Patricia A. Parham, principal of South Pointe Elementary School, describe a public/private corporate venture in which the private corporation, Education Alternatives, Inc., is directing the total curriculum program at South Pointe Elementary School, a public school in Miami, Florida.

William E. Ubinas, superintendent of District I, New York City, looks in chapter 14 at the efforts of a semi-decentralized school district in New York City as it implements the latest reform model, "choice." Community School District One, located in New York's historical Lower East Side, a port of entry for many immigrant groups and created by the 1969 Decentralization Law, is pictured as a model of the redesign of the nation's urban school.

Public Choice in Minnesota is discussed by Michael C. Rubenstein and Nancy A. Adelman of Policy Studies Associates in chapter 15. They draw on interim results from a three-year study of Minnesota's Open Enrollment and High School Graduation Incentives (HSGI) programs. Results show that the Open Enrollment program enables a relatively small number of students to attend nonresident schools for academic reasons, but it has not served as a catalyst for systemic change among the state's public schools.

REFERENCES

Chubb, J. E., and T. M. Moe. (1990) *Politics, Markets, and America's Schools.* Washington, D.C.: The Brookings Institution.

———. (1991) "The Private versus Public School Debate," *The Wall Street Journal,* July 26, p. A1.

Deming, W. E. (1982) *Duality, Productivity and Competitive Position.* Cambridge, Mass.: M.I.T. Press.

———. (1986) *Out of the Crisis.* Second edition. Cambridge, Mass.: M.I.T. Press.

National Commission on Excellence in Education. (1983) *A Nation at Risk.* Washington, D.C.: U.S. Government Printing Office.

The New York Times. (1993) "Study Says Half of Adults in U.S. Can't Read or Handle Arithmetic." September 9, p. A1.

Newsweek. (1991) "The Best Schools in the World," December 2, pp. 50–64.

Young, T. W., and E. Clinchy. (1992) *Choice in Public Education.* New York: Teachers College Press.

I

CONCEPTS

2

An Economic View of the Effectiveness of Public and Private Schools

David Beers and Jerry Ellig

Recent years have seen an outpouring of public concern over the quality of primary and secondary education in the United States. A steady stream of reports from the nation's schools has documented a 25 percent national high school dropout rate, high proportions of high school graduates who are functionally illiterate, and three decades of falling test scores. Parents and community leaders have voiced outrage that the public schools are not only failing in their educational mission, but are increasingly becoming breeding grounds for drug abuse, violence, and crime. Many in the business world see the decline of primary and secondary education as a major factor behind the nation's eroding productive capacity and faltering competitive position in the world.

Education officials at all levels have been accused of responding slowly at best to what many call a national crisis. During the decade since a landmark report by the Commission on Excellence in Education described American education as a "rising tide of mediocrity," few signs of improvement and many signs of further decline have materialized. Accusations notwithstanding, public school leaders have overseen the implementation of many of the most persistently called-for proposals for school reform. The ever-present call for more funding has been met by tripling real per-pupil expenditures from their 1960 levels. The demand for greater teacher professionalism has motivated a 50 percent increase in average teacher salaries since 1960, adjusted for inflation. Class sizes have fallen by a third since the mid-1960s, and most states have continued to raise graduation requirements (Myers 1990, 2). If the declining quality of public education continues, it is not wholly for lack of reform efforts.

In recent years education reformers, like their counterparts in policy-making circles across the nation, have been forced to reexamine their traditional assumption that higher spending and tighter regulations mean better education. The link between rules and resources on the one hand and performance on the other appears to be nonexistent in the case of public education. The traditional approach evidently does not get at the fundamental causes of the nation's learning malaise.

From an economist's perspective, reasons for declining educational quality in the public schools are not hard to find. Many public school systems are centralized, bureaucratic monopolies. Their customers are assigned to them by virtue of geography, not choice. They must pay for public education regardless of whether they are satisfied with the product or whether they choose an alternative such as private schooling. In general, reward systems within the public schools are only loosely tied to performance. As a result, school systems have few incentives to deliver quality education.

Furthermore, those schools and individual teachers that are still committed to quality and innovation usually find they have little freedom to craft the types of educational programs that will satisfy parents and students. Too many of the crucial decisions for creating a productive learning environment are made by large, centralized bureaucracies that are immersed in political, rather than educational processes.

It wasn't always this way. In 1945, the United States had more than 100,000 independent school districts, compared to less than 16,000 today (Chubb and Moe 1990, 141). Smaller districts meant smaller bureaucracies, so that parents and teachers, rather than school system officials, exercised greater control over what went on in their schools. Smaller districts also gave parents some degree of choice among public schools, since it was easier to move to a district with good schools. Multiple districts within a single city promoted healthy competition and produced ever-higher benchmarks for measuring the effectiveness of the schools.

All that has changed during the past fifty years, as education policymakers opted for consolidation and centralized administration. In a very real sense, we have tried to run public schools the same way the Soviets tried to run factories, and now we're paying the price. That sounds like strong language, but it's not just the view of academic theorists.

Consider the following comments from public officials, community activists, and independent researchers across the nation:

- "[E]ach school district enjoys a monopoly position with its 'consumers,' the citizens who live within its boundaries. And the vast majority of school districts do not permit interdistrict transfers. In the parlance of business, that would be known as 'conspiracy in restraint of trade.' Like the teachers who work for the schools, the students and families who are their customers must accept what the educational bureaucracy deigns to offer" (David T. Kearns, former deputy secretary of education and former chairman of Xerox, and Denis P. Doyle, Hudson Institute, in *Winning the Brain Race*).

- "The lesson of public-private comparisons is not that private schools are better than public schools. It is that market pressures encourage the development of better schools more than political pressures do" (John E. Chubb, The Brookings Institution, and Terry M. Moe, Stanford University, *The Wall Street Journal*, July 26, 1991, p. A12).

- "The public school system is a rule-driven monopoly, like the post office and the Soviet Union. It's a failed concept. To run the most important function we have with a failed system is inexplicable" (Joe Alibrandi, chairman of Whittaker Corp., *Fortune*, January 14, 1991, p. 52).

- "I don't know how we ever got into a situation of telling parents where they have to send their kids to school. In China, I can see, but not here" (Lamar Alexander, former secretary of education, *The Wall Street Journal*, April 5, 1991, p. A14).

- "The people who have money already exercise choice. It's time the rest of us have a way of forcing the regular schools to improve" (Beverly Williams, community activist, Watts, California, quoted in *The Wall Street Journal*, May 3, 1991, p. A10).

Across the nation and across the political spectrum, people concerned about America's schools have come to see the failure of public education as symptomatic of the institutional principles by which it has come to operate. Furthermore, they have seen the best avenue for reform as one which replaces the bureaucratic and democratic control of the schools with elements of market control: consumer choice, competition, and decentralized decision making. Proposals made in this spirit include "school-based management," the creation of "magnet schools" that parents and students may choose as alternatives to the regular public schools, and "open enrollment" programs that permit students to enroll in any school within the district. Some of the boldest plans would permit parents to put the money spent on their child by the public school system toward tuition at a private school of their choice.

As a contribution to this dialogue, this chapter offers an overview of the economics and history of "educational choice," from the fundamental justifications for government involvement in schooling to modern studies on educational effectiveness and actual case studies of choice-based reforms. While few proponents of educational choice have advocated complete privatization of the government-run public school system, this article also examines that "extreme" example of educational choice, with which the United States has had extensive historical and modern experience. The legacy of private education, surprising to many who associate private schools with elitism and upper-middle-class culture, makes the strongest case that the objections to choice-based reforms of the public schools are ill-founded.

PUBLIC SCHOOLING AND ECONOMIC THEORY

Rising public concern over education reveals that most people appreciate the benefits that a strong educational system brings. Most people would probably rather live in a society where everyone has at least a basic knowledge of reading and writing skills, mathematics, geography, history, ethics, and other such things that one must understand to function well in an advanced civilization. Nevertheless, the mere fact that something is desirable does not suffice to show that the government must either fund it or directly provide it. In general, if people want something and are willing to pay for it, we can count on profit-seeking entrepreneurs to find a way to give it to them at a reasonable cost.

Of course, there are exceptions to every generalization. Economists have suggested several reasons that the private market might not provide enough quality education. (See High 1985 for a summary.) These arguments have given intellectual legitimacy to the progressive replacement of the competitive market for education with a government-run monopoly. The three most common are external benefits, imperfect information, and wealth redistribution.

External Benefits

Education does not just benefit the person who acquires it; the educated person benefits others as well. In many cases, individuals and firms voluntarily subsidize others' education because they recognize these benefits. Businesses, for example, fund various types of employee training, and sometimes even general education, because well-educated employees are more productive. Even if an employer is unwilling to make this type of investment in its employees, employees have an incentive to invest in themselves, because their higher productivity will let them earn higher wages. Parents, meanwhile, have obvious reasons to invest in the education of their children.

When the link between investment in education and external benefits to a specific set of people is clear-cut, voluntary market activity can be expected to provide an adequate amount of education. However, when the external benefits of education are widely dispersed, voluntary cooperation to subsidize education may lead to under-investment, because everyone has an incentive to let others provide the subsidies and enjoy the resulting benefits for free. In this scenario, education will be under-provided. Therefore, government involvement is thought necessary to ensure that everyone will contribute their share of the education subsidy.

The above theory sounds quite reasonable, but it does not automatically imply that the government should establish a school system. Under-provision occurs because of free-riding; government can solve the free-rider problem simply by spending tax money on schooling. External benefits may thus justify government subsidies for schooling. To make the case for government operation of schools, one must demonstrate that government provision is the least costly way of providing the types of education that parents and students want.

The policy implications usually drawn from the theory of externalities also depend on some very difficult empirical issues. To say that education is under-provided implies that additional resources channeled into education would produce benefits that outweigh the costs. (Buchanan and Stubblebine 1962) This is not simply a matter of calculating a net return in an accounting sense. The cost of spending more tax dollars for education in the broadest sense is the value of the benefits foregone by not spending those dollars for other important needs. The practical problem of measuring these opportunity costs is intractable, to say the least, and arguments for public funding of education often skip lightly over this issue.

The presumption that educational subsidies produce substantial benefits beyond what the unsubsidized market produces is simplistic as well. The problem is a familiar one from international experience with nationalized industries: it is difficult to say exactly what gets subsidized when government finances schools, and there is a strong likelihood that it's bureaucracy, not education. The choice between degrees of public and private financing of education is not simply a matter of more or less resources for education, but an institutional change as well. Schools funded by private tuition payments must look to their customers to guide and measure their progress, whereas schools funded by tax revenues have no such constraint. Separated from accountability to the customer, publicly funded enterprises tend to cater to other interests both within and without their administrations, and school districts are no exception. Even those within the system who earnestly look to students and parents for the standards of their success find that their continued survival within the system demands conformity to regulations and policies that are rational from a bureaucratic but not an educational stand-point. All this calls into question the common assumption that the presence of external benefits from education justifies the institution of a government-run or government-subsidized school system.

Imperfect Information

The discussion of external benefits implicitly assumes that people are generally well-informed about the benefits of education and the options open to them. Employers and employees, for example, know how various types of education will enhance productivity. Similarly, parents understand various educational options well enough that they will make reasonable decisions on behalf of their children.

Not everyone agrees with these propositions. The idea that parents or students will make poor choices, due to lack of good information, provides another possible justification for government provision of schooling. In this view, the consumers cannot be trusted to identify their own best interests, and so they cannot be permitted to choose among different schooling options. Instead, the government establishes school systems, staffed by experts who make these choices for the consumers. (See West 1970, xxx–xxxii; West and McKee 1983, 1114.) Parents and students are, of course, consulted, and parents can even elect a school board to oversee the experts, but the ultimate decisions about what constitutes quality education are left in the hands of experts.

The above theory evokes strong visceral reactions, both pro and con. On the one hand, most of us resent the implication that we cannot be trusted to make our own educational choices. On the other hand, we deeply mistrust others' ability to make wise choices on their own behalf—especially when those others are of a different social class or race. To keep the discussion focused on the genuine economic issues, we need to examine the incentives and information available to both the consumers and the experts.

In the first place, parents and students actually have much better information about schooling than many policy commentators assume. Most parents may not be very good at second-guessing teaching methodologies, but they can certainly judge results. The performance of a school's students on standardized tests, and the more general performance of its graduates after they leave, both provide significant information about a school's educational effectiveness.

Second, it is not always clear that giving the experts a monopoly necessarily leads to the best expert judgment. Indeed, educational experts may well disagree amongst themselves—even about teaching methods. The sensible approach is not to argue about whether experts' or parents' judgment is better, but to create an environment that encourages educators to use their best judgment and rewards them when they create value. Economic theory suggests that government-run monopolies will perform very poorly on this score. Therefore, imperfect information is not a compelling rationale for preventing parental choice.

Wealth Redistribution

A third economic argument sometimes advanced for public schooling is that education offers lower-income people an opportunity to get ahead. Most people would like to help those who are less well-off, and having the government provide education helps ensure that they receive an important type of assistance. Public education thus becomes a type of wealth redistribution whose goal is to reduce or eliminate the need for other types of income support in the future.

Like the previous two arguments, this one provides a possible rationale for government subsidies but little rationale for direct government provision of education. In fact, the record suggests that public schools have often failed to aid the worst-off in our society. In some cases, the public school systems have arguably made life worse for the very people they are supposed to help. Thus, it should come as no surprise that some of the most vigorous proponents of school choice represent lower-income, inner-city parents who seek at least some degree of the freedom to choose their own schools that many upper-income families already enjoy.

PRIVATE EDUCATION IN U.S. HISTORY: LESSONS FOR TODAY

The early history of private schooling provides a stark contrast to the common theoretical arguments for government provision. Before the advent of public school systems, education was widely demanded and supplied in the United States—even for the poorer working classes. Establishment of government schools did not necessarily expand the amount of education offered. Public education sometimes displaced private education; at other times, public school systems deliberately stifled competing private education. In addition, government provision altered the quality of education. Many working-class parents actually viewed public education as an inferior product, because public schools did not promote the culture, language, or religious values that they believed to be important.

Early American Schools

A thriving educational marketplace existed in the United States prior to extensive government involvement in education. Carl F. Kaestle's study of New York City schools suggests that the city was well-served by private educators for a century before the first government funding became available in 1795. Private schoolmasters' records suggest that between 1760 and 1780, tuition averaged 8–10 shillings per quarter, "low enough to be within the means of many workers of the middling sort" (Kaestle 1973, 4–5). In 1795, fully 52 percent of children between the ages of five and fifteen were enrolled in the city's common pay and charity schools. Kaestle (1973, 51–53) estimates that 80–90 percent of the population must have received schooling, since few people actually attended school for twelve years. This result is impressive, given the income levels of the era.

Private schooling was hardly confined to New York. During the colonial era, private schools became so numerous in New England that many governments sought to regulate them—or even prohibit them. In 1670, for example, the town of Stamford, Connecticut, agreed "to put down all petty schools that are or may be kept in the town which may be prejudicial to the general school" (quoted in Small 1969, 312). Contradicting the idea that such regulation helped promote quality education, historian Robert Seybolt (1971, 101–2) noted that colonial schoolmasters had strong incentives to pay close attention to their customers' needs:

> It is a significant fact in American education that the curriculum developed most rapidly in the private schools, that the curricular response to popular educational demands was initiated by private, rather than public enterprise. . . . In the hands of private schoolmasters the curriculum expanded rapidly. Their schools were commercial ventures, and, consequently, competition was keen. . . . Popular demands, and the element of competition forced them not only to add new courses of instructions, but constantly to improve their methods and technique of instruction.

After the Revolutionary War, cutbacks in public support for education in New England spurred the growth of academies—educational institutions supported in whole or in part by tuition. In 1789, Massachusetts enacted a law requiring that only towns of 200 or more families must support a town grammar school; previously, towns of more than 100 families had been required to do so. This measure meant that only 110 towns would now have to support grammar schools, compared to 230 previously (Brown 1970, 216). In that same year, New Hampshire freed most of its towns from their obligation to support a secondary school (Middlekauff 1971, 133–36). Parents responded by turning to private schools. Middlekauff (1971, 136) notes, "They hired more private masters than ever before, and established academies with fat endowments, fine buildings, and complicated administrative apparatus. In short, their zeal for education seems to have been greater than ever, but it was now a zeal channeled into private education."

Teachers also found the private academies more to their liking. According to Grizzel (1923, 28), "Many of the prominent New England schoolmasters were attracted by the spirit of freedom of the academy and left the public Latin grammar school and district school, starting private schools or academies." In Massachusetts in the 1830s, the academies offered instruction in languages, mathematics, geography, arithmetic, orthography, history, rhetoric, philosophy, surveying, astronomy, composition, navigation, surveying, algebra, geometry, trigonometry, grammar, reading, declamation, writing, and needlework (Lottich 1962, 250).

There were 163 academies in New England by 1830; by 1850, there were 1,007 (Grizzel 1923, 31). In Ohio, 210 academies had been established by 1851 (Lottich 1962, 240–41). Indiana had 131 academies by 1850, located in seventy-eight of the state's ninety-two counties (Mock 1949, 4). In that year, there were also 1,815 academies in eleven southern states, with an enrollment of 70,546 students (Knight 1919, 23–32). In his study of southern academies, Edgar Knight (1919, vi) suggested, "The prestige and popularity of these private and denominational efforts accounted in large part for the long delay in establishing public high schools in the Southern States."

Although modern use of the term "academy" sometimes brings to mind college preparatory schools for the elite, the early American academies sprang up largely to serve the middle class:

> The academy age was, in fact, the age of transition from the partially stratified colonial society to modern democracy. Perhaps the most marked feature of that transition was the growing importance of a strong middle class. The rise of the academies was closely connected with the rise of this middle class. The academies were by no means exclusively middle-class schools at the start, and they became something very different from that at a later period. But it is one of their glories that they were in the earlier days so bound up with the higher interests of the common people (Brown 1970, 228–29).

In short, the historical evidence suggests that before the advent of widespread public schooling, Americans took a keen interest in acquiring education. The demand for education was not confined to the rich. The supply of schooling was extensive, despite the fact that government aid was meager, sporadic, or non-existent.

URBAN CATHOLIC SCHOOLS

Discussions of public education often assume that schooling is a homogeneous good. The market is thought to under-provide education, so government steps in to increase the amount provided. In reality, direct government provision of education can drastically alter its quality as well. The natural tendency of centralized bureaucracies is to standardize service, even when the needs served and the talents available are diverse. Large school districts must try to be everything to everybody, but in the end they tend to weed out whatever educational practices diverge from the least common denominator among their constituents. At least some citizens then find themselves taxed to pay for a product that they believe to be inferior. Even if their tax payments are less than the tuition they would have otherwise paid, this policy can make citizens worse off, because the reduction in cost may be more than offset by the reduction in quality. The history of urban Catholic schools in New York, St. Louis, and Chicago provides a striking example of this phenomenon.

The 1840s and 1850s saw an influx of German and Irish Catholics to America, followed later by fellow church members from Eastern Europe. Many of these immigrants saw public schools as an overt attempt to impose nondenominational Protestantism on their children and deprive them of their cultural heritage. Public schools often used the King James version of the Bible, encouraged students to read the Bible without instruction, and sometimes displayed a nativist bias in their choice of texts (Kaestle 1973, 151–54). In 1852, New York Archbishop John Hughes complained that American public schooling was "Socialism, Red Republicanism, Universalism, Deism, Atheism, and Pantheism—anything, everything, but religionism and patriotism." Robert Cross (1965, 197–98) commented, "Such a fantastic image of public education in the era of Horace Mann and William McGuffey reflected how deeply this prominent Irish-American was alienated from American institutions."

By 1850, it was clear that Catholic schools would receive no public support in New York City. Hughes announced that henceforth, the official archdiocesan policy would be that schools should be built before churches (Lannie 1968, 225). New York's Catholics, primarily poor and unskilled laborers, responded in dramatic fashion. By 1854, twenty-eight New York City Catholic schools had an enrollment of 10,061 children, rising to 12,938 in 1857 and 15,000 in 1862 (Lannie 1968, 256). By comparison, there were approximately 100,000 Catholics in New York City in 1850, about 20,000 of them between the ages of five and fifteen. Thus, it seems clear that most children received at least several years of schooling, in spite of the fact that poor families desperately needed their children to enter the work force (Kaestle 1973, 146).

In midwestern cities like St. Louis, Milwaukee, and Cincinnati, culture drove the establishment of private schools as much as religion did. Even before the advent of compulsory education, German immigrants led the way in establishment of private schools that would teach the German language as well as English. In St. Louis, for example, public school enrollment did not exceed Catholic school enrollment until 1850. In 1860, for every student of German descent in a St. Louis public school, there were still four in private and parochial schools (Troen 1975, 57).

Ethnicity also helped promote the growth of Catholic education in Chicago. Parish churches and their schools did not just serve particular geographic areas; some neighborhoods had several Catholic churches and schools to serve different ethnic groups. As in New York, the Germans and Irish led the way, followed by diverse others. By 1930, there were Catholic elementary schools affiliated with Polish, Bohemian, French, Lithuanian, Italian, Slovak, Croatian, Slovene, and African-American parishes (Sanders 1977, 45).

Chicago also followed another pattern typical of cities with large Catholic populations in this era: the poorest immigrants were the ones most likely to choose parochial over public schools. According to James Sanders (1977, 80), "In every poverty zone, the proportion in Catholic schools exceeded that for Chicago as a whole in 1890." Many of the poor lived in wards 5–9, where seventeen Catholic schools educated 40 percent of all children—even though free public schooling was available. Sanders (1977, 79) describes this phenomenon in striking detail:

> The workers settled near industrial and commercial sites. Here, in the shadow of belching smoke stacks and near the squeal of dying pigs the laborer could slog without cost through the mud of unpaved streets to his long day's work. In these areas—the older, residentially blighted commercial sections surrounding the city center, along the branches of the river, near the noisy railroads, around the stockyards, and in the southeast Chicago industrial areas adjoining the Calumet River—one found most of the Catholic population. It was on this infertile soil, where people lived in "conditions as bad as any in the world," according to contemporary accounts, that the Catholic parochial school system had its roots.

By 1912, 90 percent of Catholic families in the stockyard district were sending their children to parochial schools (Sanders 1977, 85).

Inner-City Private Schools Today

As heavily monopolized as the American education industry is today, and as much as taxpayers must now pay to support the government-run school systems, private schools still carve out a niche for themselves in the market. Interestingly, the frontier for private education has not only been with schools for children of upper-middle-class families that have always been able to afford better options than the public schools, but with schools for children of impoverished, predominantly minority, inner-city families. Chicago's contemporary experience with private neighborhood schools emphasizes that private education is not a fragile flower easily trampled by adverse socioeconomic conditions, but a hardy weed that springs up relentlessly through any crack in the sidewalk.

The Chicago public schools have experienced dropout rates among minorities of nearly 50 percent, and a solid majority of students graduate without basic skills (Ratteray 1986, 1). Among the parents of these inner-city youth, there is a widespread conviction that the problem has not been with the communities these schools serve, but with the public school system itself. Many of even the poorer families have preferred to pay for their children's education rather than leave them in the failing public schools, and entrepreneurial members of these communities have built a substantial network of neighborhood private schools to satisfy this demand. One observer of these independent schools noted,

Parents from low-income neighborhoods are continually seeking independent schools to help their children survive the schooling process, often doing so under great financial hardship. While there are many influences that tend to hamper the growth of these institutions, the schools continue to thrive (Ratteray 1986, 1).

Indeed, as of 1986 nearly fifty such private institutions operated in Chicago, most located in the areas of the city least effectively served by the public schools: the poorest, minority-dominated neighborhoods. In fact, compared to private schools in nearby middle-income neighborhoods, the schools in the poorest areas have the highest enrollments, the longest waiting lists, and the greatest need for expanded facilities (Ratteray 1986, 2). With tuition ranging in 1986 from as little as $270 per year to as much as $3,000, inner-city independent schools in Chicago have an average enrollment of 200 students. Some are supported by neighborhood churches that offer facilities, but few receive financing from these sources or have curricula that are controlled by them. Many are supported through fundraising or volunteer work by parents, alumni, and other members of the community.

Most importantly, independent schools in Chicago are creating productive learning environments. Typically they have sound academic programs, committed faculty, staff, and parents, and they meet state and local standards for accreditation. Some have strong, specialized curricula in areas like mathematics and sciences. At one such school for grades kindergarten through eight, the students compete in city-wide and state-level competitions in these areas and score two or more years above national norms on standardized tests.

LESSONS FROM THE PRIVATE SCHOOL EXPERIENCE

This brief foray into the history and present reality of private schooling casts grave doubts on the assertion that a government school monopoly is necessary to ensure that students receive the right amount of education. Ever since the colonial period, America has had a thriving, private educational marketplace. By the 1800s, education was no longer just for the rich and upper middle class. The working classes and the poor demanded schooling, and the marketplace usually supplied it at affordable prices. In addition, free public schooling came to be viewed as a burden by the very people it was supposed to help—immigrants and the poor. It was these groups who took the lead in establishing private and parochial schools in an attempt to preserve religious and cultural diversity. Later, inner-city African-American and Hispanic groups took the lead in building independent private schools to meet the needs of their communities. If quality education has been "under-provided," it has not been for lack of demand.

THE PROBLEM WITH PUBLIC EDUCATION: TOO LITTLE MONEY, OR TOO MUCH BUREAUCRACY?

Both historical and modern experience with private education in the United States belie the traditional arguments used to rationalize government-run public schools. Certainly, the heavily monopolized public education system has failed to meet the varied demands of its diverse clientele. Are government schools *as such* actually less effective at the basic job of educating children than their private counterparts, or do they just lack the funding and strict standards of the private schools? More to the point, can it be empirically demonstrated that monopoly school districts run by political bureaucracies are inherently less effective by virtue of their bureaucratic structure?

These questions strike at the heart of recent debate over public school reform. When standardized test scores, graduation rates, and literacy rates began to slide in the 1960s, American educational reformers sought objective evidence about the cause of the decline. From academics in the social sciences came statistical analyses of data on the performance of American schools. A great deal of research into school effectiveness took the form of statistical models that tested for the correlation of some measure of educational "output" with various variables considered to be "inputs" into the education process. Output was typically measured in terms of students' test scores or earnings after graduation, while inputs included in these models varied widely from study to study.

Some researchers examined the effects of the schools' physical assets, such as the size and age of the school building, the quality of the science labs, and the number of books in the library. Many others tried to specify the various human variables in the education equation, such as class size, socioeconomic status of students, racial composition of the school, and the experience, salaries, education, and verbal ability of the teachers. Of course, many studies attempted to ascertain a quantitative relationship between expenditures per pupil and academic performance within school systems.

The results of this intensive research program were disappointing for those who hoped that specific policy reforms and planning recommendations could be derived from the estimated parameters in these models. The authors of a Rand Corporation survey of nineteen of these studies concluded flatly, "Research has found nothing that consistently and unambiguously makes a difference in student outcomes" (Averch et al. 1972, x). Another author summarized his overview of this literature in a similar vein:

No measurable school resource or policy shows a consistent relationship to schools' effectiveness in boosting student achievement. The specific school resources that have a "statistically significant" relationship to achievement change from one method of analysis to the next, from one sort of school to another, and from one type of student to another. While it is always possible to invent explanations for all this after the fact, it is never possible to predict much about such differences in advance (Jencks et al. 1972, 96).

Research during the 1970s and 1980s made use of better data and more sophisticated methodology, but was no more conclusive about what factors made schools work—or what accounted for the continuing decline in SAT scores. One of the most comprehensive surveys of educational achievement studies was performed by University of Rochester economics professor Eric Hanushek (1989). Surveying 187 such studies, Hanushek found very few that established significant connections between student performance and many of the factors traditionally assumed to increase school effectiveness. As summarized in Table 2.1, higher expenditure per pupil, better education of teachers, higher teacher salaries, larger teacher/pupil ratios, and enhanced administrative inputs generally were found to have no effect on student achievement.

These findings might suggest that schools simply do not make a difference in the cognitive development of students. Education researchers, by and large, rejected this interpretation. Most studies of school effectiveness indicated that schools did make a significant difference in that average gains in achievement differed widely from one school to the next. Certain schools had quite a lot of learning going on, while certain others had very little.

When John Chubb of The Brookings Institution and Terry Moe of Stanford University published their pathbreaking study *Politics, Markets, and America's Schools* in 1990, they were among the first social scientists to demonstrate statistically what many teachers and parents had known for years: that success in education has less to do with the easily measured inputs and proclaimed standards of the schools than with those harder-to-quantify characteristics that

Table 2.1
Inputs and Outputs in Education: What the Studies Show

INPUT	Increases Student Achievement	Reduces Student Achievement	Makes No Difference
	No of studies	No of studies	No of studies
Teacher/Pupil Ratio	14	13	125
Teacher Education	8	5	100
Teacher Salary	40	10	90
Spending per Student	11	4	54
Administrative Inputs	7	1	53

Source: Eric Hanushek, "The Impact of Differential Expenditures on School Performance," *Educational Researcher*, May 1989. Table reproduced from *Choice in Education: Opportunities for Texas*, Education Task Force Report (Texas Public Policy Foundation and National Center for Policy Analysis, March 1990).

define the organization and internal culture of the school. Using the largest comprehensive data set yet collected on American high schools and their students, Chubb and Moe found that, next to student aptitude, the quality of the school organization accounted for more of the difference between successful and unsuccessful schools than anything else. Factors like school economic resources and racial composition were found to have no effect on student achievement gains. Schools with effective organizations saw achievement gains over the last two years of high school that were one-half to two-thirds of a year beyond those occurring in schools with poor organizational cultures (Chubb and Moe 1990, 139–40).

The qualities of schools with healthy organizations are no great mystery. Successful schools, say Chubb and Moe, generally exhibit commitment to a clearly articulated academic mission, motivated leadership, teacher professionalism and participation in decisions, staff harmony, and disciplinary fairness, among other things. Less obvious, though, are the ways that these elements can be brought about in practice. Chubb and Moe's most significant finding was that desirable organizational qualities are not the result of policies imposed on schools through school boards, upper administration, or unions—the usual arbiters of educational reform. In fact, as shown in Table 2.2, it is precisely the schools with the greatest freedom from such bureaucratic interference that tend to have the most effective organizations.

Chubb and Moe found that private schools tend to enjoy the most autonomy from external bureaucracies, to be organized effectively, and to post among the

Table 2.2
Bureaucratic Control and School Organization[a]

Characteristic	Ineffective Organization[b]	Effective Organization[b]
Schools with above-average level of school board influence	52.5%	37.3%
Schools with above-average level of administrative constraint	68.1%	39.4%
Schools with above-average level of personnel constraint (union influence)	45.0%	8.2%

[a]Sample weighted to achieve a nationally representative sample of public and private high schools.
[b]Schools with "ineffective" or "effective" organizations ranked in the bottom and top quartiles, respectively, using an index composed of ten desirable organizational characteristics.
Source: John Chubb and Terry Moe. (1990) *Politics, Markets, and America's Schools*. Washington, D.C.: The Brookings Institution, pp. 152–156.

largest achievement gains. Of the schools which performed in the top quartile of their sample, 38 percent were private, while only 2 percent of the low performance schools were private. Statistically speaking, knowing whether a particular school chosen at random is public or private predicts its performance better than any other variable tested in their study. Smaller, suburban public schools that manage to avoid creating layers of educational bureaucracy also tend to perform well.

Most public schools, however, have a hard time creating an organization that maximizes students' learning opportunities. One reason for this is that attempts by education policymakers to effect reforms within the existing system of bureaucratic control deprive the public schools of the very autonomy they need to improve their organizations. Such control is inherently at odds with the teacher professionalism, responsive leadership, personal commitment, and staff loyalties that define well-organized schools. Another reason is that institutions of centralized control can, at best, aim for what appears to be the "one best system" for their varied constituency. Bureaucracies are well-suited to enforcing uniform standards among many organizations, but rigid, uniform regulations don't address the individualized problems faced by schools. The effectiveness of a school in any given district has far more to do with its ability to respond to the unique demands of its customers and the distinctive problems that it encounters than with its conformity to the policies of other schools in the district. Centralized control, even if guided by democratic principles, prevents school systems from responding to the varied needs of the communities they serve and exacerbates the problems their policies are meant to solve.

It isn't enough for policymakers to command school boards to "decentralize" or "avoid bureaucracy." Instead, we need to change the institutional environment that most public schools find themselves in, so that individual schools will have both the freedom and the incentive to take initiative and develop productive learning communities. Private schools in the market operate in such an environment. Educational choice plans are designed to provide for public schools the same kind of independence and rewards that have impelled the private schools toward excellence.

CHOICE AND DECENTRALIZATION IN OPERATION

As the perception has grown among education experts and the general public that the political monopoly in the American education industry is the source of the problem, not the means to a solution, many public school systems have begun introducing plans for decentralization and choice. While the blueprints for these reforms differ in important respects, they share some common principles. All share a common goal of giving parents and students the opportunity to choose their own schools—that is, they deregulate the demand side of the education market.

Nine states now have "open enrollment" policies, which give parents the option of choosing which public school their children will attend within the district, or sometimes within the state. Funding follows each student to whichever school he or she attends. The proliferation of "magnet" and "alternative" schools across the nation is an example of the choice principle implemented on a more limited scope. Many have been created with the specific needs of urban minority children in mind, having distinctive philosophies and specialized curricula. Usually these institutional reforms were adopted as powerful tools for voluntary desegregation, based on the commonsense idea that the new schools of choice would draw "customers" who had chosen to go there rather than being assigned according to the neighborhood they lived in. While magnet and alternative schools typically offer choices only to a small proportion of a district's students, they exhibit many of the desirable qualities of schools in open enrollment systems and in private schools: healthier organizations, increased parent support, more satisfied faculty and students, higher achievement scores, and lower dropout and absenteeism rates (Chubb and Moe 1990, 209).

The most extensive choice plans concentrate on giving parents the financial means to choose private as well as public schools. Milwaukee, Wisconsin, hosts one of the most ambitious programs of this type. In 1990, State Rep. Polly Williams—a former state chair of the Rev. Jesse Jackson's presidential campaigns—led a coalition of Democrats and Republicans to secure passage of a bill allowing up to 1,000 Milwaukee children from low-income families to enroll in nonreligious private schools. The state pays these schools $2,500 per student, less than half the cost of educating them in Milwaukee's public schools.

When the choice concept expands to include private schools, which operate in a full-blown market context, not only is the demand side of the market freed to motivate the improvement of the schools, but the supply side of the market is brought to bear as well. Healthy competition among schools to achieve better, more attractive programs is enhanced by giving visionary educators greater freedom to start their own programs and their own schools with a minimum of bureaucratic interference. Choice proposals will fail to achieve their full potential unless schools are freed to develop the kinds of schools parents and students *want* to choose—even if it involves starting whole new schools with innovative concepts. Including private schools in choice-based reforms is an excellent way to achieve this, but not the only way.

One of the boldest and best established exercises in educational choice has been carried out in Manhattan's Community School District Four in East Harlem, New York. It is an excellent case study for examining the potential of public sector choice: it probably represents the most thorough application of the concept in the United States; it has eighteen years of experience operating as a choice-based system, and according to the conventional wisdom about education, it has had the demographic odds severely stacked against it. If choice works in District Four, it is hard to see how it couldn't be at least as successful in other school systems. The population of the district is roughly 65 percent Hispanic, 34 percent African-American, and 1 percent non-minorities. Of the twenty-six poverty areas in New York City, East Harlem has the eighth highest percentage of welfare recipients. More than half of the families in the district are headed by single parents (Chubb and Moe 1990, 212). Furthermore, in 1973, before choice was implemented, District Four ranked last in mathematics and reading among the thirty-two school districts in New York City (Fliegel 1989, 96).

By 1989, District Four ranked sixteenth in the city in test scores, had 64 percent of its students reading at or above grade level, and attracted close to 2,000 students from neighborhoods outside of East Harlem. The district's Benjamin Franklin High School, which graduated only about 7 percent of its students in the early 1970s, today sends 96 percent of its students to college (Hood 1989, 21).

The transformation of East Harlem's schools followed some radical changes in the basic assumptions about public schooling—but educators, parents, and community leaders were desperate for radical change in the community. Beginning with three small alternative schools, teachers and administrators began to create a network of highly individualized schools that parents and students could choose among. Spurred by the surprising success of these schools, the system of alternative schools began to expand rapidly. Much of this expansion was due to the district's policy of encouraging motivated, innovative teachers to propose their own programs and start their own schools, with the district's involvement and consent. By 1981, all the traditional neighborhood junior highs in East Harlem had been replaced by a remarkable variety of small alternative schools with individualized philosophies and curricula to meet every educational need. Schools that are unable to attract enough customers are put out of business by the district, freeing up resources for innovators with more promising ideas or better leadership.

In addition to permitting both the demand for and supply of education to motivate and check the quality of the competing programs, the district granted the schools a substantial amount of freedom to control their own admissions and to make their own decisions about programs and methods. By giving parents, students, and teachers wide domains for choice, these schools have been able to inculcate a sense of ownership and pride in their programs. This has enhanced teacher professionalism, parental involvement, and the discipline and motivation of the students. It has also minimized the need for many of the cumbersome rules and regulations used to enforce order in the typical public school (Fliegel 1989, 97). In short, District Four's program of school choice nurtured just the kinds of school organizations that Chubb and Moe found to be decisive factors in effective schooling.

CONCLUSION

The evidence of Chicago's inner-city private school system shows that parents need not be *given* educational choices by the public school system; they can create their own. Privately funded independent schooling is certainly safer from the threat of bureaucratic creep than even the best public sector choice system. Even East Harlem's District Four has shown its vulnerability in recent years to the reassertion of traditional controls by new leadership whose commitment to the concept of choice was less firm (Fiske 1989, B8). Since, for better or for worse, public education appears to be here to stay, parental choice represents the most promising institutional reform available for the public schools. With the authority for vesting most substantive educational decisions in individual schools and families rather than public authorities, the result is less a reform of education policy than it is a process for continuously developing new reforms and testing them in the market. Far from being a subversive proposal, educational choice is really the American formula for progress put to work in our schools.

REFERENCES

Allen, Jeanne, and Michael L. McLaughlin. (1990) "A Businessman's Guide to the Education Reform Debate," Heritage Foundation, *Backgrounder* No. 801.

Averch, Harvey A., Stephen J. Carroll, Theodore S. Donaldson, Herbert J. Kiesling, and John Pincus. (1972) *How Effective is Schooling?* Santa Monica, Calif.: RAND Corporation.

Brown, Elmer E. (1970 [1902]) *The Making of Our Middle Schools*. Totowa, N.J.: Littlefield, Adams, and Co.

Buchanan, James M., and W. Craig Stubblebine. (1962) "Externality," *Economica*.

Chubb, John, and Terry Moe. (1990) *Politics, Markets, and America's Schools*. Washington, D.C.: The Brookings Institution.

Cross, Robert D. (1965) "Origins of the Catholic Parochial Schools in America," *American Benedictine Review*, Vol. 16, pp. 197–98.

Education Task Force. (1990) *Choice in Education: Opportunities for Texas*. Dallas: Texas Public Policy Foundation and National Center for Policy Analysis.

Ellig, Jerome, and Jack High. (1988) "The Private Supply of Education: Some Historical Evidence," In *The Theory of Market Failure: A Critical Appraisal*, edited by Tyler Cowen. Fairfax, Va.: George Mason University Press.

Fiske, Edward B. (1989) "The Alternative Schools of Famous District 4: Accolades and Better Attendance Are Not Enough," *The New York Times*, November 1 1989, p. B8.

Fliegel, Sy. (1989) "Parental Choice in East Harlem Schools," In *Public Schools by Choice*, edited by Joseph Nathan. St. Paul: The Institute for Learning and Teaching.

Grizzell, Emit D. (1923) *Origins and Development of the High School in New England before 1865*. Philadelphia: Macmillan.

Hanushek, Eric. (1989) "The Impact of Differential Expenditures on School Performance," *Educational Researcher*.

High, Jack C. (1985) "State Education: Have Economists Made a Case?," *Cato Journal*, Vol. 5, No. 1.

Hood, John M. (1989) "Miracle on 109th Street," *Reason*, May 1989.

Jencks, Christopher, et al. (1972) *Inequality: A Reassessment of the Effect of Family and Schooling in America*. New York: Basic Books.

Kaestle, Carl F. (1973) *The Evolution of an Urban School System: New York City 1750–1850*. Cambridge: Harvard University Press.

Knight, Edgar W. (1919?) *The Academy Movement in the South*. Chapel Hill, North Carolina. Reprint from *High School Journal*, Vol. 2, No. 78, and Vol. 3, No. 1, publisher unknown.

Lannie, Vincent P. (1968) *Public Money and Parochial Education*. Cleveland: Case Western Reserve University Press.

Lottich, Kenneth V. (1962) "Democracy and Education in the Early American Northwest," *Paedagogica Historica*, Vol. 2, No. 2, pp. 240–41.

Middlekauff, Robert. (1971 [1963]) *Ancients and Axioms*. New York: Arno Press.

Mock, Albert. (1949) "The Midwestern Academy Movement: A Composite Picture of 514 Indiana Academics, 1810–1900," Butler University, unpublished.

Myers, William C. (1990) "The ABC's of Educational Choice," *Essays on Our Times*, No. 5, p. 2.

Ratteray, Joan Davis. (1986) "Access to Quality: Private Schools in Chicago's Inner City," *Heartland Policy Study*, No. 9, pp. 1, 2.

Sanders, James W. (1977) *The Education of an Urban Minority: Catholics in Chicago, 1833–1965*. New York: Oxford University Press.

Seeley, David S. (1985) *Education through Partnership*. Washington, D.C.: American Enterprise Institute.

Seybolt, Robert F. (1971 [1925]) *Source Studies in American Colonial Education: The Private School*. New York: Arno Press.

Small, Walter H. (1969 [1914]) *Early New England Schools*. New York: Arno Press.

Troen, Selwyn R. (1975) *The Public and the Schools: Shaping the St. Louis System, 1838–1920*. Columbia: University of Missouri Press.

West, E. G. (1970) *Education and the State*. London: Institute of Economic Affairs.

West, E. G., and Michael McKee. (1983) "De Gustibus *est* Disputandum: The Phenomenon of 'Merit Wants' Revisited," *American Economic Review*, Vol. 73, No. 5, p. 1114.

3

Why Educational Choice: The Florida Experience

Tom Feeney

The present effort will draw upon the experience of one legislator dedicated to school choice to provide a guide for drafting legislation and referenda and subsequently organizing support for the enactment of such reforms.

School choice is nothing new. Wealthy families have always enjoyed the ability to locate in school districts with superior public schools, or afford tuition for private alternatives. Nobel prize winning economist Milton Friedman should be given credit for being a generation ahead of his time in his visionary arguments for school choice for all families. In both *Capitalism and Freedom* and *Free to Choose*, Professor Friedman argued persuasively in favor of the merits of choice, and predicted many of the disasters and crises which we now face in our public schools system (Friedman 1962; Friedman and Friedman 1980).

Nonetheless, the drafter of legislation or referenda supporting the choice concept has a unique problem: no American state has ever experimented with a comprehensive school choice program. In one sense we can look to our system of higher education as a model. In higher education we provide public and private competition; we supplement private schools through grants, scholarships, and vouchers (such as the GI bill); we underwrite the cost of public education; we provide complete choice to any eligible student to choose the school that he/she attends; and as a result, America arguably has the finest university system in the world. However, the university model is not perfect in that not every individual goes on to any form of post-secondary education, transportation is not provided, public school students have to pay a portion of the cost of their education, and the purpose of K–12 schooling differs in degree from the purposes of higher education.

CONSTITUTIONAL AND LEGAL ISSUES

Because of vehement objections from the education establishment to any form of school choice that includes private competition, any ambitious school choice program will be challenged subsequently in the courts. The drafter should seek assistance from competent experts to ensure that the legislation enacted will stand a good chance of withstanding subsequent attacks by public school administrators or teachers' unions who oppose choice.

The constitutional questions involved will fall into two categories, federal and state. Most experts believe that a comprehensive school choice program including private and religious instruction can be drafted to withstand federal constitutional attacks. The U.S. Supreme Court has issued a number of opinions that provide guidance on the constitutional issues involved and most court observers feel that the existing "Rehnquist" court will view the federal Constitution in a light even more favorable to school choice proponents if tested.[1]

Essentially, the U.S. Supreme Court has indicated that any legislation involving state funds to private and religious schools must withstand the so-called "Lemon" test.[2] The test sets forth three requirements: any legislation must have a "secular" purpose; it must have as its "primary effect" an outcome that neither inhibits nor advances religion; and it must not foster "excessive entanglement" between government and religion. Supreme Court Chief Justice William Rehnquist noted the "catch-22" of the decision "whereby aid (to religious schools) must be supervised to ensure no entanglement but the supervision itself is held to be an entanglement."[3]

Nonetheless, constitutional scholars have predicted that a properly drafted statute will likely withstand a federal constitutional challenge, if it includes the following considerations:

1. Does not provide general subsidies directly to schools

2. Provides funds only on the basis of parental decision to enroll a child

3. Makes non-religious schools equally eligible to participate with religious schools

4. Creates no financial incentive to attend religious schools

5. Limits government regulation to ensure secular educational objectives are accomplished

6. Keeps direct government involvement with schools as minimal as possible

7. For non-religious private schools, requires schools receiving funds directly or through vouchers to abide by a policy of non-discrimination on the basis of race, national origin, gender, or handicap (Heritage, Feb. 18 1992)

In some states, the state constitution will create more difficult problems. Many state constitutions provide specially for a state-funded public school system. The federal Constitution never mentions either education or public schools. Additionally, state constitutions may be more specific in prohibiting state funds to benefit individual religions. Contrary to popular belief, the federal Constitution does not require a "wall between church and state." Some state constitutions may be significantly more problematic for the drafter of legislation on these and other matters.

For instance, in my home state of Florida, Article I, Section III of the State Constitution provides that "No revenue of the state or any political subdivision or agency thereof shall ever be taken from the public treasury directly or indirectly in aid of any church, sect, or religious denomination or in aid of any sectarian institution." Additionally, Article IX, Section 1, provides for a "uniform system of free public schools" and Section 6 prohibits spending money raised for public schools for any other purpose. While case law provides school choice proponents with hope that school choice will be held constitutional,[4] state law presents dilemmas that are unique and separate from federal problems.

In short, the drafter should first review the general federal constitutional requirements for any school choice legislation. Second, the drafter must consider carefully state constitutional difficulties that may be unique to the state. Even where a state constitution may read identically on the pertinent issues to the federal Constitution, a state court could legally decide that its constitution requires more stringent standards than federal courts have established in reviewing the constitutionality of choice systems. Thus, even the political disposition of the state supreme court may become an important factor to the drafter.

In the event that the drafter concludes that due to state constitutional difficulties he cannot accomplish his objective, the only choice is to amend the state constitution, either by referendum, or other permissible means.

What Type of "Choice System"

I have not defined previously what "choice" means. It turns out that so long as they get to define it, virtually *everyone*, including teachers' unions, administrators, and other opponents of comprehensive choice programs, can support choice. Myron Lieberman describes the general "modes of privatization" available in the education system as follows:

1. Contracting (with independent contractors)

2. Vouchers (a comprehensive public/private school choice system)

3. Load shedding (government withdrawal from providing educational services)

4. Franchising (private organizations given monopoly privileges to provide a service)

5. Subsidies to non-governmental suppliers (government payments to private educators)

6. Voluntary service (volunteers provide education, such as home schooling)

7. Sale of government assets (transfer of property rights from government to private sector)

8. Leaseback arrangements (schools lease private property on which they intend to provide services) (Lieberman 1989, 6 and 7)

While this writer will address the most comprehensive form of private and public school choice, the drafter may wish to implement pilot programs or experiments with a much more limited range of choice.[5]

Fly-by-Night School Problem

The drafter will want to consider the problem of "fly-by-night" schools. Suppose legislation provides for vouchers in the amount of $2,500 for a private school. If a private school is admitted to the program and accepts 100 students, it will receive $250,000 for admitting those students. How will your legislation prohibit the proprietor from taking the quarter of a million dollars and running to the nearest racetrack or Mexico? Among other resolutions, the state could release the funds gradually, or require the school to provide bonds or letters of credit. Additionally, once the schools have established a history of performance some of these requirements could be eased.

In the city of Milwaukee, where State Representative Polly Williams passed a voucher program that has had some immediate positive effects on poor minority students in the Milwaukee school system,[6] one of the participating private schools went out of business in the first year. Obviously the students went back into the public school system, so the students themselves were probably no worse off than before the choice system. Choice critics delighted, however, in pointing to the failure. Unfortunately, funds, time, and energy were indeed wasted.

Admissions Criteria

Can participating private schools "select" their clientele? Can they require a certain standard of academic achievement? Can they require that parents volunteer time or review student homework?

Can participating schools discriminate against students and if so, on what basis? Does a private school have to be fully equipped for blind students, disabled students, at-risk students, or special needs students?

With respect to discrimination, the federal and state constitutions and laws should be consulted at a minimum. Discrimination on the basis of race, creed, and national origin should most certainly be prohibited. However, discrimination based on religious affiliation presents an interesting question. Suppose a certain synagogue-affiliated school wishes to admit only members of the Jewish faith, or perhaps only members of that particular synagogue. There is a question as to whether or not this is federally permissible, and if so it may require very specific statutory language. One alternative is to permit organizations to reserve spaces for their own members first, but then to prohibit any such discrimination after admission spaces open up to non-members. The constitutional issues involved have not been resolved.

Another interesting question concerns discrimination on the basis of sex. Inner-city schools have experimented increasingly with "Afro-Centric" education for troubled black male students. No one would deny that our school system has failed this category of students miserably. Perhaps radical approaches are necessary, and experiments are certainly desirable. The drafter has serious constitutional and policy considerations facing him in crafting the "admissions" criteria. Again, the constitutional issues have not been resolved, and the ultimate answer will probably differ state to state.

Amount of Scholarship

The "voucher" or "scholarship" amount is a critical consideration. Recently, Pennsylvania had a legislative fight over a full-fledged school voucher plan, that would have permitted parents to receive $900 for children to attend private schools if they so desired.[7] The Milwaukee figure was $2,500 per student but was only redeemable at non-sectarian schools. A proposed California referendum provides up to $2,500 per student.

My own view is that a fixed dollar amount fails to take into account several important considerations. On average it is more expensive to educate a high school student than a third-grader (because of the requirements for supplies, athletic fields, science laboratories, specialized teachers in curriculum, etc.). Most states recognize certain categories of children who are "at-risk" of dropping out or failing school and provide subsidies for their special needs. Clearly programs for the learning-disabled and for the emotionally troubled, handicapped, or blind students require additional funds.

My own belief is that a carefully tailored proposal would take into account the current costs of educating the individual children in the public schools system and provide a percentage of the dollars that would be spent in public schools.

The State of Florida has a complicated formula it calls the Florida Education Finance Program (FEFP). It recognizes differences in the costs of educating students based on their grade level, learning disability, handicaps, and many other intricate factors. Florida also takes into account the difference in the cost of living between small rural counties that are relatively inexpensive and the more expensive urban centers.

I recommend that you review your state's funding formula, and propose a percentage (perhaps 50 percent) of what is being spent on similar children in the public school system. I believe this is equitable, and it also permits you to deflate some of the favorite arguments of the "educrats" who will attack school choice proposals.

For instance, I may not be able to assure that private schools will fill the market to meet particular niches such as education for blind or disabled students. I can, however, provide market incentives for them to do so. Poor and minority students are more likely to be labeled as "at-risk." They generally cost our public schools more to educate. Choice opponents will charge that private schools will wish to select only the cream of the crop, and ignore minorities and difficult to educate children. If, however, a "normal" child entitles a private school to a $2,500 scholarship, and an "at-risk" child entitles it to $3,500, there are market incentives for schools to cater to specific needs across the spectrum. If your choice opponents argue that the funding mechanism is unfair, then their quarrel is with the state's funding formula, not with your choice proposal.

Subsidizing Existing Private Students

Obviously a program of any nature whatsoever can be attacked if it requires additional state funding. If, for instance, you devise a formula that provides that as student A moves from a public school to a private school, we will spend only 50 percent of what we would have spent in the public schools, there are demonstrable savings. There may be costs associated with administering choice systems and related expenses, but they should be significantly less than the 50 percent savings engendered by the selection of a private school or a public school.

However, in the United States today approximately 10 to 15 percent of K–12 children are already in private schools. In the initial years of a choice system, before market forces have permitted the private sector to develop the supply to meet the new demand for private education, only a small percentage of public school students may actually transfer to private schools because of space limitations. To the extent that the existing private school children who heretofore have not received scholarships are funded through the system, there could be substantial start-up costs.

Assuming your state is not in a position to fund such an expensive program in today's recessionary environment, I have a suggestion. I believe that the goal of a school choice program, in general, is to spur competition that will result in an increased supply of unique and exciting private and public experiments in education, and ultimately improve the public school system. If I thought school choice would merely subsidize existing private schools, I would not be terribly excited about it. Some have made equitable arguments that parents of private school students pay taxes and yet receive no educational benefits. This is true, but my real interest is to improve education for all students, and provide choices and opportunities for parents at all socioeconomic levels.

The key is to create a demand by providing economic power to people who have not had it before. When that demand is created, the marketplace will provide suppliers to meet the demand. I believe that the desired results can be obtained by phasing in scholarship amounts for most students. For instance, in year one of the program a student may be eligible to take only 10 percent of the state's base allocation for that student to a private school. In years two through five, that amount could be increased by 10 percent a year, until 50 percent of the funds that were being expended in the public school system make up the scholarship amount. This significantly decreases the start-up costs, and there are no long-term adverse effects on the desired results, which are to spur creation of new schools through market demands. In my bill, I have created an exception for "at-risk" students (generally poor and disproportionately minority). I would give these children the full value of the scholarship *immediately*. Few of them are in private schools, and very few are having their needs met adequately by the existing public school system. Not only is this equitable, but it provides wonderful arguments to refute the charge that choice is designed to create an "elite" system. [8]

Requirements for Participating Private Schools

A key hot-button question for both opponents and supporters of choice is, What if any additional regulations will be imposed upon the private schools that decide to participate and accept scholarships? Public school defenders argue that private schools should have to meet the same cumbersome regulatory and statutory requirements that have been imposed over the years on the public school system. This completely defeats the ultimate purpose behind introducing market forces into the government monopoly system of public schooling in America.

I am convinced that the only way to assist public schools in shedding the enormous bureaucracy that former U.S. Secretary of Education William Bennett refers to as "the blob," and the mandates, rules, regulations, and requirements that have done more to impede the flexibility of professional teachers than anything else, is to inject market competition into the system. If one accepts that general premise, then the idea is to refuse to permit any significant additional governmental requirements on participating private schools. Ultimately, public schools will be forced to reallocate resources to the classroom and away from the growing bureaucracy in order to compete, and all schools will have market incentives to constantly improve, as opposed to the existing bureaucratic monopoly wherein preservation of the status quo is the primary goal.

Additionally, private schools that are interested in choice will be very concerned about this issue. They are jealous of the discretion they have to meet the needs of parents and schoolchildren and are very cognizant of the devastating effects additional government rules, regulations, and bureaucracy have had on the public schools. A bill should be crafted to provide a certain *minimum* level of requirements, and *prohibit* any additional government requirements.

For instance, we have already addressed the question of admissions policy and discrimination. In general, I was surprised at how few problems most private schools had with these provisions. Most now are prohibited from discriminating based on race, creed, or national origin, and the shocking statistic is that parochial schools in the Northeast are more likely to be integrated along racial and ethnic lines than their public school counterparts (Coleman 1987, 148). Moreover, private school administrators are thrilled to point out their successes with children public schools had long since written off.

However, when you begin to discuss curriculum matters (sex education, textbook selection, multicultural education, the theory of evolution versus creation, etc.), you infringe upon the academic freedom that virtually every private school is so proud to possess. The dilemma as to what additional requirements if any, the private schools should be forced to meet is probably the most difficult and troubling as we breach the gap from the theory of introducing market forces into education and the reality of doing so.

I proposed in my bill that private schools would be required *only* to file a report with certain information (no inspections, no state policing, no bureaucracy, no regulators). The idea is that true and effective accountability in any system runs to clients (parents) and not through a cumbersome bureaucracy dominated by special interests (Chubb and Moe 1990).

Such a report from participating private schools would include the following:

1. Teacher credentials (I do *not* require teacher certification that has prohibited many talented and able individuals from participating in teaching)
2. Record of the incidence of crime and drug abuse
3. A basic curriculum including history, geography, English, math, and science is taught
4. The program of instruction
5. Student achievement data

Transportation

A key element with respect to the logistics of implementing choice and the cost thereof, is the question of providing transportation. Will students who desire a public school other than the one to which they are normally assigned receive free transportation to the desired school? Will students attending private schools be provided with public school transportation? In an ideal world, each student should be provided with transportation to the school that his or her parent has selected as the optimal school for meeting that student's needs. This is not a practical solution in most situations. If no transportation is provided, choice opponents argue that upper-class suburbanites will have parents with vans or station wagons to provide transportation to their choice of schools, whereas inner-city, poor students will once again be confined to the poorest schools.[9]

The State of Minnesota has enacted both an inter- and intra-district public school choice plan, where students are provided with transportation within the district or to the district lines. Since the system is relatively new, there is little reported evidence about the effectiveness of the transportation program.

Once again the choice of this author is to opt for market forces. The higher scholarships available to "at-risk" and poorer students provide opportunity and incentives for private schools to locate near large populations of those students, generally in the inner city. Alternatively, private schools could provide transportation from targeted neighborhoods, and this would be paid for within the price of the scholarship.

Obviously there are a great deal of alternatives between the one extreme of transporting any child to wherever he or she decides to attend, and not providing any transportation whatsoever. The transportation question is another significant question in drafting a bill designed to work as well in reality as it does in theory.

Information Center

Meaningful choice for parents means informed choice. A review of the marvelous success of the East Harlem School District choice experiment demonstrates that poor, single parent families *can* make great choices, even if limited to just public schools (Hood 1989). Information is critical. A method for dissemination of information about individual schools is vital to meaningful choice. Typically, college selection is based on a vast array of information about the school's size, curriculum, cost, faculty, student body, discipline policy, location, etc. Why should poor parents not be enabled to select a K–12 school that meets their child's needs with the same freedom wealthy parents do? To do so, a choice system must facilitate the flow of meaningful information about schools in the choice system.

PASSING YOUR CHOICE LEGISLATION OR
REFERENDUM

Almost two decades ago, Nobel prize winning laureate Milton Friedman, standing outside the front door of a small one-room schoolhouse, discussed the inevitable failures that result when government controlled monopolies attempt to provide services or goods. Both efficiency and quality suffer. He argued that this was true in education as with other services, and he predicted the continuing decline (this was about 1975) in student achievement and the increase in costs. He discussed bureaucratic versus parental control of decisions that affect children, and argued (persuasively, I thought) that essentially, education was too critical "to be left to the government." During my campaign for state representative in 1990, when asked what my single top priority was, I routinely answered "giving parents more choice in terms of where and what their children learned." I recall specifically discussing choice in front of the teachers' union lobbyists, who, at the time, seemed to believe that the idea had so little chance of becoming policy in the political environment they controlled, that it was not worth debating with me. At the time, they certainly showed no evidence of thinking my proposals would get any serious discussion by the politicians they had, in many cases, helped to place in office.

Shortly after my first election, I was asked by our local newspaper, *The Orlando Sentinel*, to write a New Year's column indicating what my priority concern would be. I wrote a column in the editorial page decrying the sad state of education in the United States and in Florida, and indicating that I would fight for school choice and competition. For the most part the media and policy makers initially ignored the proposals. Increasingly, constituents and citizens throughout Central Florida began contacting my legislative office urging support. Along with a few energetic friends, I began reviewing policy works by groups like the Manhattan Institute, The Heritage Foundation, The Heartland Institute, the Cato Institute, and others, and we designed an educational choice program for Florida which I filed as my first bill in the Florida House of Representatives.

In the following year, some remarkable things happened. A black state representative from the city of Milwaukee, Wisconsin, mother of two, and former welfare recipient teamed up with Republican Governor Tommy Thompson to initiate a private school choice plan for inner-city minorities. Professors Terry Moe and John Chubb wrote a book for The Brookings Institution that decimated the education establishment in explaining why students achieve and why some schools are effective in educating students. Minority columnists like William Raspberry openly called for choice experiments, especially among public schools (but even including private schools).

The issue was no longer an issue controlled by free market economists and conservative Republican politicians.

The President of the United States, along with Secretary Lamar Alexander and the former secretary of education, Bill Bennett, essentially began arguing that choice was imperative to improving the plight of schools in America. Jeb Bush, son of the former president (also the former secretary of commerce for the state of Florida), agreed to lead a group of citizens in Florida in pushing for choice legislation or a referendum. A Florida free market oriented think tank, The James Madison Institute, published some marvelous papers by Florida State University Professor James Gwartney urging the adoption of school choice in Florida (Gwartney 1991 & 1992). The James Madison Institute, with help from Jeb Bush; Stanley Marshall, the former Florida State University president, and others, formed a statewide organization called Floridians for Educational Choice. The American Legislative Exchange Council (A.L.E.C.), a group of almost 3,000 state legislators interested in public policy matters, began advocating choice as the necessary first step in reforming American education.

In the meantime, back in the legislature, I began as one of forty-six Republicans in a 120-member Democrat controlled House. My choice legislation was D.O.A. I had been fortunate to be assigned to the public schools committee. (It's an appropriate name since we deal very little with the needs and achievement of students. The majority of the committee seem very concerned about protecting a growing class of state employees: making sure they are comfortable, happy, and free from ANY competition. Declining student achievement in Florida and the highest dropout rate in the country is not something most committee members enjoy discussing.)

Along with a few other "mavericks" I routinely distributed copies of reports concerning skyrocketing school costs, the number of administrators, the number of statutes and rules, the effect of mandates on teachers and schools, dropout rates, and student achievement. When I first began discussing the need for "choice" on the public schools committee, some of the members reacted as though I were speaking in a foreign language.

Slowly, but surely, some of the more open-minded members acknowledged that we did have serious problems in education. They acknowledged that we were spending ever increasing sums of money, and that standardized test scores were declining. Most members continued to believe that the way to rectify these problems was by issuing new mandates, passing new rules, new regulations, and new statutes to "force" teachers and schools to do better through bureaucratic control of the school establishment.[10] Of course more money was the *sine qua non* of school improvement. No amount of charts, graphs, or statistics showing costs spiraling, with test scores declining, would jar some of the legislators (let alone the education lobbyists) from insisting that money was primarily the answer.

It would be too cumbersome to describe choice efforts in Florida for the past year and a half, since we have waged battle after battle with increasing success. Based on my experience and observing the maneuvering between choice proponents and choice opponents, I have some suggestions for policy makers who are considering advocating choice.

Think Tanks and Research Organizations

By now almost every major think tank in the country has visited the issue of school reform, and almost universally the answer among these groups (other than those controlled by the education establishment) has been a move toward significantly greater school choice. At the national level, The Brookings Institution, The Heritage Foundation, the Cato Institute, and many others across the political spectrum have become full-fledged supporters of school choice.[11] In individual regions and states, think tanks have tailored choice proposals to the unique and specific needs of their states. The James Madison Institute in Florida has been instrumental in providing research and data that consistently keeps the Florida education establishment on the defensive. The Manhattan Institute in New York, The Heartland Institute in Chicago, and other organizations located in your state or region can be of invaluable and immediate service to you, not only in providing intellectual and research support, but also in assisting you to network with other individuals in your state. I strongly suggest that before you definitively set out any particular choice proposal, some of these organizations be contacted.

The American Legislative Exchange Council has created an education task force which does an outstanding job of staying on top of developments in school choice on a state-by-state basis.[12] The U.S. Department of Education has established a "Center For Choice" which also can be instrumental in "networking."[13]

Minority Leaders and Organizations

Most people are surprised to learn that support for school choice is even greater in the minority community than it is among Caucasians. A 1990 Gallup poll on education found support for public school choice among 72 percent of minorities and 62 percent of the general population (Gallup poll, June 1990). Vouchers for private schools are supported by 50 percent of Americans, but over 57 percent by Blacks and Hispanics (Gallup/Phi Delta Kappa [PDK] poll 1991). While most mainstream minority leaders have ties to the education establishment that discourage them from supporting choice, columnists like William Raspberry[14] and Clarence Page have presented fair commentary on the potential benefits of choice to minorities. State Representative Polly Williams has championed choice as an alternative to failing inner-city public schools (Innerst

1990). In my state, a bright and independent minded black freshman, Representative Darryl Reaves, has evolved to the position that choice experiments should be undertaken to empower parents of poor children.

In addressing concerns of minorities, you should be careful to point out that resegregation of the school system is neither the intent nor the effect of choice proposals. In areas where school desegregation orders are in effect, choice can be limited to assure that student ratios are not undermined. Increasingly, as State Representative Polly Williams puts it, minorities are more concerned with "education, not integration."

In Florida, the Hispanic community has been especially supportive of choice. Representative Carlos Valdes of Miami, who represents a Hispanic community, is my prime co-sponsor of comprehensive choice legislation. There seem to be a number of reasons that much of the Florida Hispanic community supports choice. Ties to the Catholic church, the debate within the Hispanic community as to whether Hispanic children should be taught primarily in their native language until a certain age or immediately taught in English, and most of all, Cuban experience with government control of societal functions at the expense of individual freedom, all combine to provide ample reasons for Hispanic citizens to support choice.

Minority communities often (despite their leadership) are naturally fertile grounds for school choice support. Real life has forced them to look at alternatives to the existing system.

Civic Organizations

Activists and community leaders have been extremely fortunate in Florida to have an organization, by the name of The Floridians for Educational Choice, which is led by Jeb Bush and Tommy Bronson, a prominent Democratic businessman. The F.E.C. works closely with The James Madison Institute and other research groups to coordinate the dissemination of research and information vital to the public. It has begun to develop county-by-county organizations to push for school choice in Florida. It makes the intellectual and economic case for choice and does so effectively since it is non-secular and has no "ulterior motives" beyond improving educational opportunity for all Florida's children. Encourage formation of such an organization in your state by working with think tanks, business and civic leaders, and supportive politicians.

Religious Groups and Sectarian Schools

Massive political grass roots support can be established once private religious schools and religious institutions provide their endorsement. These organizations should be carefully consulted with respect to their concerns about choice legislation. Catholic schools have a tradition in the northeastern United States of cooperating with the public school system and accepting public funds for certain functions. They tend to be comfortable, supportive, and open toward choice proposals.

Some conservative Protestant organizations often are reluctant to endorse choice proposals. This is primarily due to their fear of "strings" being attached to public dollars. Any choice proposal should permit private schools to "opt-out" of the system, and should include prohibitions against unwarranted government intrusion into those schools that do participate. Even the most conservative religious leaders are sympathetic to the tragic plight of our public school system, and recognize the need for more parental control and choice in all schools for moral as well as academic reasons (Coons 1992). Some fears may only be overcome after choice legislation is enacted and analyzed carefully by religious educators. Even the most cautious religious educators can be persuaded that choice proposals can have important positive effects on the rest of society, so long as their schools are not forced to participate.

Non-Sectarian Private Schools

Increasingly, private schools are developing that do not have affiliations with any specific religious organizations. Whittle Communications, Inc., has induced former Yale University president, Benno Schmidt, to lead its effort to establish 1,000 for-profit schools by the year 2010 in the United States. Educational Alternatives, Inc., is a private company that works with public schools to "privatize" individual curriculum needs or even fund individual schools for school districts. You should be certain to contact the representatives of all facets of private education, including non-sectarian, Jewish, parochial, other Christian and non-Christian religious schools, *before* you draft your final proposal. Their input can be crucial in securing support for your proposal.

Business Organizations

The U.S. Chamber of Commerce has been increasingly supportive of public/private choice alternatives.[15] A 1989 poll sponsored by the Allstate Insurance Company found that business executives gave American public education a "C–" (Foltz 1990). Organizations such as The Heritage Foundation have increasingly provided businesses with arguments to demonstrate that genuine reform and education cannot take place without competition and choice.[16]

While few business organizations need to be convinced that the American school system is in difficult straits, not all are excited about taking on the powerful education establishment. There is some significant reluctance to enter the fray with both feet, apparently for the same reason that most politicians shrink from the choice fight: fear of retribution from teachers' unions and the education establishment. Business representatives will almost uniformly attack the failing system privately but are often frightened to "offend" the people in control of the system. While individual businessmen and women will become key supporters of your efforts, many business organizations may need to be consistently prodded before they will lend support. Appearances from articulate choice supporters like Bill Bennett, Jeb Bush, Professor Terry Moe, and others may be the best approach to building support (and backbone) for choice among business organizations.

Teachers Unions

The Wall Street Journal has alleged that teacher "unionization has provided teachers with perverse incentives to put their paychecks ahead of education." (*The Wall Street Journal*, December 9 1991). Indeed, the president of the American Federation of Teachers, Albert Shanker, has acknowledged that "when school children start paying union dues, I'll represent their interests." Shanker's union has generally been more forthright and progressive in supporting school reform than the other major national union, The National Education Association (Gwartney, Marshall, Sobel 1992, *Backgrounder*, No. 6).

Union leaders should not be confused with their entire membership. Large numbers of teachers disagree with many of the more radical positions of the union leadership, and in many areas large numbers of teachers are not even members of the union, generally for philosophical reasons. I believe as the union leadership continues on a more radical bent, this trend will grow.

As a child of two outstanding public school teachers, I can assure you that not all teachers are afraid of competition, or proposals like merit pay (which the union vehemently opposes). Most teachers do not put their interest above those of the students. My office gets calls almost daily from teachers supportive of my efforts for education reforms. Even the union leadership will acknowledge that the mandates and bureaucracy have handcuffed their members. Teachers should be convinced that true professionals are not controlled by bureaucratic or regulatory mandates from government organizations, or are even unionized. Models like the Medical Association, the Bar Association, or Certified Public Accountants are the professional models of organization that teachers should strive for. Those models combine a great deal of market competition, but also the professional responsibility and the freedom from administrative micromanagement that teachers need. Financial and professional rewards for quality teachers will be inevitable in a choice-based system where accountability runs to clients (as does accountability for lawyers, doctors, and accountants), not to government administrators and politicians.

Finally, teachers who can be persuaded to review actual choice programs, such as the one in East Harlem, will understand that choice and flexibility for parents and students also provide choice and flexibility for teachers. To the extent that choice plans can encourage major corporations like I.B.M., Exxon, Xerox, and others to establish their own competitive private schools, competition for selection of the best, brightest, and most energetic teachers should dramatically increase financial incentives and other rewards for the better teachers in the system.

Notwithstanding the fact that many individual teachers may be somewhat or even altogether supportive of properly crafted choice proposals, expect aggressive opposition from teachers' unions to any real choice proposals. When Oregonians for Educational Choice placed a school choice plan on the Oregon ballot, teachers' unions expended millions of dollars to defeat the proposal by running TV adds that showed "Nazi teachers" indoctrinating students. In the California referendum movement scheduled for this fall, choice proponents report that unions organize "rings" around petition gatherers to prohibit free discussions with citizens to solicit their signatures. The union spent millions fighting this proposal. Since teachers' unions represent not only "teachers," but in many cases, bus drivers, maintenance personnel, curriculum advisors, and many employees in the education establishment, union leadership has every incentive to protect the government monopoly in education regardless of its failures. Bigger (and more expensive) really is better for union leaders.

Finally, the biggest threat to the union leadership from school choice can be illustrated by the fate of one famous teacher in East Los Angeles. In his book *The Devaluing of America: The Fight for Our Culture and Our Children*, former U.S. Education Secretary Bill Bennett documents the story of Jaime Escalante, the teacher who was made famous in the movie *Stand and Deliver*. Escalante was so successful in teaching poor kids from the Mexican-American barrio of East Los Angeles, that about 25 percent of all Mexican-American students in the entire country who passed the advanced placement calculus exams one year came from the high school at which he taught.

Escalante refused to accept his students socioeconomic status, their language difficulties, or class sizes that reached seventy students as excuses for failure. His success removed excuses from other school board members and teachers for failure. As a result, according to Bennett, "union representatives helped organize a vote by the teachers that ejected [Escalante] as Garfield's mathematics department chairman in 1990" (Bennett 1992).

Like Escalante, choice threatens to remove excuses for failure from the existing school system. Therefore, those who control the system are terribly afraid of even the most minor choice experiments for the poorest children in the poorest schools. If you don't believe that self-interest is the reason "educrats" oppose choice, try a pilot program for 300 of the poorest children in the worst schools of a 300,000 student city system. I did—it failed narrowly thanks to union opposition and threats toward politicians.

Parent Organizations

Leaders in the PTA often have a very comfortable relationship with principals, administrators, and union representatives. While PTA leaders are sometimes hesitant to challenge their friends in the system, individual parents who may be disgruntled, for a wide array of reasons, with the existing system, will provide a marvelous source of grass roots support and manpower for choice initiatives. They can help write letters to the editor, challenge waste in the existing system, and speak with neighbors and friends about the need for reform of the existing school system. Efforts can be made to bring school choice spokesmen to meet with groups of parents to talk about the merits of choice and the opportunities for not only providing the choice of public/private schools, but improving the existing public school system in response to the competition. When faced with the ultimate question,"Why shouldn't families decide what school is best for their child?" parents support choice. PTA "leaders," however, are comfortable with the relationship they have cultivated with the establishment.

CONCLUSION

In summary, the better your specific proposal is designed, the less ammunition you give the opponents of school choice, and the better you are able to sell this exciting new idea. If your plan provides market incentives for private schools to meet the requirements of special needs children, including blind and physically handicapped children, you have anticipated an argument.

If you provide relatively greater sums for "at-risk" or inner-city children, you dispel the notion that you are trying to create an "elite" private school system. If you phase in the costs of the programs of the mainstream students, you cushion the initial start-up cost of school choice. Finally, crafting your proposal to make certain that your natural allies (parochial schools, business leaders, parents, and inner-city minorities) support the specifics of the plan, has insured the overwhelming grass roots support that you will need to overcome the entrenched government bureaucracy that has failed to meet the needs of so many of our American school children in the past generation.

As *Time* magazine pointed out:

No social experiment is more worthy than for an entire state—with significant minority population—to embark on a true test of unrestricted CHOICE, complete with the participation of private, parochial and for-profit schools. The risks are grave, but so are the consequences of continued educational mediocrity (*Time*, Sept. 16 1991).

Only a true statewide test of choice can provide an answer to the question of whether choice is really the answer to our education dilemma in America today.

NOTES

1. The recent U.S. Supreme Court opinion prohibiting prayer at high school graduations surprised court observers and may be problematic, but the majority opinion keyed in on the "coercive" aspects that attended a situation where only one graduation exercise takes place, and individuals who desired to attend were "forced" to join in the prayer or at least stand in silence during the prayer. See *Lee vs. Weisman*, 60 L.W. 4723 (U.S. 1992). Such coercion would not accompany situations where parents chose sectarian or non-sectarian schools.

2. *Lemon vs. Kurtzman*, 403 U.S. 602, 612–613 (1971).

3. Ibid.

4. *Nohrr vs. Brevard County*, 247 SO 2d 304 (Florida 1971).

5. For instance, at South Point Middle School in Miami, Florida, the school board has hired the services of a private corporation known as Educational Alternatives, Inc., to run the school as an experiment.

6. University of Wisconsin 1991.

7. 1992 Pennsylvania Legislative Session. In the 1992 Pennsylvania legislative session, the House of Representatives successfully passed the choice initiative. However, the two-week time delay before the state Senate took up the measure gave plenty of time to the choice opponents to garner enough votes in the Senate to kill the choice initiative.

8. This is a charge that I consider patently ridiculous since only the wealthy now are able to exercise such choices, and only the elite are guaranteed the opportunity for educational excellence.

9. Actually this argument merely reflects the reality of the existing public school system, where most well-off families procure satisfactory education, and poorer families cannot.

10. The Soviet Union took a similar approach to improving its agricultural output from 1917. Socialist failures in that particular sector of their economy were written off, annually, as unusually bad weather conditions.

11. American Enterprise Institute, The Brookings Institution, American Enterprise Institute, The Heritage Foundation, The Heartland Institute, The James Madison Institute, Cato Institute, Adam Smith Institute, American Legislative Exchange Council, Manhattan Institute for Policy Research, Sequoia Institute, Urban Institute.

12. The American Legislative Exchange Council's president is Sam Brunelli, and its Educational Task Force Director is Patty Farnan. (202)547–4646.

13. U.S. Department of Education's "Center for Choice." (202) 401–1307 or "choice hotline" at 1–800–442–PICK.

14. See Raspberry 1991, in references.

15. See Center for Workplace Preparation and Quality Education 1991, in references.

16. Heritage, December 21 1990. The Heritage Foundation address is 214 Massachusetts Avenue, N.E., Washington, D.C. 22200–4999. It has done a number of *Backgrounder* newsletters, emphasizing important developments and notorious arguments in favor of choice.

REFERENCES

Allen, Jeanne, and Michael J. McLaughlin. (1990) "A Businessman's Guide to the Education Reform Debate," The Heritage Foundation, *Backgrounder*, No. 801, December.

Ball, G. Carl, Jerry Hume, Sam H. Ingram, David T. Kearns, Tom Peters, Donald J. Roberts, and Thomas F. Roeser. (1990) "In Search of Educational Excellence," *Policy Review*, Fall, p. 54.

Bennett, William. (1992) *The Devaluing of America: The Fight for Our Culture and Our Children*. New York: Summit Books.

Boaz, David. (1991) *Liberating Schools—Education in the Inner City*. Washington, D.C.: Cato Institute.

Bolick, Clint. (1991) "Choice in Education: Part II, Legal Perils and Legal Opportunities," The Heritage Foundation, *Backgrounder*, No. 809, February.

Bracey, Gerald. (1991) "Why Can't They Be Like We Were," *Phi Delta Kappa Magazine*, October, pp. 104–117.

Center for Workforce Preparation and Quality Education. (1991) "The Business Stake in Educational Choice," *Occasional Paper No.1*, Washington, D.C.: U.S. Chamber of Commerce, February.

Chubb, John E. (1992) *School Reform and the Need for School Choice*. Washington, D.C.: The Brookings Institution.

Chubb, John E., and Terry Moe. (1990) *Politics, Markets, and America's Schools*. Washington, D.C.: The Brookings Institution.

Coleman, James S. (1990) "Do Students Learn More in Private Schools Than in Public Schools?" The James Madison Institute for Public Policy Studies, *The Madison Papers*, No. 4, p. 148.

Coleman, James. (1987) *Public and Private Schools*. New York: Basic Books.

Coons, John E. (1992) "School Choice as Simple Justice," *First Things*, April, p. 15.

Foltz, Rose G. (1990) "Big Business Is Backing You," *Learning*, February, p. 65.

Flanigan, Peter M. (1991) "A School System That Works," *The Wall Street Journal*. February 12.

Friedman, Milton. (1962) *Capitalism and Freedom*. Chicago: University of Chicago Press.

Friedman, Milton, and Rose Friedman. (1980) *Free to Choose*. New York: London, Martin, Secker and Warborg.

Gwartney, James D. (1990) "A Positive Program to Improve Florida's Schools," The James Madison Institute for Public Policy Studies, *Backgrounder*, No. 2.

Gwartney, James D., J. Stanley Marshall, and Russell S. Sobel. (1992) "Comparing Spending and Performance in Florida's Public Schools and Colleges," *Backgrounder*, No. 6.

The Heritage Foundation. (1992), "Business/Education," *Insider*, #20, May.

Hood, John M. (1989) "Schools Compete, Parents Choose, Students Thrive . . . As Harlem Goes So Goes the Nation?" *Reason*, May.

Innerst, Carol. (1990) "Minorities Overwhelmingly Favor Public School Choice," *The Washington Times*, August 24, p. A3.

Lieberman, Myron. (1989) *Privatization and Educational Choice. New York: St. Martin's Press*.

Myers, William, and Michael Schwartz. (1990) "School Reform—Minnesota's Educational Choice Program Earns High Marks," *Beaumont, TX ENTERPRISE*, October 29, p. 5B.

National Commission on Excellence in Education. (1983) A *Nation at Risk: The Imperative for Educational Reform*. Washington, D.C.: U.S. Government Printing Office.

Niskanen, William A.(1991) "The Performance of America's Primary and Secondary Schools," *Liberating Schools*. Washington, D.C.: Cato Institute.

Raspberry, William. (1991) "Give School Choice a Chance, Starting with the Public Schools," *The Orlando Sentinel*, January 4, p. A10.

Schlager, Kenneth J., and Hector S. MacDonald (1989) "An Entrepreneurial Approach to Science Education," *A Heartland Policy Study*. Chicago: The Heartland Institute, August 16.

Shapiro, Walter. (1991) "Tough Choice," *Time*, September 16, p. 54.

Singal, Daniel J. (1992) "The Other Crisis in American Education," *The Atlantic Monthly*, November, p. 59.

University of Wisconsin. (1991) "The Milwaukee Parental Choice Program," *Madison Study*, November 27.

U.S. Department of Education, Center for Educational Statistics. (1987) *The Condition of Education: A Statistical Report*. Washington, D.C.: U.S. Government Printing Office.

———. (1991a) "Restoring Parent Power in America's Schools," *The Education Voucher and Tuition Tax Credit Book*. Chicago: The Heartland Institute.

———. (1991b) "Unions vs. Education," *The Wall Street Journal*, Editorial Board, December 9.

———. (1992a) Center for Choice in Education, *Public Opinion on Choice in Education*. Washington, D.C.: U.S. Government Printing Office, March 18.

———. (1992b) "Choice in Education—Legal Perils and Legal Opportunities," *Backgrounder*, Part II. Washington, D.C.: The Heritage Foundation.

Uzzell, Lawrence A. (1989) "Education Reform Fails the Test," *The Wall Street Journal*, May 10.

4

Private School Choice: An Ineffective Path to Educational Reform

Albert Shanker and Bella Rosenberg

The most widely touted reform for American education these days is so-called private school choice which would allow public dollars to follow students to private and parochial schools. Private school choice was at the heart of the Bush administration's education agenda, and it was the only education program on which Mr. Bush campaigned during the 1992 presidential election. It has been the subject of an increasing number of education hearings, bills, and referendum initiatives in an increasing number of states. It has even been considered at the local level. In Milwaukee, Wisconsin, private school choice exists in the form of a state-initiated "experiment" that allows a small percentage of the district's low-income students to use state education dollars at non-sectarian private schools that have agreed to participate in the program.

This is not the first time that the public has been asked to subsidize the tuition costs of families who choose, and whose children are chosen by, private schools, nor is Milwaukee the only place in the nation where public dollars support students in private schools. In fact, private and parochial schools get a considerable amount of public assistance for large-ticket items like student transportation and Chapter 1. What distinguishes this movement for public aid to private education from all others is that this one is being marketed almost exclusively on the basis of education reform and improvement—indeed, as *the* education reform that would make any others unnecessary.[1]

The argument is as follows. Students in private schools achieve at much higher levels than do public school students. Private schools, particularly Catholic schools, accept students just like the ones attending public schools and do a far better job of educating them. This should be no surprise. Private schools

don't have bureaucracies, teacher unions, tenure, desegregation orders, affirm-
ative action, or due process in student expulsion cases to contend with; they are
subject only to the discipline of the market. Therefore, in order to overcome the
crisis in education and for the sake of fairness, we should allow all parents, and
especially poor parents, to use public funds to send their children to private
schools.

Are the claims of private school choice supporters solid? Do private and
parochial schools really work with the same children and get far better results?
According to the 1990 National Assessment of Educational Progress math
examinations, the answer is *no* on all counts (National Assessment of Educational Progress [NAEP] 1992).

NAEP's national study of math achievement, which covered fourth-, eighth-,
and twelfth-graders, contained private school data and thus allows us to
compare public and private school performance to an extent never before
possible. The results indicate that there is virtually no difference in the performance of public and parochial and other private schools; students in *all* our
schools are achieving at disastrously low levels. Hence, under so-called private
school choice, if half or even all of our public school students were to choose
and be chosen by private schools tomorrow, we'd still be a nation at risk.

What, specifically, do the 1990 NAEP math results tell us about public and
private school performance? The most logical place to start is with the twelfth
grade, where we can make some judgments about the value added by a public
or private school education. The first thing to notice is that there is only a six-
or seven-point variation in average scores among seniors in public, Catholic,
and other private schools. That's not much of a difference, and it is certainly
not evidence of the superiority of private over public education.

It is true that a little over half of seniors in private schools achieve at the 300
level, which means they can handle content that NAEP says is typically
introduced by the seventh grade: decimals, fractions, percents, elementary
geometry, and simple algebra. This is a few percentage points better than the
public school figure, but, again, it hardly proves the excellence of private school
education. The real point is that both school sectors performed miserably.
Approximately half of our graduating seniors, from both public and private
schools, cannot do the kind of math they should have mastered before they even
entered high school.

For still worse news, let's look at the proportion of graduating seniors who
achieved at or above level 350, which NAEP terms an indicator of readiness to
handle college-level math. It is 5 percent in the public schools and 4 percent in
both the Catholic and other private schools. Five percent is nothing to cheer
about, but 4 percent is even worse. It is of course plausible that this public school
figure is higher than the private school figure only because public schools have
a higher dropout rate; more of the kids who would score poorly are gone. If one
adjusts for that, the result is that 4 percent of students graduating from public

school are prepared to do college math—the same number as the students graduating from Catholic and other private schools (see Table 4.1).

The terrible results are even more shocking when you compare them with the achievement of students in our competitor nations, where 20 to 30 percent of students meet standards that are at least as high as NAEP's 350 level in order to get into college. Given those standards, 95 percent of our public *and* private high school graduates would not be admitted to college anywhere else in the industrialized world.

"Okay, so there's not much difference between the performance of public and private schools in the twelfth grade, and their students are in a dead heat at NAEP's highest level," private school choice supporters might say. "But look

Table 4.1
Average Proficiency and Percentage of Students at or above Four Anchor Levels on the NAEP Mathematics Scale by Type of School

	Percent of Students	Average Proficiency	Percentage of Students at or Above			
			Level 200	Level 250	Level 300	Level 350
GRADE 4						
Public Schools	88 (1.2)	214 (0.9)	70 (1.3)	10 (0.8)	0 (0.0)	0 (0.0)
Catholic Schools	8 (1.1)	224 (2.0)	83 (2.6)	16 (2.2)	0 (0.0)	0 (0.0)
Other Private Schools	4 (0.8)	231 (2.8)	89 (3.8)	22 (3.4)	0 (0.0)	0 (0.0)
GRADE 8						
Public Schools	89 (1.3)	264 (1.2)	97 (0.5)	66 (1.3)	13 (1.3)	0 (0.1)
Catholic Schools	7 (1.1)	278 (2.6)	100 (0.2)	84 (2.6)	22 (3.4)	0 (0.2)
Other Private Schools	4 (0.7)	274 (2.4)	100 (0.5)	80 (3.8)	18 (2.9)	0 (0.0)
GRADE 12						
Public Schools	90 (1.3)	295 (1.1)	100 (0.1)	90 (0.7)	45 (1.4)	5 (0.6)
Catholic Schools	6 (1.1)	302 (3.0)	100 (0.0)	96 (1.2)	54 (4.5)	4 (1.0)
Other Private Schools	4 (0.8)	301 (3.1)	100 (0.0)	97 (1.1)	51 (4.8)	4 (1.8)

The standard errors of the estimated percentages and proficiencies appear in parentheses. It can be said with 95 percent certainty that for each population of interest, the value for the whole population is within plus or minus two standard errors of the estimate for the sample. When the proportion of students is 0 percent, the standard error is inestimable. Although percentages less than 0.5 percent are rounded to 0 percent, a few eighth-grade public school students (0.2 percent) and Catholic school students (0.1 percent) reached Level 350.

DESCRIPTION OF NAEP LEVELS:

Level 200: Simple additive reasoning and problem solving with whole numbers; content typically covered by 3rd grade.

Level 250: Simple multiplicative reasoning and two-step problem solving; content typically covered by 5th grade.

Level 300: Reasoning and problem solving involving fractions, decimals, percents, elementary geometry, and simple algebra; content introduced by 7th grade.

Level 350: Reasoning and problem solving involving geometry, algebra, and beginning statistics and probability; content generally covered in high school math courses in preparation for the study of advanced math.

Source: The State of Mathematics Achievement: NAEP's 1990 Assessment of the Nation and the Trial Assessment of the States. Washington, D.C.: U.S. Department of Education, National Center for Education Statistics, June 1991. Table 2.6 and Executive Summary, pp. 6–7.

at the fourth- and eighth-grade average scores. There's a spread of ten to seventeen points there and a clear case of private school superiority."

Let's say, then, that it makes more sense to concentrate on results one-third or two-thirds of the way on the education process instead of on the end results. From this perspective, the NAEP results tell us that the longer students stay in private schools, the worse they do, and the longer students stay in public schools, the better they do. Rather than constituting proof of private school superiority, this seems more like evidence that public schools add more value to their students than do private schools.

The small differences between public and private school performance in all the grades become more shocking when one looks at how different public school students are from the youngsters who attend Catholic and other private schools. Contrary to what private school choice supporters claim, especially about Catholic schools, the students public and private schools educate are not alike. In fact, given the dramatic differences in their socioeconomic status and in the courses they take, to name just two factors, what's surprising is that private school students didn't leave public school students behind in the dust.

The basic difference is that private schools can and do select their students and turn away applicants who do not meet their standards. For example, 71 percent of Catholic high schools require an entrance exam, as do 43 percent of other religious schools and 66 percent of independent schools. Moreover, 71 percent of Catholic high schools cite student discipline as their chief admissions criterion, and 80 percent require that entering students have successfully completed their previous year of school (National Center for Education Statistics 1987). In other words, these schools are not obliged to take all comers, as public schools must, and they are free to get rid of students who do not work out, who generally end up in the public schools.

In the sample of students tested by NAEP, about 50 percent more private school youngsters than public school youngsters have parents who were college graduates. For the nation as a whole, the difference between public and private school students in level of parent education is even more dramatic: 30 percent of parochial school children's parents and 57 percent of the parents of children in other private schools graduated from college, in comparison with 19 percent of public school students' parents (see Figure 4.1).

If there is anything education research tells us, it is that higher education translates into higher incomes and both are strongly associated with higher academic achievement. Even on the basis of family income alone, private school students should have performed dramatically better. According to the latest national figures, about three times as many public school students as private and parochial school students had family incomes under $15,000, while twice as many parochial school students and more than three times as many other private school students had family incomes of $50,000 and more (see Figure 4.2). Consider, too, that private schools in the NAEP sample and

Figure 4.1
**Parental Education Levels of Elementary and Secondary Students in Public,
Parochial, and Other Private Schools**

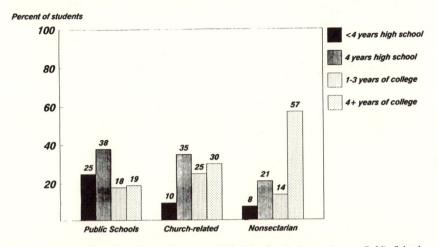

Source: *Private Schools in the United States: A Statistical Profile with Comparisons to Public Schools.*
Washington, D.C.: U.S. Department of Education, National Center for Education Statistics,
February 1991, Figure 3-6, p. 47.

Figure 4.2
**Family Income of Elementary and Secondary Students in Public, Parochial,
and Other Private Schools**

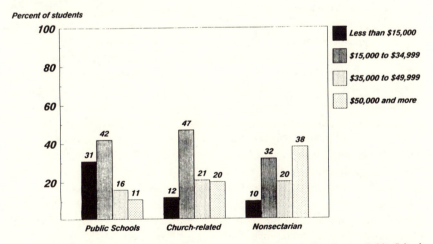

Source: *Private Schools in the United States: A Statistical Profile with Comparisons to Public Schools.*
Washington, D.C.: U.S. Department of Education, National Center for Education Statistics,
February 1991, Figure 3-5, p. 46.

nationally are dramatically underrepresented in rural and disadvantaged communities, where the nation's poorest youngsters live, and that poverty is strongly associated with lower academic achievement.

Socioeconomic status makes a big difference in student achievement, but school counts too. There are big differences in what public and private school students take in school. For example, 81 percent of the private school seniors and only 56 percent of the public school seniors in the NAEP sample were in an academic track. Taking more academic courses, like having better-educated and wealthier parents, is strongly associated with higher scores, so how come public and private schools had an identical record in the percentage of students they produced who were prepared to handle college-level math? Why were the average scores of private school seniors so close to those of public school seniors?

In fact, these considerable differences between the family and academic backgrounds of public and private school youngsters explain why, when you look only at *average* scores, private school students do somewhat better—though well below what you would expect, given their advantages. When you compare the NAEP scores of public and private school students who have similar family backgrounds and who have taken similar courses—when you compare apples with apples—their achievement is almost identical.

For example, when you compare the scores of public and private twelfth-graders whose parents have similar education levels, the sector differences become even narrower (see Figure 4.3). Consider the results when eighth-graders are matched according to the math courses they have taken. Public school students who have had pre-algebra score 274 and private school students score 273. The results are similar for eighth-graders who have taken algebra, except that public school students score four points better than students from private schools: 298 as opposed to 294 (see Figure 4.4).

A similar result occurs with comparison of the scores of public and private school seniors who have taken similar courses (see Figure 4.5). Among those who have gotten only as far as Algebra I, private school students score slightly better; and among those who have taken more advanced courses, public school students score slightly better. There are no big differences in achievement; there is no "private school advantage." Since these comparisons by courses taken did not factor in the big differences in public and private school students' backgrounds, the proposition that public schools are adding more value to their students than are private schools becomes even stronger.

Though the 1990 national NAEP results in mathematics have been largely ignored, they are not an anomaly. The results of the 1990 NAEP science examination tell the same story. The average scores for twelfth grade private school students are slightly better. Comparison of the achievement of public and private school students in grades nine through twelve who have taken science courses reveals no difference (NAEP 1992, Table 3.8, p. 73).

Figure 4.3
Mathematics Achievement at Grade 12 by Level of Parental Education,
Public and Private Schools

Source: National Assessment of Educational Progress, American Federation of Teachers.

Figure 4.4
Average Overall Mathematics Proficiency by Students Taking Similar Courses:
Grade 8

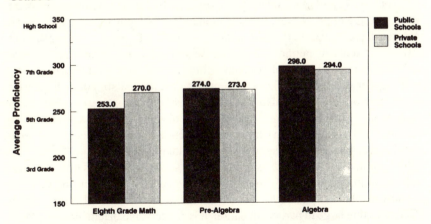

Source: National Assessment of Educational Progress, American Federation of Teachers 1990, Student
Data.

Figure 4.5
Average Overall Mathematics Proficiency by Students Taking Similar Courses: Grade 12

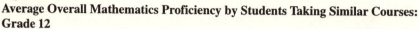

Source: National Assessment of Educational Progress, American Federation of Teachers, 1990, Student Data.

Although the 1990 mathematics and science examinations were the first time NAEP reported out public-private comparisons, it was not the first time that NAEP collected private school data. In 1988, Chester E. Finn, Jr., who now works on Christopher Whittle's Edison Project and who was then assistant secretary of education, presented unpublished public-private school comparisons from the 1986 NAEP reading, history, and literature examinations to the annual meeting of the National Association of Independent Schools. Finn noted what we have found here: that there was little difference in achievement between students in public and private schools. According to Finn, private (including parochial) school students scored only about an average of four points higher than public school students on reading and six points higher on history and literature. He also said that the soon-to-be-released 1986 math exams would show similar results. "There's a differential," he said, according to *Education Week*, "but it's a very small differential, in an area where the public school performance is scandalously low" (Goldberg 1988, 1).

Finn pointed out that twice as many private school students as public school students taking the tests had parents who were college graduates and that this probably explained the slightly higher average private school score: "With differences that large in parent education, it is conceivable that there's no school effect showing up here at all." His advice to the private-school audience? "You need to improve faster than the public schools if you expect to continue to have people paying an average of $6,200 a year for day schools . . . in order to get a presumably better educational product."

Even James S. Coleman, whose 1981 analysis of public-private school performance is cited as the premier source of scientific evidence of private school superiority, warned that "one should not make a mistake: Our estimates for the size of the private-sector effects show them not to be large" (Coleman 1981, 19). A small army of other researchers has shown that the small private school edge found by Coleman disappeared when differences in students' family background and course taking were examined.

John Chubb and Terry Moe are the authors of *Politics, Markets, and America's Schools* (1990) and the present-day purveyors of "objective proof" of private school superiority. Lots of politicians and op-ed writers have repeated their findings as gospel, and many individuals have become converts to public aid for private education on their authority. As their peer reviewers and even a few statistics-savvy journalists have pointed out, Chubb and Moe's study of public and private high schools also fails to find a private school advantage once students' background characteristics and academic courses are taken into account.

The failure of Chubb and Moe's analysis to yield them support for their conclusions is not particularly surprising. The evidence they use comes exclusively from the "High School and Beyond Study," the same data that failed to yield Coleman sizable private-sector effects. Moreover, despite the considerable print they expend on discussing why their handling of this data is an advance over other researchers' methods, Chubb and Moe ignore virtually all that has been learned about how to work responsibly with this deeply flawed, if not worthless, data set. What they do instead is highly unorthodox. A short list includes: combining elite private and other private schools along with Catholic schools in a way that automatically conferred a private school advantage in their public-private analysis; constructing a school organization measure comprising fifty variables, making it almost impossible to single out the effects of any one variable; pioneering the use of a dependent variable that measures achievement change in a way that exaggerates high and low performance differences—and then conceding, in a footnote in the back of their book, that this has no substantive meaning; and reporting results in terms of average differences between schools in the highest quartile of performance (87.5th percentile) and the lowest quartile (12.5th percentile), which makes for very extreme comparisons. John Witte forcefully points out that "*they never directly test the differential effect of public and private schools on achievement. . . .* [P]rior studies either ran separate regressions for public and private school students, or analyzed all students together but included a variable indicating whether the student was in a public or private school. They did neither." Methodological pyrotechnics notwithstanding, Chubb and Moe still fail to prove their hypothesis. *All* of their variables taken together explain only about 5 percent of the variation in achievement; and even when they ask what would happen if we moved students from a school in the lowest quartile of effective organization to the highest, the answer is they'd get less than one more answer correct on a 115-item test (Witte 1991, 21; Rosenberg, December 1990-January 1991; Shanker and Rosenberg, Winter 1991; Witte 1990).

Valerie Lee and Anthony Bryk suggest that Chubb and Moe fail to prove the superiority of private schools because they let their preference for market control of schools influence the way they look at the data: "Chubb and Moe have artfully employed extensive, but not always solid, empirical evidence to support a policy argument to advance some preconceived notions about American schooling." They call the "popular acceptance of this book as a source of scientific evidence to support its policy recommendations . . . unfortunate" (Lee and Bryk 1992, 3).

The latest pieces of evidence debunking the private school superiority myth both come from Milwaukee. The first concerns Catholic schools and is especially noteworthy because Catholic and other private schools are not required to report their students' test scores to the public. When Catholic schools do on occasion, it is always in terms of average scores aggregated at the district or national level. The *Milwaukee Journal*'s religion reporter, Marie Rohde, persisted in asking the Milwaukee archdiocese to provide a finer breakdown, and her request was eventually granted. In a story that ran in the *Journal* on August 1 1991, Rohde reported that "minority students enrolled in Milwaukee's Catholic elementary schools suffer the same lag in achievement test scores as their counterparts in the public schools, according to test results made public for the first time." The test was the same one used by the Milwaukee public schools, the Iowa Test of Basic Skills. The scores, Rohde continued, "run counter to longstanding claims by most Catholic educators that they are doing a superior job of teaching disadvantaged children." In fact, while the scores of public school minority students have been stable, those of minority children in the Milwaukee Catholic schools have declined.

According to Rohde, John Norris, superintendent of the Catholic schools, blamed the gap on "socioeconomic factors" and said that test scores of Catholic and public schools "should not be directly compared." Two years earlier, when the archdiocese used a different test from the one used by the public schools and reported out the scores without breaking them down by race or individual school, it had no qualms about making such a comparison. "The bottom line," Norris said, is that "in our system we perform better than the national average, and we are dealing with minority people in an inner-city situation." The real bottom line is that averages can obscure as much as they illuminate. In this case the higher scores of advantaged Catholic school students masked the poor achievement levels of minority Catholic school students, most of whom were concentrated in separate schools.

The other piece of evidence from Milwaukee comes from its much vaunted, state-initiated voucher experiment. The product of a coalition between Polly Williams, a Democratic state legislator from Milwaukee and the former chair of Jesse Jackson's presidential campaign in Wisconsin, and Governor Tommy Thompson, a conservative Republican, the Milwaukee voucher program began in September of 1990 and was open to a maximum of 1,000 low-income children in a district where about 60,000 children met the law's definition of poverty. Religious schools were excluded from the program, and only seven of twenty-one eligible private schools volunteered to participate. The voucher was worth $2,500, paid out of the public schools' budget.

Estimates of how many families applied for the voucher vary from 600 to 750 families, but in the end 341 students were accepted by the seven private schools. By June, 249 students remained, in part because one school, which had been a religious school until shortly before the program began, went bankrupt and its 63 voucher students returned to the public schools. The following September, 86 of the remaining 249 voucher students did not return to their private schools.

According to the first-year evaluation of the program, while the parents of the participating students met the low-income criterion, they also tended to be more educated than either the Milwaukee public school parents on the whole or the low-income public school parents. Voucher parents had also been more active in the public schools and more dissatisfied with them than the average public school parent. Their involvement in the private schools was even higher than it had been when their children attended public schools, and their satisfaction levels were greater. Why so many of them did not return their children to the private schools begs further exploration.

What about the achievement of the voucher students, the prime justification for the experiment? During the recent presidential campaign, Mr. Bush often used the Milwaukee program as an example of what vouchers can achieve for poor children. In fact, though one-year evaluation results do not make for conclusive evidence, the Milwaukee results do nothing to support the contention that private schools do a better job of educating low-income students than public schools. There were no dramatic gains in achievement among the voucher students, and their performance was about equal to that of the low-income students in the Milwaukee public schools (Witte 1991).

Private schools may have something to teach public schools. For instance, public schools could stop giving students a choice of curriculums—they choose easy ones—and insist that they take more academically challenging courses, the way they do in Catholic and other private schools. The public school system also could start heeding the message that many parents, especially poor minority parents, have been trying to convey when they remove their children to Catholic and other private schools: Teachers can't teach and students can't learn when a handful of violent or disruptive students is allowed to terrorize the school community. Something needs to be done for those students, but right now the failure of many school boards to face up to the issue means that public school youngsters who want to achieve and who are a majority are being held hostage by a small destructive minority. Private schools do not tolerate that, and neither should public schools.

Private schools also have a lesson to teach policymakers and the public about children in poverty. As the NAEP results indicate, most of the private school advantage in average scores is due to a more advantaged student body. In fact, the results of NAEP and other assessments demonstrate that childhood poverty is not only bad for America morally and socially but educationally, as well. Of course, many poor children do very well in school, and education continues to be a major route out of poverty. Poverty, especially when it is accompanied by family and community disintegration, is associated with lower academic achievement. Overcoming childhood poverty might not solve our crisis in education, but it would take us a good stretch down that road.

Would permitting public dollars to follow children to private and parochial schools turn our education system upside down? Would it destroy neighborhood schools and transform public education into a system for the have-nots? Would it violate the separation between church and state to the detriment of both? Could it lead to public money going to cult schools, radical schools (of the left and the right), and crassly commercial schools thrown together by people out for a quick buck? Would it mean less accountability in education because private and parochial schools, unlike public schools, are not required to report publicly their test results or their finances? Might it sanction a school system stratified by class, religion, ethnicity, and race and thereby undermine our pluralistic democracy?

The risks involved in public aid to private education are substantial, and they are not balanced by any evidence of educational benefit. In fact, the results of NAEP and other national studies show that if we want American children to meet world-class education standards—or even be able to do seventh-grade math by the time they leave high school—then shifting tax dollars to send them to private and parochial schools will not help.

If private schools do not outperform public schools, then those who have charged that bureaucracy or teacher unions or desegregation orders or democratic control is chiefly responsible for our crisis in education had better look elsewhere because private schools are not constrained by any of these. On the other hand, it also means that public schools cannot blame their dismal performance chiefly on the deterioration of families and communities. Even if they were to get the kinds of students private schools have—hand-picked and with parents who are relatively well-educated and motivated to spend money on schooling—and even if they, like the private schools, were to have smaller class sizes or more flexibility in removing troublemakers, private school test scores indicate that student achievement would still be at a level that is far below world standards.

The results of the public-private school comparisons may be surprising, but they are not really shocking. Public and private schools by and large have the same textbooks, the same curriculum, the same tracking methods, the same internal organizations—and the same indifferent standards.

Public and private schools also have students who are subject to the same incentives for working hard in school—that is to say, very few. College-bound students in both public and private schools know they'll be able to find a college that will accept them, no matter how poor their grades are or how little they know, as long as they have a high school diploma and, usually, money. The one exception is students, in either school sector, who hope to attend elite universities; they have to work very hard indeed.

As for going to work from high school, students in both public and private schools know that employers don't ask to see high school transcripts and don't even offer decent jobs to high school graduates until they are twenty-four or so, if then. A student who has worked hard at rigorous courses will be competing for the same poor job at the same low pay as a student who has filled his schedule with soft courses that he barely passed. These bad lessons are being learned by students in public and private schools alike.

Why aren't parents making sure youngsters apply themselves? Whether children are in public or private schools, most parents won't be successful at pressuring them to work harder when the children can tell them, "I've already done what I need to do to get what I want."

As for teachers, they have a hard enough time, under the best of circumstances, persuading students that history or physics or even regular attendance is "relevant" to their future lives. When the students can say, "I don't need that to get into college or to get a job; it doesn't count" or "Taking that course will pull my average down," the battle is lost before it starts.

One solution is for American businesses to link getting jobs with high school achievement and for colleges to do the same thing in setting admission standards. Elementary and secondary schools would then have support for upholding standards. Parents and teachers would have support when they say, "Unless you turn off the television set and work harder, you're not going to make it." Our students would have evidence that working hard and learning something are essential to getting what they want. At the very least, they would see a reason to achieve, and because they're no less able than students in our competitor nations, they would.

The poor outcomes of both public and private education also indicate that there is not much to the argument that the competition which school choice would produce would serve as an excellent accountability system. The argument is that parents would make school decisions on the basis of educational excellence; hence bad schools would fail and good schools would thrive and be replicated. There are parents who choose private schools and who keep their youngsters there despite, as NAEP tells us, their mediocre performance, and this suggests that if school choice produces accountability, it is not primarily or always on the basis of educational quality and outcomes.

Choice may be an excellent incentive for schools to work hard to attract customers but it is no substitute for designing school-wide incentives in which there are rewards for improving student achievement and consequences for failure.

The idea of an accountability system for schools that involves rewards and consequences is radical and controversial, and it would need to be tested to see what works, when, and how. The idea of an accountability system based on private school choice is also radical and controversial, and the NAEP and other results tell us it would not work. It is very clear that even if the public rejects private school choice, it will not put up with the status quo in public education. Either there will be a new kind of accountability system in education that both the public and educator can believe in, or some crazy accountability scheme that will not be good for education will be imposed on us.

The private school choice packages that are being pushed across the nation will not help kids find out that they need to work in school to get what they want, just as they must on the athletic field and in the world of work. They will not stimulate schools to focus on improving student achievement and to experiment with new ways of doing so. They will not produce greater accountability in education, and they will undoubtedly yield less. They certainly will not eradicate the effects of childhood poverty. They will not solve the crisis in education because that crisis afflicts public and private schools alike.

NOTE

1. An earlier version of this article by Albert Shanker appeared under the title of "Do Private Schools Outperform Public Schools?" in the Fall 1991 issue of *American Educator*, the magazine of the American Federation of Teachers. Another by Albert Shanker and Bella Rosenberg appeared in *The Choice Controversy*, edited by Peter W. Cookson, Jr. (Newbury Park, Calif.: Corwin Press 1992).

REFERENCES

Chubb, John E., and Moe, Terry M. (1990) *Politics, Markets, and America's Schools.* Washington, D.C.: The Brookings Institution.

Coleman, James S. (1981) "Response to Page and Keith," *Educational Researcher*, Vol. 10, pp. 18–20.

Coleman, James S., Thomas Hoffer, and Sally Kilgore. (1981). *Public and Private High Schools.* Washington, D.C.: National Center for Education Statistics, U.S. Department of Education.

Goldberg, Kirsten. (1988) " 'Gravest Threat' to Private Schools Is Better Public Ones, Finn Warns," *Education Week*, March 9, p. 1.

Lee, Valerie E., and Anthony S. Bryk. (1992) "Science or Policy Argument? A Review of the Quantitative Evidence in Chubb and Moe's *Politics, Markets, and America's Schools.*" Paper prepared for conference on School Choice: What Role in American Education? sponsored by the Economic Policy Institute, October 1, Washington, D.C., p 3.

National Assessment of Educational Progress. (1991) *The State of Mathematics Achievement: NAEP 1990 Assessment of the Nation and the Trial Assessment of the States.* Washington, D.C.: National Center for Education Statistics, Office of Educational Research and Improvement, U.S. Department of Education.

———. (1992) *The 1990 Science Report Card: NAEP's Assessment of Fourth, Eighth, and Twelfth Graders.* Washington, D.C.: National Center for Education Statistics, Office of Educational Research and Improvement, U.S. Department of Education.

National Center for Education Statistics. (1987) *Private Schools and Private School Teachers: Final Report of the 1985–86 Private School Study.* Washington, D.C.: U.S. Department of Education.

Rohde, Marie. (1991) "Minority Test Scores at Catholic Schools Mirror Lag in City," *Milwaukee Journal,* August 1, p. 1.

Rosenberg, Bella (1990–1991) "Not a Case for Market Control," *Educational Leadership,* December/January, Vol. 48, No. 4, pp. 64–65.

Shanker, Albert, and Bella Rosenberg. (1991, Winter) *Politics, Markets, and America's Schools: The Fallacies of Private School Choice.*" Washington, D.C.: American Federation of Teachers.

Witte, John F. (1990) "Understanding High School Achievement: After a Decade of Research, Do We Have Any Confident Policy Recommendations?" August 30–September 3, paper presented at the 1990 Annual Meeting of the American Political Science Association.

———. (1991) *Public Subsidies for Private Schools.* Madison: University of Wisconsin-Madison.

5

Public Schools by Contract: An Alternative to Privatization

Paul T. Hill

John Chubb and Terry Moe's critique (1990) of public education has caught on: even people who cannot accept their vision of a school system run by private entrepreneurs and funded by public vouchers agree that the problems they set out to solve—public schools' preoccupation with rule-following and tolerance of low performance—are real. Despite widespread agreement about what is wrong with public education, it is proving extremely hard to create a critical mass of support behind privatization or any other method of reform.

Despite over ten years of ferment at federal, state, and local levels, the public school system continues as before, as a bureaucracy that tolerates innovation on the margins but isolates and destroys any changes in its fundamental ways of doing business. Recent experience validates the old political adage, "You can't beat something with nothing." Chubb and Moe are the only people to have proposed an alternative whole-systems concept, showing how large numbers of schools serving the whole public school population could be established, staffed, managed, evaluated, and improved, all without a large public service bureaucracy. Other current reform proposals, such as national standards and tests and radical new designs for individual schools, accept the principle of a bureaucratically run public education system. Even the charter schools concept, which would let groups of students and teachers "opt out" from the public school system, creates exceptions rather than reforming the system as a whole.

In its purest form, privatization of schools means total private ownership and supervision. Private organizations would design and manage schools and be funded only through tuition paid by parents. Government would have no relationship with schools, except to provide vouchers or other forms of subsidies that help parents pay their children's tuition. Aside from licensing schools for health and safety, government agencies would have no responsibility for staffing, supervising, or guaranteeing quality control in the schools. Market forces, and the self-interested initiative of people who own and staff the schools, would force a concern for quality and efficiency. Good schools would attract many tuition paying students, make money, and could sustain themselves and even expand or open new branches. Bad schools would attract few students and go broke.

Schools would be forced to attend to student needs and parent preferences, rather than to the requirements of a centralized bureaucracy. Funding would be explicitly based on attendance, not on opaque staff allocations. Teachers and principals would have a strong incentive to collaborate, to press one another for good performance, to weed out weak staff members, and to work as hard as necessary to build their school's clientele. Teacher pay and job security would depend on contribution to the school's performance, not on longevity or accumulation of degrees.

Privatized schools would compete for students, and in doing so they would be forced to differentiate their products, both in quality and type. Some schools would try to be excellent in a safe, conventional way, while others would provide innovative services or appeal to particular tastes in subject matter or pedagogy. Product differentiation would help parents and students know what to expect from a school. They would know whether they were likely to enjoy it and be willing to do the work it requires. They would also have little trouble knowing whether the school had kept its promises. Accountability would therefore be direct and immediate: schools that delivered would keep their students, and those that did not would be abandoned.

These consequences of privatization fit the current consensus about what makes an effective organization. Even more to the point, they possess the known ingredients for an effective school: clear and distinctive missions, simple organization, a strong commitment to defined student outcomes, and a strong ethic of collaboration and mutual dependency among staff. They also make demands on students. As the growing research on magnet schools makes clear, students who choose a particular school (even if they consider it their least-bad alternative) have a greater incentive to meet its requirements than students who are just assigned on the basis of neighborhood.

This chapter presents an alternative systems concept that builds on Chubb and Moe's idea but makes one major change. Like Chubb and Moe's prescription, this chapter suggests that schools be operated by private organizations, receiving public funds and enjoying considerable discretion in hiring and curriculum, and living and dying on their own performance. Unlike Chubb and Moe, however, it suggests that schools be funded via contracts with public authorities rather than by subsidized tuition payments. Contracting for schools has two advantages over pure privatization: first, it lowers the cost of entry into the school business, thereby ensuring a plentiful supply of schools that are worth choosing; and second, it provides mechanisms that privatization alone does not provide, ensuring non-discriminatory admissions to schools and allowing public authorities to move quickly to close and replace schools that fail to educate their students.

After a critique of the pure-privatization model, the paper shows how contracting for schools would work, and how it would solve the problems implicit in the Chubb and Moe plan.

CRITIQUE OF VOUCHERS

Of all the criticism leveled against the privatization concept, the most important one concerns the supply of schools. Privatization assumes that entrepreneurs, drawn by the possibility of lucrative tuition payments, would offer alternatives to unpopular schools. In the long run, weak schools would be eliminated, strong ones would appear in their place, and all schools would feel the pressure of competition to maintain quality.

Choice plans, whether all-public or public-private, have a glaring problem. Subsidized tuition payments may increase parents' capacity to demand better schools, but it is not clear from where alternatives to the existing bad schools are to come. They do not exist now, and giving public school students access to the existing private and parochial school systems will not solve the supply problem. Even in New York City, where the Catholic schools educate over 100,000 students and constitute the twelfth largest school system in the country, there is no room for the 1,000,000 public school students. Few other cities have even that large a supply of privately run schools.

Starting a school is not cheap or easy. Aside from the capital costs of school buildings and equipment, the requirements of curriculum selection, staff selection and training, and quality control are imposing. Whittle Communications, whose Edison Project is developing a system of for-profit schools, will spend over three years and tens of millions of dollars designing a prototype school and its staffing and management plans. Whittle expects to recoup its investment by opening a large number of schools and taking small profits from tuition, but the front-end costs are enormous. Despite its announced intention to charge tuitions comparable to the average per pupil expenditure of the nation's public schools, the Edison project is now raising its tuition estimates and planning to use a great deal of time donated by parents and community members.

Some other private organizations have curricula, staffing and training methods, and school management teams up and running. Religious organizations, such as the Hebrew schools, the Friends schools, some Protestant denominations, and several Catholic religious orders (e.g., the Jesuits and the Sisters of the Sacred Heart) have made the capital investment necessary to create and sustain networks of consistently high-quality and moderate-cost schools. These, and secular organizations such as Montessori, could supply new schools with up-front costs lower than Whittle's. Their capacities are small. None of them runs more than a few dozen schools nationwide, and a doubling of the total effort (far more than any of them could manage in less than a decade or so) would not produce enough new schools to solve the supply problem of even one major city, let alone the whole country.

Other well-known organizations devoted to school improvement, such as Ted Sizer's Coalition of Essential Schools and James Comer's community schools network, provide staff training but they do not assemble or manage whole schools. They are stretched thin dealing with 150 or 200 schools nationwide. Even under the most ambitious scenarios they could not be expected to become the proprietors of more than a few score schools nationwide. A final demonstration of the high front-end costs of new schools comes from the experience of charter schools. In Minnesota, groups of parents, teachers, or other concerned citizens can petition to run a publicly supported school that is independent of the local education agency. After nearly three years, fewer than a dozen groups have been able to create the shared vision and organizational arrangements necessary to start a charter school.

The foregoing does not mean that there is no alternative to the current public school system. It does mean that schools are not easy to start and that the opportunity to fund a school by collecting tuition vouchers may not be attractive enough to elicit a strong supply of alternatives.

A weak supply response may not be a serious problem in suburban and small-city school systems. Many such systems have essentially sound public schools that would almost certainly become more efficient and effective in the face of competition. Even the threat of competition might stimulate greater effort to make the current schools more attractive to parents. The addition of a small number of private competitors has had a salutary effect in many such school systems, and it is surely a good thing.

Big-city school systems present a different problem. They have few schools that would be considered good by even the present standards of suburban and small-city public schools and many more that are failures by any standard. In the nation's largest cities, the typical comprehensive high school graduates less than half of the students who enter it in ninth grade, and daily attendance rates are often barely 50 percent. Only a small minority of their students even encounter the complete curriculum that is offered to all students in suburban and small town schools. Many big-city systems already have a form of choice, in open enrollment policies that allow students to enroll in any school that has room for them. Choice has little meaning, however, in the absence of a supply response. New York City's open enrollment policy is rendered virtually meaningless by the fact that the non-selective magnet schools to which all students may apply get ten to thirty applications for every seat. The majority of students who choose a school other than the one in their neighborhood end up back in the school they tried to leave.

Privatization may look at first like the perfect alternative to a public school system that either will not or can not respond to an overwhelming demand for a different kind of school. However, the rigors of urban education are likely to discourage most entrepreneurs. Who could be confident in staying solvent running a school in an area burdened by violence, strikes, students' ill health, and family instability? What profit-seeking investor would choose to build a school in a core urban area when he might collect just as much tuition in a far less stressed suburb?

Though many of the most insistent critiques of privatization are stated in terms of equity and civil rights, they all reflect a concern for the supply problem. The fears that good schools will discriminate against the poor and that children whose parents are not aggressive consumers will be consigned to the worst schools are based on the implicit assumption that the supply response will be inelastic; even though parents will have a greater capacity to demand good schools, good schools will be so scarce that the most important choices will be exercised by the desirable schools, not the parents. Foes of privatization predict that schools will discriminate on admissions, grading, and teacher hiring, all to make themselves as attractive as possible to the middle class.

Should the facts bear out any of the fears outlined above, pure privatization is not likely to survive. Lawsuits based on unequal distribution of publicly funded benefits would lead to the imposition of new regimes of regulation. It is not far-fetched to think that schools accepting government-subsidized tuition payments would come under court-ordered regulation of their admissions, expulsion, grading, promotion, curricula, and teacher hiring and compensation. Chubb and Moe admit that pure privatization entails these risks, and they call for limited public regulation and oversight, including licensing of schools, to protect students and avoid devastating scandals.

THE CONTRACTING ALTERNATIVE

This section takes on the challenge of how to obtain the benefits of privatization while solving the supply problem defined above. A solution must, like privatization, free the schools from micromanagement by political bodies; allow development of schools with specific approaches to education, so that staff members can feel responsible for what they produce and parents can hold them accountable; and give teachers and principals a strong incentive to collaborate, press one another for good performance, weed out weak staff members, and work as hard as necessary to build their school's clientele. To avoid the problems described above, a solution must also contain a supply mechanism that creates new schools in the place of ones that have failed, and is as sensitive to failure in schools serving low-income and minority students as in schools serving the privileged.

The solution suggested here is a hybrid of privatization and more standard government-run institutions. Schools would be run by private organizations under contract with local public education agencies. To the degree possible, as described below, schools would be independent enterprises, operating under applicable state and local laws and the terms of explicit contracts specifying what kinds of instruction was to be delivered, to and by whom, and to what effect. As in a privatization scheme, students and teachers would choose and be chosen by schools: no one would have an automatic right to administer, teach in, or attend a particular school. In contrast with private firms operating under a privatization scheme, contractors would not have to build or equip schools, and they would be guaranteed a minimum level of income for the duration of the contract. Contracts would, however, specify that schools failing to attract a minimum level of enrollment, or failing to produce the specified student outcomes, could be closed and their contractors released.

In effect, contracting for schools is a way of re-inventing public education, rather than eliminating it. (See Osborne and Gaebler 1992, for a discussion of re-inventing government.) A public school would be one run under contract with a local education authority, not, as presently, a school both owned and operated by a public authority. Contracting would work as follows:

- Any private organization, profit-making or non-profit, would be eligible to enter into a contract to manage one or more schools. Likely contractors could include universities, civic groups, businesses, church groups willing to provide non-sectarian instruction, and ad hoc organizations put together expressly to serve a particular group or use a particular instructional method.

- A contractor would be guaranteed a fixed amount per pupil, plus a management fee. In return, the contractor would staff and manage a school, using curricula and instructional approaches specified in the contract.

- Contractors would use public school buildings at no cost, and the local public education authority would provide a negotiated amount for utilities, incidental repairs, and maintenance; capital expenditures not specific to the contractor's instructional methods would be made by the public education authority.

- Contractors would hire teachers, either on the open market or from a register of certified teachers, depending on the terms of the contract. State and federal wage and hour laws would apply. Decisions about hiring, promotion, and assignment of individuals would be made by the contractor, subject only to applicable state and federal laws and regulations.

- Each school's processes and standards for student admission would be set by its contract. In general, to avoid charges of discrimination, schools would admit by random selection from the list of all who apply.

- Schools would publish their demands and expectations for students, and their methods for helping students who encounter academic trouble. The school could expel any student who refused to meet the published demands, but in doing so the school would have to show that it met its contractual obligations for assisting the student.

- School contracts would include specific agreements on the kinds and levels of student outcomes expected, and the methods whereby those outcomes would be assessed. Contractors who failed to provide instruction as promised, or whose students' outcomes were low and not improving as anticipated, could be fired or faced with new contract terms.

Under such a scheme, a local public authority would retain a number of functions. Its basic job would be to maintain a portfolio of contracts serving two objectives: first, to ensure that the local system as a whole offers a range of approaches and services that matches the diversity of needs of local children; and second, to ensure that no child receives a low quality education. It would pursue both objectives via contracting. The local authority would identify the need for particular kinds of schools, identify contractors potentially able to provide such schools, solicit proposals, and negotiate contracts. It would also continuously evaluate contractors' performance, both to prepare for the time when a contract must either be renewed or re-competed, and to identify contractors who were not delivering on their promises or, for any reason, failing to produce positive student results.

Central offices would not wither away entirely. They would still need to provide fair, unbiased information about school performance to local public authorities and the community. Central offices would also help local public authorities to assess needs for new types of schools and to identify promising potential contractors. Many of these functions could also be performed by contractors, though not the same ones that operate the schools. It is essential, however, that the evaluation and contractor identification process could not be neglected or performed for free, as they would be the main mechanisms by which the public was assured that its children were being well cared for and its money carefully used. Central offices would not need to be large. New York City's world record of nearly six central office administrators per public school would be unchallenged; central office staffing in a contract system could more nearly resemble that of the New York City Catholic schools, which employ fewer than one administrator for every five schools.

Not all the central office administrative reductions would translate into net cost savings. As in the private and parochial school systems, schools run under contract would have responsibility for their own staff development and quality control. These functions, which are now centrally administered, and therefore unresponsive to individual schools' needs, would be performed by the contractors themselves. Though some cost reductions are likely, contracts must include reasonable funding for staff training, self-assessment, and adoption of promising new teaching methods and technologies.

One important technique for both reducing the size of central office staffs and guaranteeing the efficiency of schools' self-improvement efforts is contracting with intermediary organizations that would run multiple schools. Universities, teachers' unions, social service agencies, churches willing to provide non-sectarian instruction, and private firms like Whittle Communications' Edison Schools could operate several local schools under one contract. They might run all the schools in a given neighborhood or region of the city, or run a network of elementary, middle, and high schools all based on a common approach or philosophy. These organizations could be responsible for school self-evaluation, staff development, and quality control; they would also have a strong interest in making sure that their stronger schools help their weaker ones. As Celio (1993) has shown, the use of such networks, provided by the religious orders of nuns, priests, and brothers is one of the secrets to the Catholic school's success and low cost. Like the religious orders, such intermediary organizations could develop distinctive curricula, conduct the research and development (R&D) necessary to improve their methods, train staff to use a common approach to instruction, and adjust staffing to compensate for individual schools' needs and weaknesses. Dealing with intermediary organizations would also simplify the work of local public authorities, which would then have to supervise and evaluate a far smaller number of contractors.

Several existing organizations are qualified to manage multiple schools, including Education Alternatives, Inc., which now plays exactly that role in Baltimore and three other cities; the Edison Schools; educational reform networks run by Brown, Johns Hopkins, Yale, and Stanford universities; school design teams sponsored by the New American Schools Development Corporation; and local Catholic, Jewish, African-American, Protestant, and Lutheran school systems. A school system that wanted to deal exclusively with intermediary organizations would have to search for providers and entice some by promising long-term initial contracts. The potential providers exist, and most, especially the religious school systems, would find the per pupil funding available from local public authorities lavish and enticing.

Public funds for schools would continue to be raised from a combination of local and state taxes and federal grants. The local public authority would pay contractors by combining funds from all sources. Contracts would, in the vast majority of cases, be based on a standard local per pupil amount. A local school board would be free, however, to negotiate a slightly higher than average per pupil rate for schools in the lowest income areas, where children frequently need extra supportive services and small classes are often necessary.

The issue of extra funding for schools in problem areas is a well-established battleground in public education. Since 1964, the federal and state governments have provided "categorical" grants to pay for extra services to low-income, handicapped, and language minority children. These grants can add as much as 20 percent to a school's funding. However, as several recent studies and lawsuits have shown, the schools that get most of the categorical grant money are frequently short-changed in the distribution of other resources. Because the highest-paid senior teachers cluster in middle class schools, schools in low-income areas of a school district often have younger, less experienced, and cheaper staff members, many of whom can teach only because they have been granted waivers of normal certification requirements. The result, as was demonstrated in the 1992 Los Angeles case, *Rodriguez v. Anton*, is that local spending in low-income area schools is often only one-half to one-third of what is spent in higher-income areas. The categorical grant funds that cluster in the low-income schools are too small to equalize funding. Thus, despite a declared policy of providing extra resources to the neediest schools, most localities in fact give them much less.

By bringing all schools up to true equality of funding, contracting will dramatically increase the funding for schools in the most troubled inner-city areas. The first contracts negotiated for such areas could, therefore, be based on the district-wide average per-pupil expenditure. If, in future contract negotiations, it became clear that competent providers can not operate in those areas without supplementary funding, higher per-pupil rates could be negotiated. A local public authority that held contracts with several intermediary organizations could also require every such organization to run a specified number of schools in low-income or otherwise troubled areas. This would guarantee that capable organizations could not evade the toughest problems. It would create an incentive for all contractors to develop competency in dealing with multi-problem students. Most, wanting to avoid being responsible for a school with a bad reputation, would make sure that none of their schools was considered a "dumping ground" for troublesome students and staff.

Precedent for Contracting

The ideas described above are uncommon in public education, but common elsewhere. Perhaps the best example is the "GOCO" system under which the Department of Defense sponsors laboratories and special production facilities that are Government Owned, Contractor Operated. This arrangement gives the government flexibility to hire senior scientists and engineers who lack the seniority to win civil service positions, and to make rapid changes in the management and staffing of low-performing units. It also allows key government R&D units to hire extremely capable professionals who will not accept the limits on income and working conditions typically imposed on the civil service. It also attracts contractors who have great technical and managerial competence but lack the capital to purchase expensive buildings and equipment.

GOCO is not without its problems. In any enterprise, some contractors make mistakes, and others come to treat their contracts as entitlements. In the Department of Defense scheme, some incumbent contractors and their rivals lobby Congress to gain the advantage in competitions. Nonetheless, the government enjoys far greater flexibility—and typically gets substantially superior performance—from GOCO facilities than from wholly government-operated ones.

In the defense sector, GOCO ensures that capable providers will work on problems of public concern. Without GOCO, many senior defense analysts are convinced, private commercial pursuits would capture virtually all of the most capable scientists, engineers, and managers.

In education, contracting could have similar consequences. Contractors could offer premium salaries for the most outstanding teachers and create career ladders that would attract and hold the ablest people. Local authorities would enjoy the flexibility created by temporary commitments to individual contractors, and parents and children would benefit from the competition among potential school providers.

Compared to pure privatization, government contracting for schools would reduce the size of school entrepreneurs' front-end investment. If competition were based on performance alone, with per pupil costs fixed, contractors would have strong incentives to invest in their staffs and programs, not to cut costs by skimping on quality control and product improvement. Perhaps most importantly, schools would be freed from the burden of civil service employment. Good teachers could be well-rewarded, and highly productive young teachers would be sought after, not rejected because older teachers will not leave their safe, tenured civil service positions. Teachers' unions might still have important roles, serving as brokers to find the right match between teachers and schools, and training teachers whom schools reject as deficient. Teacher unions would operate as professional craft organizations, protecting their members' interests in dealing with the contractors who run individual schools, rather than negotiating highly prescriptive industrial-style contracts with central school boards.

How Contracting Improves on Privatization

Contracting has all the advantages of privatization: it creates school flexibility and accountability, eliminates the bureaucratic gamesmanship that leads to gross inequities in school funding, makes school staff members collaborators in a market enterprise, and casts the teacher unions as professional associations, not industrial organizers. It also creates a range of knowable alternatives for parents and students.

Unlike privatization, it provides public authorities with leverage to avoid scandal and run a stable school system: they can require race- and sex-neutral admissions, accept only those contractors who will work to help disadvantaged as well as able students, and cancel and replace contracts that fail to provide the services promised or fail to educate large numbers of students. Most importantly, contracting provides the leverage to solve the supply problem that is endemic to pure privatization. It can attract multiple providers by lowering the barriers to entry, and it allows public authorities to offer premiums for work in difficult neighborhoods or to match good contractors to troubled schools on an "assigned risk" basis.

How Contracting Might Be Tried Out

Though a few public school systems have contracted for a few schools, the ideas outlined here have never been used as the basis of a whole school system. Though good providers exist, they could not suddenly gear up to run hundreds of schools next year. Even if the existing potential contractors decided to collaborate in providing all the schools for a whole school system, they could not hope to take over any major city's schools.

The existing providers could, however, make a very big dent in any city's supply of failed schools. As this author has suggested elsewhere (Hill 1992) contracting could have a quick impact on even as large a city as Los Angeles if it were used as the way to redevelop the lowest-performing 5 percent of the city's schools. While even finding contractors to take responsibility for thirty schools (1/6 of the city's 600) would be difficult, it could be done. The key is to begin with organizations that are already running successful schools, including churches and ethnic organizations (including African-American Christian schools). Another source of potential contractors are the staffs of existing public magnet schools. Many of the religious schools are closing down schools every year, and could readily supply teaching and administrative staffs to run nonsectarian schools under public contract. Others, including the public magnet schools, could "hive off" staff and students to reproduce new variants of their existing models.

Innovators and reformers from outside a community could also be enticed in. Profit-makers like the Edison Project and Education Alternatives are ready to go. Principals and teachers who have developed new school models under foundation grants—from, for example, RJR Nabisco, General Electric, and Panasonic—and under state model school programs—like Washington State's Schools for the twenty-first Century—could be placed under contract to recruit and train teachers and open a school on the site of a failed existing school.

The decision of even one major city school system to turn around its worst schools through contracting would elicit an immense new supply of people with school ideas, ready to do the work and take the risks that contracting entails. A decision to promote contracting, made by several big-city mayors, or the governors of a few urban states, would produce great interest among educators and unprecedented amounts of development funding from foundations and the federal government. The supply mechanisms assumed by the contracting approach will provide the supply of good alternatives that must exist if choice is to work, but they require a commitment to try contracting for several years, in a large number of schools.

The people whom education insiders call "stakeholders"—teacher union leaders, parent advocacy organizations, the civil rights bar, and the suppliers of educational materials—are likely to see contracting as an even bigger threat than privatization. It will make it harder for these groups to influence education everywhere by negotiating a policy or consent decree with the local superintendent and a few key school board members. For many stake-holders, anything that inconveniences their adult supporters is perforce harmful to children.

Reform is inconvenient. There is no way America's schools can improve unless the adults who work in them do their jobs differently. The stakeholders have blocked privatization by raising the specters of discrimination against the poor and weakening of the First Amendment. Contracting, by reinventing public education, not eliminating it, will not be so easy to fight. Many of the people who blocked privatization might even join the contracting movement, especially if it is clear that many of them—union leaders, principals' organizations, and experts employed by school system central offices—might get a chance to make a better school. The steady and insistent support for reform must come from parents and members of the business community who know that good schools are places where adults make binding commitments about what they will do for children and have real incentives to deliver.

REFERENCES

Celio, Mary Beth. (1993) *Building and Maintaining Systems of Schools: Lessons from Religious Order School Networks*. Santa Monica, Calif.: RAND Corporation.

Chubb, John E., and Terry E. Moe. (1990) *Politics, Markets, and America's Schools*. Washington, D.C.: The Brookings Institution.

Elmore, Richard. (1986) *Choice in Public Education*. Santa Monica, Calif.: RAND Corporation.

Hill, Paul T. (1992) "Urban Education," *Urban America: Policy Choices for Los Angeles and the Nation*, Vol. 5, pp. 127–51. Santa Monica, Calif.: RAND Corporation.

Osborne, David, and Ted Gaebler. (1992) *Reinventing Government*. Menlo Park, Calif.: Addison-Wesley.

II

ALTERNATIVE PLANS

6

Three Privatization Models for Public Schools

Thomas H. Kean

This chapter focuses on three private sector efforts that have the potential to improve both public and private schools for the next century. Each varies slightly in its approach, but all seek radical change in the way traditional schools operate.

Education Alternatives, Inc., a private, for-profit group, works within the confines of the current public school system. This organization "co-manages" the schools with the existing staff and hopes to do away with many of the bureaucratic bottlenecks in order to save money and make the school a more efficient operation.

The Edison Project, a private, for-profit company, is set up to create brand new schools, separate from public schools, as the only way to correct the ills of the current system. These new schools will cost the same to operate as public schools, will be equipped with state-of-the-art technology, and will use a variety of new teaching methods.

The New American Schools Development Corporation, chaired by the author, is a private, non-profit effort backed entirely by the business community. NASDC has brought together the best and brightest educators to create new learning environments. These designs will operate within the public sector, but they will not look like the schools of today. Each design will combine what works in public education today with new techniques, and the goal is ultimately to allow every community to select among a variety of designs to suit its needs.

Ten years after the release of the report *A Nation at Risk*, the public school in America still faces peril. I fear it may end up like the dinosaurs of millenniums past. Dinosaurs, once the biggest creatures around, defied all predators. When

the environment changed, these massive animals could not. Only those creatures clever and innovative enough to adapt survived. What have dinosaurs to
do with the privatization of the public school?

Effective public schools seem to be a dying breed. We read endless statistics
and articles announcing that American children cannot keep up with their
counterparts worldwide. In fact, students today fare poorly in our own country.
They reach adulthood unable to read or write well and without the critical
thinking skills needed for productive citizenship.

Corporate leaders have long been concerned about the public education
system's ability to graduate competent students, and they have grown thoroughly dissatisfied. They regard the system as unable or unwilling to adapt to
the needs of the twentieth century, let alone the twenty-first. They witness
schools producing graduates for jobs that no longer exist . . . schools ignorant
of technological advances or the global economy . . . schools still teaching
children the way they did 100 years ago and structured on the agrarian calendar
of that time.

For years businesses have tried to influence school reform through volun-
teerism and philanthropy. According to a 1993 study by the Conference Board
and the Points of Light Foundation, 74 percent of businesses focus their
volunteer programs on education as compared with 47 percent on health, 41
percent on the environment, and 41 percent on the homeless. A 1992 *Fortune*
survey indicated that 28% of the Fortune Industrial 500 and the Fortune Service
500 gave one million dollars or more to education. These projects cover the
gamut of school needs. Burger King Academies aim at dropout prevention.
Chevron Accelerated Schools help youngsters who fall behind their classmates.
Martin Marietta sponsors teacher development courses at the University of
Tennessee.

Many of these projects have produced real gains in learning and in improved
relations with communities. Corporate leaders complain that the public schools
are still mediocre. Even as they acknowledge some improvements, only about
one in ten believe that their involvement has made a big difference. Now they
are trying to get more involved.

RJR Nabisco sparked a trend with its $30 million Next Century Schools,
which funds a handful of schools with radical ideas for transforming public
education. In 1992, three new efforts came to the fore—the New American
Schools Development Corporation, the Edison Project, and Education Alternatives, Inc.—marking an even more pervasive role for the private sector in public
education.

NASDC is a private corporation encouraging and funding the design of new
public schools. Edison and Education Alternatives offer more traditional forms
of privatization.

You might compare EAI to the management firms hired to run prisons whose
Departments of Corrections found themselves unable to handle the overflow—

in cost or space—when prison populations doubled in the 1980s. These firms proved that the private sector could build and maintain correctional facilities at lower cost and higher efficiency than government; EAI claims it will do the same for school districts.

The Edison Project, the brainchild of controversial media magnate Christopher Whittle, compares with the mail delivery revolution, in which Federal Express and other companies have offered better services than the public got from the U.S. Postal System. FedEx has flourished and the Post Office has added overnight service and other amenities just to keep up.

Whittle gained notoriety with his Channel One, a ten-minute current-events program broadcast daily to thousands of classrooms nationwide and supported by two minutes of commercials. Channel One has turned a number of educators against Whittle. Typical is writer Jonathan Kozol, who has called him "very dangerous for American education." Kozol said of the Edison Project, "You don't improve the public water supply by selling Coca-Cola."

BETTER MANAGEMENT FOR BETTER LEARNING

Education Alternatives, a five-year-old for-profit venture, attempts public school reform from within. It rests on the belief that while learning environments must improve, the public school should survive. EAI operates in the school itself, contracting with school boards to buy services. In one sense, EAI extends a practice already employed by many public schools for food and bus services. The company also moves into previously uncharted territory.

EAI tries to direct a higher percentage of a school's budget to instruction and teacher training through better management. EAI may hire one company to operate the plant and another to analyze spending and employ staff more efficiently. The savings, minus a percentage for EAI, revert to curriculum development. Some of the savings support Tesseract, a progressive approach to education intended to provide more individual attention to students. One teacher, helped by an intern, works with up to thirty youngsters and develops "personal educational plans" that set goals for each student. Tesseract integrates computers and real-life experiences into the curriculum. EAI assumes day-to-day management, trains teachers in Tesseract, and promises measurable gains in student achievement—all for the per-pupil amount the district already spends.

EAI sounds too good to be true, and perhaps it is. The company has yet to turn a profit and a new client, the Baltimore school system, has had problems. Some critics say that the firm moved too quickly. The Baltimore teachers' union boycotted many of the teacher training sessions. Still, these setbacks may simply demonstrate the cost of trying to improve schools from within. A deeper understanding of the school culture and the school as a work place may help

EAI solve its problems. I consider it promising, nonetheless, that EAI has dedicated a large part of its efforts to training teachers.

A LIGHTBULB INSTEAD OF A CANDLE

Chris Whittle ought to escape some of EAI's setbacks, since the Edison Project tries to fix schools from the outside. Whittle and a small cadre of high-profile advisers plan to create a powerful incentive for public schools to improve. He envisions for-profit, private schools so successful that public schools will have to improve just to stay in business. He also promises to share his technological advances with the public schools.

Edison Project schools will remain open at least twelve hours a day, twelve months a year. Parental participation is in, central bureaucracy is out. Technology runs through every act of learning. Whittle envisions that all students will have computers and printers that will connect them to "every book that a student might need, every film, every speech, every image that can be accessed electronically."

The Edison Project rests at the other end of the privatization spectrum from EAI. Whittle will not take over a group of schools or even one school; rather, he has set out to create 1,000 brand new schools by 1996 that will cost as much as the country's average per-pupil expenditure—about $5,500 as of 1992 and rising.

The notion of starting from scratch appeals. Whittle won't encounter the burdensome system of school boards and district offices. He'll have no trouble with teachers' unions because teachers hired will have already signed on to the system. I assume that Whittle will train the teachers in the technology he hopes to use, although he has not made that point clear. In fact, we know little yet about Edison Project plans. Whittle has only recently hired his team.

What makes Whittle so sure he can create new schools? Won't they simply mirror the selective private schools that exist? How will he replicate each of these new schools? These questions still await answers, but the return-on-investment concept that the Edison Project promotes should be given a chance.

Whittle must answer a more pressing question: how will parents afford his tuition? He pledges that one-fifth of all students will receive full scholarships, but that leaves 80 percent paying $6,000 or more a year. Many have assumed that Whittle will have to rely on the use of vouchers unless he hopes to establish 1,000 schools open to all but affordable to few. However, both President Clinton and his Secretary of Education, Richard Riley, have opposed vouchers. Riley told a Senate committee, "I am 100 percent convinced that it is not good for public schools. The bottom half would be terribly disserved to pull large amounts of dollars out of the public schools."

Edison Project schools will suffer from the need for vouchers to make them affordable to the average American family. While I believe we ought to experiment with vouchers, the New American Schools Development Corporation represents a different alternative.

BREAKING THE MOLD

NASDC, a private corporation for which I served for two years as Chairman of the Board, will develop the ideas and let communities, without charge, choose a suitable model from this research and design project. NASDC is a non-profit organization funded entirely by business. There is no profit or shareholder responsibility. It is dedicated to improving *public* schools through *private* means.

NASDC had its birth in the Bush administration. It was on the cutting edge of President Bush's four-pronged "America 2000" strategy which encouraged cities and towns to adopt the six national education goals, map a strategy to meet them, draft a report card to mark progress, and create a "break the mold" school. NASDC was asked to develop an array of new schools more conducive to learning. Communities would be free to choose the learning environment best suited to their needs.

What intrigued me when the President asked me to chair NASDC was the prospect of radical, systemic change. The President wasn't asking us to clean out the barn; he wanted a new barn. We were charged with fixing the schools by completely revamping them. There would be no sacred cows in this barn, either. Every aspect of a school would be on the table, from how the year is structured to how classes are organized to how student learning is measured.

In the fall of 1991 we went to work. Calling upon the advice of a board that included philanthropist Walter Annenberg (who committed $10 million to the enterprise), Louis Gerstner, now chairman of IBM and then CEO of RJR Nabisco and the instigator of Next Century Schools, and the heads of corporations like AT&T and Eastman Kodak, we created a Request for Proposals (RFP) and challenged the brightest minds in America to give us their ideas for the best schools in the world.

Nearly 700 proposals came to NASDC by February of 1992. The NASDC formed an Education Advisory Panel, led by the former New Jersey Commissioner of Education, Saul Cooperman, to oversee the evaluation process. The original batch of 686 proposals was reviewed by a group of 180 "readers" chosen for their expertise in education, management, public relations, business, and technology. They judged designs against four criteria: 1) their likelihood for enabling all students to reach the national education goals set by President Bush and the nation's governors and thus to attain world-class standards; 2) the quality of their plans for assessing their own performance; 3) their potential for widespread application; and 4) their cost-effectiveness (all New American Schools were expected to operate at the normal cost of running a school).

Readers pared the list to about 200, and the Education Advisory Panel honed in on about twenty-five designs. In July of 1992, the Board selected eleven for funding. Two of the eleven designs have since been denied further funding and a third is operating on first-year funds because of a late start in implementation.

A brief description of the current designs demonstrates the breadth and diversity of NASDC approaches:

The Los Angeles Learning Centers. This plan links each young student with older students, parents, teachers, and a community volunteer throughout grade clusters. Three grade clusters will carry the students through grades four, eight, and twelve, and the classes will be ungraded.

Teachers also learn, and the classroom will involve the family, the work place, the city, the neighborhood, and the health and social services (called a "Moving Diamond" of support). Because one out of every 100 students in this country is enrolled in Los Angeles County schools, it is essential that this program works.

The traditional sense of "after school" programs will end, since the centers will be open daily from the early morning until the evening, for fifty weeks of the year. The curriculum will center on English, science, history, mathematics, geography, and languages other than English. About one day per week will be allocated to teachers so they can continue their own learning, solve student needs, and create plans with their fellow teachers.

Students are to be taught how to solve real-world problems and how to connect what they learn across disciplines. Transition-to-work programs during the final two years of upper school will devote per-pupil resources to support training possibilities. Opportunities to learn away from school will be available, such as the use of multilingual neighborhoods of the area for foreign language practice.

A site-based Management Council made up of teachers, parents, students, and the Center principal will decide issues of curriculum, discipline, community relations, students' rights, and budget. State-of-the-art technologies will be available to the teachers and students who can learn from systems widely used in business to gain administrative efficiency.

Health and social services will be linked by integrating the experience of thirty agencies currently planning services within L.A. County. Through the cooperation of the students, teachers, parents, and older students, the "Moving Diamond" plans to provide in-depth learning for young Los Angelenos.

The Co-NECT School. Emphasizing math and science, the Co-NECT Schools will attempt to prove that technologies can form a communication environment where better learning can take place. Students will initiate projects that investigate local, national, and global issues and gain knowledge in all subject areas, achieving where they otherwise would have failed. Multimedia and interactive video technologies will be used in almost every activity that the students perform.

Clusters of six teachers and up to 100 students will be the focus of all academic activities. Teachers will advise the students for several years, and each teaching team will be self-governing and responsible for all parts of the school's operation.

Co-NECT encourages students to maintain their independence. They map their progress through the maintenance of resources and portfolios, and with the assistance of parents and teachers, focus on long-term goals and on how much effort is necessary to achieve these goals.

A computer-based network will link school community members with one another and with various resources and tools. Through the connection to the National Science Foundation (NSF) internet regional network, the program gives students a means of communication with scientists working on research projects all around the world. Assessing the students' work will involve rating their portfolios, their progress in the five core areas, and their abilities and attitudes toward life and work.

The Modern Red Schoolhouse. Using technology, the Modern Red School-house program aims to bring "classical education" back into the schools. Students will study five core subjects (math, science, history, geography, and English) and bring personal accountability to an "old fashioned" idea about schooling. The model will cover seven school districts in rural, urban, suburban, and Native American communities and boasts of former Secretary of Education Bill Bennett as one of its design team members.

Students will undergo self-paced learning, which enables them to meet standards based on their effort, ability, and prior attainment. They will negotiate with the school and their families an Individual Education Contract (IEC), a kind of educational road map for the student over a period of time. Students will be grouped into multi-age, multi-year "homerooms" headed by teacher/advisors.

Schools will have their own characteristics, including flexible daily and yearly schedules, the elimination of traditional grading formats, and autonomy from the district. Principals will take the role of CEO and the instructional staff will comprise master teachers, associate teachers, teachers' aides, and volunteers from all backgrounds. Students and teachers will attend the schools by choice and a random "draw" from students interested in a particular school will determine enrollment.

The schools will assess student progress at three transitional levels (primary, middle, and upper), and devise ways to report student achievement to parents, students, and the community. Technology will enable the school to communicate more effectively with families and allow for instruction, management, and communication between the home, community, and school. Parents will be able to keep track of their school through databases, community access television, and electronic bulletin boards, and they will have a two-way communication link with the teachers to discuss their child's progress.

The National Alliance for Restructuring Education. Marc Tucker, president of the National Center on Education and the Economy, heads this design team, which will apply lessons learned from industry's Total Quality Management movement to improve the outcomes and achievements of public schools. By 1995, the National Alliance hopes to have 243 "break the mold" schools in seven states working with an outcome-based curriculum in core subject areas.

The National Alliance will incorporate the curricular standards adopted by the New Standards Project, which will release its first tests (for English language arts and math) by 1994–1995, with other discipline areas to follow. This examination system has been created to measure the quality of work through portfolios, exhibitions, and projects.

Teachers will be encouraged to design their own curricula from a growing bank of teacher-oriented research information and updated curricular models. Teachers will serve as the students' collaborators and are the chief designers of the education programs. New teachers will work side-by-side with master teachers. The principal will facilitate teachers' efforts more than simply enforce rules made elsewhere.

Business will play a vital role. An effort will be made to find industrial corporations with expertise in quality management to offer technical assistance to the schools. Apple Computer will lend assistance through its Apple Classrooms of Tomorrow to bring computer-based technologies into the curriculum. The design will also include a new work transition program to be created by the Commission on the Skills of the American Workforce.

Roots and Wings. Using the term "neverstreaming" as its focal point, Roots and Wings intends to help all children succeed in the regular classroom by giving them the best early tools in school. Led by Johns Hopkins University researcher Robert Slavin, and based in rural St. Mary's County in Maryland, it will serve children from infancy through age eleven. Children will work on real-life problems during the elementary grades and pursue activities relevant to their own communities through a program called Worldlab. Each subject will be related to the Worldlab simulations, and cooperative learning and integration techniques will be used.

At-risk students will receive family support services, tutoring, assistance in the classroom, and other services. There are no official grades in the schools, and students are grouped across age lines based on their interests and accomplishments.

Parents will participate in the school program by way of a family support team at each location. Parents can choose to send their children to any of the four schools. Each school has a facilitator, who will coach teachers, oversee the staff's efforts, and make sure that each child is succeeding. Backing up the facilitator will be a School Improvement Team, a group which will ensure that the school's particular needs are met by the Roots and Wings design.

Each student will have a "passport" that records that student's accomplishments during his or her time at the school, or at one of the other schools in the same district. The passport can aid the school in deciding student placements and progress in the nongraded blocks.

The College for Human Services. The premise that students learn best when they connect what they are learning with the real world is the intention of the Audrey Cohen College design team. Each semester, students will study a "Purpose" with a substantial body of knowledge and a socially important thrust (for instance, "We Work for Good Health"). Core subject lessons will allow the students to explore each semester's purpose, using the applied learning concept.

The curriculum contains three elements. *Purpose*, the first, is the broad area of activity around which the student is learning over a period of time. In the second, classes are organized around *Dimensions*—critical perspectives from which knowledge is examined and acted upon. The third element, *Constructive Action*, allows the student to use what he or she is learning to plan and act in the world outside of the classroom.

Each day, children will go into the community to learn how to take action in an integrated atmosphere. Educational programs and internships will be organized by community organizations outside of academia. Likewise, families can become sources for the learning process. Parents and parent surrogates will interact with children from the first learning stage.

The curriculum will be planned by the teachers as a team. Principals will become "educational brokers," marshalling classroom and community resources to help students achieve their *Purposes*, while finding themselves more involved in everyday educational activities.

Besides employing audio and video resources for gathering information in the community, students will have telecommunication tools they can use to contact other schools in the country and around the world.

In terms of assessment, the student will be expected to possess an essential body of knowledge, use critical thinking in making critical judgments, and use English language skills correctly and effectively. If these abilities are organized properly, the student will be able to progress at his or her pace to higher intellectual levels. Abilities in the *Constructive Action* area are to be assessed by teachers, by other students, and, on occasion, by people from the community.

Expeditionary Learning. Outward Bound sponsored a design that begins with the idea that to start a school is to proclaim what it means to be a human being. This team believes children will learn to think by moving through program-related voyages and adventures. The core subjects like math and science and English will intertwine with these adventures.

A student in this design would be assigned to a "watch"—a group of about a dozen students who will stay together for several years. Each watch will share responsibility for presenting research reports, solving problems, serving the school and the community, and even playing together.

A watch will join with one or two others in a "crew" and be led by an expedition guide. From kindergarten through second grade, they will have the same teacher. A second teacher will have the crew from third grade to fifth, and so on. These crews will mix ages, and older students will help younger ones.

The expeditions will take place in museums, hospitals, businesses, airports, social agencies. One expedition might develop an understanding of the bubonic plague. Crew members might write biographies of people from that time. They would use math to project life spans, or draw house plans and scale models of villages in that time. At one point they might research issues like superstition and public health—and discuss whether there are connections to the AIDS epidemic of today.

ATLAS Communities. This design was put forth by some of the nation's leading thinkers on education, including Ted Sizer from Brown University, who heads the Coalition of Essential Schools, and James Comer of Yale, who has done remarkable work in the area of student learning.

ATLAS schools will use technology in creative ways. They will support each student with a community health team that includes teachers, parents, psychologists, and social workers. Students will learn by doing. They will seek out experts in the school, at home, or a place of business. They will consult primary resources. They will carry out experiments and then communicate them with other students. A seven-year-old might work with a sixteen-year-old on a project on astronomy.

ATLAS Communities will not rely on traditional tests. Students' understanding and progress will be judged in a much different way. They will show how to use what they have learned in one area to solve a problem in another. Each student will build a portfolio of work and be examined on performances like debates or group explanations of a particular idea.

Community Learning Centers of Minnesota. Using the State of Minnesota's charter school law as a jumping-off point, this program gives teachers the responsibility for what their students learn. They have to make sure that their students meet the state standards for improvement or the school charter may not be renewed. Parents, educators, students, social service agencies, and community business agencies take responsibility for the management of each center through a representative council.

An outcome-based education is the program's goal. Students might, for example, demonstrate their writing proficiency and civics awareness by sending letters on pressing public issues to their elected officials. Students will learn cooperatively in projects such as implementing a new school service program. Students may even plan the learning activities during the day and be held accountable for the results of these exercises.

Teachers are to be in charge of the curriculum. They will be expected to incorporate modern technology into the classroom and involve parents in learning. A contract or charter will dictate measures by which to judge the center's performance in attendance, educational goals, and graduation percentages. The center will also negotiate with the school district over the degree of independent decision-making, budget decisions, learning outcomes, program freedoms in each school, and staffing arrangements. Social agencies will provide services on-site as needed.

A Community Learning Center aim is the proverbial "more with less"— more results with fewer staff so that technological equipment may be acquired within normal district budgets. Students will take an active and experiential approach to education, learning from methods such as video, role playing, field trips, and analogies. Assessment methods will be qualitative and quantitative, recording data such as graduation rates, parental enthusiasm, thinking skills, adult participation, and results of academic achievements at all grade levels.

" ... FRAMEWORKS AND EXEMPLARS ... "

The eleven New American Schools designs diverge on the methods they use to reach educational excellence, yet they share common threads:

1. Teachers take on the role of facilitator and mentor, not just lecturer.

2. Technology becomes a tool of learning, not simply an attention-grabber.

3. Students are expected to master the basics *and* to apply them to real-life situations.

4. Parents get involved directly in the learning process.

5. The school takes a more visible place in the community. Through activities like visits to the local newspaper, joint projects with the county health department, and invitations for the Chamber of Commerce president to teach a seminar, the school finds its way into the minds of community residents, if not their hearts as well.

I would be wrong to suggest that NASDC has been an unadulterated success. In truth, the organization has struggled in a number of areas during its first two years. After an initial flurry, fundraising has stalled at about $50 million. Despite steady support from President Bush, publicity for NASDC has been poor from the start, and the effort has remained a blip on the radar screen of public school reform. One project, which has since been dropped for unrelated reasons, drew the ire of Christian activists who contended that its curriculum would undermine their children's religious beliefs.

A RAND Corporation consultant in April 1993 reported several problems in the implementation of NASDC designs. The consultant's report pointed out that because some schools will only be partially operational by the fall, timely and accurate evaluation will become more difficult for those endeavors. It criticized a few of the teams that have not incorporated world-class standards thoroughly into their plans and argued that student assessment measures, particularly ones external to individual schools, remain sketchy. It expressed disappointment that secondary schools have received far less attention than primary schools, suspecting that curriculum-centered faculty in high schools are less amenable to radical changes in school structure. It described collaboration among teams as "weak."

NASDC's prospects have brightened considerably with this spring's public endorsement by President Bill Clinton. In a White House speech describing his "GOALS 2000" plan for education, President Clinton said:

> The private sector in this country has shown an astonishing willingness to become more involved in education ever since the issuance of the Nation at Risk report ten years ago. The New American Schools Development Corporation . . . has already raised millions of dollars from public-spirited business leaders. It has path-breaking design teams which are providing us with valuable lessons about how school innovations all around America can help us to reach world class standards. And it is trying to help replicate what works, which I still believe is our most urgent task.

> Through these new designs, they will be able to provide promising alternatives for schools and states as they work to reinvent their schools with the help of GOALS 2000 and other reform efforts that this administration will make. I ask all of you to support this legislation and the work of the New American Schools Development Corporation. I ask you to support it in the larger context of what we must do as a nation.

Adding to Clinton's praise, that April RAND report commended NASDC for a number of contributions to education reform, such as the emphasis on developing school faculties as teams that share a vision and a strategy; the focus on innovative uses of technology; the emphasis on continuous performance improvement; and what RAND called "organic school capacity for program development." As RAND explained, "The design teams have not tried to develop complete programs that can simply be adopted *in toto* by a school; an approach that has almost always failed in the past. Rather, they provide frameworks and exemplars that support schools in individualized development. The designs go significantly beyond organizational development processes but stop short of a complete prescription of programs. They recognize and support the professional responsibilities of teachers."

The spirit and the long-term prospects for New American Schools remain sound. Unlike EAI or Edison, NASDC is a private venture that seeks to improve public schools from the outside in and from inside out without hope of profit. Every public school in America stands to benefit from its work. As a school that adopts an NASDC design proves effective, others in the same community will be able to replicate the design in their buildings. For now, it is the best form of "privatization" around.

All these efforts to bring the private sector into the public schools have drawn criticism from educators. They point out that, for the most part, these ideas aren't new. They can cite one school or another in some district, somewhere in the country, which has already succeeded with the very ideas that privateers are touting as revolutionary.

The critics have missed the point. Across the nation, districts *are* achieving remarkable things—Harlem's District Four, Montclair in New Jersey, some of the Comer schools, Alachua County in Florida. Effective public schools remain the exception rather than the rule. Their success remains isolated, even from neighboring districts. Often they depend on a charismatic leader. When that leader leaves the scene, the district slides back toward mediocrity.

The mark of the entrepreneur is finding the best way to do something, not necessarily the newest. Should projects like Edison, EAI, and NASDC do no more than draw attention to what works, then they will have achieved their purpose.

Those interested in public education must make a choice. The status quo will no longer stand. Public school leaders must be open to new ideas. They must embrace change. If they do not, those interested in better schools will look more and more to the private sector for solutions.

If our public schools are to avoid the fate of the dinosaurs, and for the sake of our democracy I believe they must, we have to pursue every means of improvement—even those that offend our educational instincts. Edison Project advocates think competition will get us there. Educational Alternatives proponents say better management will. New American School supporters believe the basic school structure must change. All these viewpoints are right. All these paths must be traveled. A nation cannot remain at risk forever.

7

Redesigning the Financing of American Education to Raise Productivity: The Case for a Just Voucher

Peter W. Cookson, Jr.

Until recently, I thought that the efforts to deregulate public education were at their core undemocratic and probably not feasible; I still believe that public education is a fundamental institution upon which our democratic future is dependent (Cookson 1992). In the last several years I have been engaged in a national study of school choice and as a result I have come to believe that a redesign of American elementary and secondary education is not only desirable but essential. The hostility toward privatization is largely misplaced if privatization plans are driven by a sense of justice. The inequities of the public education system today are so profound that without a fundamental redesign in the way in which public and private education is funded, millions and millions of American children will be permanently excluded from the economy and from participation in society. The crisis in American education is the crisis in children's lives. Decency impels us to do everything in our power to create schools for the poor that are equal to, if not better than, schools for the rich.

From a redesign point of view, the fundamental issue is school finance. To continue to fund schools in an inequitable manner is to mandate unequal education, which condemns the disadvantaged to permanent economic dependency and social isolation. Traditionally, the most common alternative to the current method of financing education has been the school voucher. While voucher proposals vary, a voucher can be defined as an "arrangement whereby individuals are in effect handed the funds (typically in the form of a chit) to purchase the schooling of their choice outside the public sector" (Raywid 1987, 762). For a wide variety of reasons voucher proposals have been lightning rods for public controversy and, by and large, supporters of public education have lobbied hard to defeat a variety of voucher proposals.

To dismiss voucher proposals as anti-public school, however, is a serious policy error. School vouchers are simply a way of returning to families the money that they themselves have earned and given to the government in the form of taxes. Revenues derived from taxation ought not go to support public school bureaucracies that heretofore have been resistant to educational innovation and have sadly used a significant proportion of their revenues to maintain themselves, sometimes at the expense of children's education. A thoughtful system of vouchers would not weaken public education but strengthen it, because it would lead to greater parental involvement and loyalty. Public education is strong; it need not collapse in the face of competition from the private sector. A redesign of American education should include voucher provisions that provide continuing support for public schools. Private schools do not work educational miracles as it is sometimes implied. In fact, most private schools are exceedingly pedestrian from a redesign point-of-view. Privatization is a scare word among public educators, but if all that privatization means is allowing families the freedom to choose their children's schools and allowing groups of people to found new schools, then we must ask ourselves if these fears are real or imaginary. This chapter is written from the perspective of one who supports public education but who also believes that alternative forms of financing public and private education must be seriously considered if we are not to foreclose the future to millions of children. Some voucher plans are derived from economic theories about the nature of the market place (Friedman and Friedman 1980) and other voucher plans are derived from social theories about the nature of a just society (Coons and Sugarman 1992). The voucher plan that is suggested in this chapter draws its inspiration primarily from a theory of a just society, but also acknowledges that sensible and controlled competition is a method for creating more diversity in education. The fundamental principles of this redesign plan are that just schools are essential for a just society and that educational innovation is essential for a productive society.

The essential argument of this chapter is that a revitalization of American education rests on three policy postulates:

1. Every child is entitled to equal access to educational opportunity and every child one year after birth or upon entrance into the educational system should receive an "educational trust fund." The poorer the child the larger the fund.

2. Existing public and private schools may compete for students and thereby for funding, but schools that receive public funds must ensure that at least 20 percent of their admissions openings are reserved for

students who come from families whose incomes are at or below the established poverty line. While public schools will still be substantially funded through revenues raised through taxation and public gambling, at least 30 percent of each public school's income will be raised from vouchers. Public schools whose annual revenues exceed their actual expenses may retain these surpluses for school improvement.

3. Individuals and groups may create "model" schools, which can be financially supported through private contributions and through income derived from vouchers. These schools are subject to the same enrollment guidelines as other public and private schools.

The organization of this chapter is straightforward. After an examination of the traditional problems and promises of school vouchers, a proposed voucher system is outlined and discussed. Very often choice and voucher plans are appealing at an abstract level but are so vague that there is no way of telling if they would work in practice. One cannot solve educational and social problems by rhetoric alone. It is essential to offer a concrete plan that can be examined in the light of its basic suppositions about the nature of schooling and society. Policy cards should be played openly; without daring and candor, redesign will remain just another educational buzzword.

Problems and Promises of Vouchers

Throughout American history the balance between liberty and equity has teetered perilously; overall, however, the ethos of equity has been dominant in the public discourse about education. The voices of liberty have never been completely silent. Over two hundred years ago Thomas Paine proposed a voucher plan in *The Rights of Man* and Adam Smith argued for at least partial parental funding of education (Wise and Darling-Hammond 1984, 32). More recently, Stephen Arons (1983) has argued that as the "one best system," public education violates the right of free speech. John E. Coons and Stephen D. Sugarman (1992) have argued that compulsory public education violates freedom of choice as a matter of personal conscience and social justice. Milton and Rose Friedman (1980) and John E. Chubb and Terry M. Moe (1990) maintain that markets are better arbiters of the social good than are public institutions. During the 1960s, some school reformers advocated vouchers as a way of diversifying educational opportunity and helping disadvantaged families gain access to quality education. In the 1970s, the Office of Educational Opportunity and the National Institute of Education funded a voucher demonstration project in Alum Rock, a school district in California. This plan did not include private schools and only 20 percent of the parents participating in this voucher experiment chose to send their children to non-neighborhood schools (Cookson

1989; Wells 1991). As a consequence, the results of this test case did not yield any clear indication about the feasibility or desirability of vouchers as a way of providing equal educational access to students and as a method for stimulating educational innovation.

In a somewhat different vein, the Reagan administration in the 1980s proposed several tuition tax credit schemes that included some rudimentary voucher-like elements, but these proposals failed to pass either the Senate or the House of Representatives (Cookson 1989, 78). At the same time, a number of legislators were calling for "Compensatory Education Grants" for disadvantaged students, but none of these plans was passed into law, at least at the national level. In the last five years, however, the voucher movement has gained increasing momentum both in individual states and at the national level. The 1990 Oregon initiative provided every child in the state with a $2,500 subsidy to be used for tuition and expenses in private elementary and secondary schools. In 1991 a Pennsylvania statute that provided $900 "Educational Opportunity Grants" for use in private schools was passed by the Pennsylvania Senate but was narrowly defeated in the Pennsylvania House of Representatives. Supporters of a "Parental Choice in Education Amendment" in California have placed a voucher proposal that is very similar to the Oregon plan on the California ballot.

Perhaps the most well-known voucher plan to be enacted is in Milwaukee, Wisconsin. In 1989, the Wisconsin legislature adopted a voucher plan that was strongly supported by Representative Annette (Polly) Williams, an African-American Democrat and a supporter of the Reverend Jesse Jackson. Representative Williams believes that African-American children should not be bused to white schools, but that African-American families should be allowed to choose private schools in their own communities. Representative Williams expressed her views as follows, "this parentalistic idea that poor people can't make choices is ridiculous. Poor people are some of the best shoppers, most skilled at stretching a dollar, you'll ever see" (Coons and Sugarman 1992, 62). Only 1000 students may participate in this voucher plan and a study by John E. Witte (1993, 70) found that only 341 students could be accommodated by the schools which participated in the plan. While there have been questions raised about the Milwaukee voucher plan as it relates to providing quality education for African-American children, the Wisconsin Supreme Court upheld the constitutionality of the plan in 1992.

In January of 1992, a "Low Income School Choice Demonstration Project" sponsored by Senator Orrin Hatch of Utah was defeated in the U.S. Senate. This amendment would have appropriated $30 million to be used by the Secretary of Education to support choice plans in up to six locations. Sponsored projects would have to provide choice options, and these options could include religious schools. Federal funds were to be used to provide "educational certificates" to pay the tuition fees and extra transportation costs of low-income families participating in choice plans. In this regard, the Hatch proposal is very similar to the scholarship program sponsored by the Golden Rule Insurance Company which helps low-income families living in the Indianapolis, Indiana, Public School District to send their children to private schools of their choice. The Hatch proposal provides that the value of the certificates be set at the per pupil expenditure rate of the public school district where the child lives. Despite the defeat of this amendment, it is the intention of the Senator to continue to propose an inner-city school voucher plan. In the summer of 1992 educational advocacy groups in Los Angeles and in Chicago undertook lawsuits demanding that groups of low-income parents and children receive state vouchers for private school tuition (Walsh 1992).

This very brief overview of the history of school vouchers in the United States is meant to highlight the key issues that chronically appear in the debate as to whether or not vouchers will prove to be a useful way of encouraging equity and educational innovation. Traditionally, a reoccurring argument against vouchers is that public financial support of religious schools (and most private schools are religiously affiliated) is unconstitutional because such support violates the First Amendment to the U.S. Constitution, which prohibits the government from establishing a state religion. The courts have consistently maintained a very narrow construction of the establishment clause, which has meant that religious schools have not received a great many public dollars, although, private schools do derive some of their income from public sources. Another argument against vouchers is that by allowing parents to choose schools for their children, the public school system will flounder and eventually wither. For those who believe that compulsory education in state-run schools violates the right of free speech, as indicated in the First Amendment to the Constitution, this possible eventuality is not considered a liability. For those public school supporters who believe in the common school, however, the idea that the public school should pass into history is anathema. Moreover, the Fourteenth Amendment to the Constitution specifically states that no citizen may be deprived of "life, liberty or property" without due process of the law and the equal protection of the laws. In effect, the Fourteenth Amendment makes a strong case for a publicly funded school system.

Those who have advocated vouchers essentially have taken the opposite position on each of these issues. Voucher advocates believe that genuine educational freedom ought to be protected under the First Amendment by allowing for freedom of educational choice and that the establishment clause does not preclude public support of religious schools as long as all religions are equally entitled to these funds. Voucher proponents have further argued that the apparent cultural neutrality said to characterize the ethos of the public school is little more than the ideas and opinions of an educational establishment that has no more or no less bias in its thinking than private school trustees and administrators. Market oriented proponents of vouchers argue that by increasing school choice parents and children will have a far greater number of educational options and that, on the whole, parental choice, supported by vouchers, will allow educational innovation to develop. Equity oriented voucher proponents have strongly argued, as I do in this chapter, that the present method of financing education reinforces class and race segregation. The neighborhood school, far from being a common school, is in many cases a microcosm of the very social problems that the public school is supposed to alleviate.

If we were to balance the pros and cons of the voucher issue in a dispassionate manner, it is apparent that the arguments against school vouchers have lost their force because the environment in which schools operate today essentially ensures that public schools reflect the very problems that they are attempting to ameliorate. The bureaucratic structure of the public school system stifles innovation and the financial structure of the public school system reinforces educational and social stratification. The time has come to propose a redesign of American education that balances equity with liberty, innovation with stability, and opportunity with justice.

Elements of a Just Voucher System

School choice is a matter of social trust (Coons and Sugarman 1992, 3). The word trust is used here in several ways: parents and children should be trusted to make sensible educational choices, educators should be trusted to create schools that are decent learning environments for children, and the government should trust the people to make wise decisions about their own lives. Genuine school choice derives its power from a social covenant based on individual conscience and collective responsibility. True community springs from true liberty, but true liberty can only have meaning in terms of collective responsibilities. In this sense, each of us is responsible for ourselves but we also have responsibilities toward others. We have a particular responsibility toward children regardless of their parents' financial status, racial characteristics, or beliefs. One significant measure of a good society is the degree to which it reveres its children. Thus, an alternative design for education ought to begin with the very basic principles of community trust, individual freedom, and collective responsibility. These are the principles that guide the alternative design system outlined below. The three key elements of the new system are: (a) the establishment of an educational trust fund for every child, (b) a carefully managed system of school choice, and (c) the creation of "model" schools. These major components are discussed below. Subsequent to these discussions a proposal is presented in outline form.

Educational Trust Funds

A basic principle of this plan is that every child has the same right to educational opportunity as every other child. This does not mean that every child is of equal talent nor does it mean that we should expect every child to reach the same level of academic proficiency. The right of access refers to the social obligation of the community not to discriminate against a child because of his or her family characteristics or personal limitations. Thus, every child is entitled to a school voucher that can be used at a school of his or her choice or his or her family's choice. In a society that is highly stratified and where the financing of education is also highly stratified it is necessary in a redesign plan that the monetary worth of a school voucher be in inverse relation to the amount of a family's income. The poorer the child the greater the worth of his or her voucher. In effect, every child receives at birth an educational trust fund that guarantees him or her equal access to the schools of his or her choice. How these trust funds will be financed will be discussed in the proposal itself. The fundamental concept of the educational trust fund is that we, as a community, make a commitment to children that their life opportunities will not be fore-shortened for reasons of their birth.

Managed School Choice

Most market driven voucher plans attempt to deregulate the educational marketplace by minimizing the authority of the state in the regulation of schools. The California initiative of 1992 is an example of this trend. Essentially, the market model for redesigning the school system is an alternative schools model which can be found in some statewide school choice plans. The State of Minnesota, for instance, has implemented a series of school choice policies that are based on the alternative schools model. While this redesign model has many virtues, it does leave the door open to the continuing stratification of educational opportunities by emphasizing individual choice over collective responsibility. Moreover, there is evidence that the Minnesota plan has not produced the educational renaissance that its promoters have predicted (Cookson 1994, 46). The central problem of the market model of educational reform and unregulated privatization of education is that it underemphasizes the importance of the social covenant and often fails to recognize that schools are not only social inventions, they are also social interventions.

Moreover, how do schools become truly excellent? Or more specifically, how do schools become educationally productive? Do schools become better when they exclude students according to students' ascriptive characteristics or do they become better when they include students because of their achievement characteristics? In the 1980s I had the opportunity to conduct research in over 100 American private schools. Those schools that had become co-educational in the

1970s, and had become more racially and ethnically diverse, outperformed more traditional schools on a variety of student outcome measures. Diversity sparks intellectual imagination and encourages healthy competition. The argument that schools become more effective when student bodies become homogenous has not been empirically demonstrated nor is it socially desirable. In a society that is becoming increasingly multicultural it is imperative that students learn to tolerate and rejoice in diversity. Equity drives excellence.

Recent research has indicated that controlled school choice in such different communities as Cambridge and Fall River, Massachusetts, and White Plains, New York, has resulted in greater parental involvement, racial balance, and school autonomy (Cookson 1994, 55–64). Controlled choice has not resulted in more regulation. Almost all parents are able to place their children in their first school of choice in a controlled choice design. A key element in a just voucher system is that a family may invest their child's educational trust fund in schools that they choose with the provision that schools accept at least 20 percent of their students from homes whose families incomes are at or below the poverty line established by the federal government. The 20 percent commitment ensures that a publicly funded school does not discriminate against the disadvantaged and positively commits itself to the educational promise implicit in diversity. It is not the obligation of the taxpayer to support schools that are socially elite or racially divisive.

Historically, most voucher plans were designed in a manner that allowed parents the financial capacity for choosing a private school for their child. In a system of carefully managed choice, however, it is imperative that public education be partially protected from the uncertainties of the marketplace. It is both unfeasible and undesirable to deregulate the public school system entirely. The redesign of American education should strengthen the public sector, not weaken it. To this end, public schools in a just voucher system would continue to receive revenues that were raised through taxation and state operated gambling. However, these revenues would only cover 70 percent of a public school's operating budget. The remaining 30 percent would have to be raised by attracting voucher students. A public school that receives educational trust funds from students must ensure that 20 percent of its student body is composed of students whose families incomes are at or below the poverty line. It is important to remember, however, that these students receive larger vouchers than other students and are thus economically attractive to public schools. The key incentive for public schools to recruit voucher students, especially voucher students from disadvantaged homes, is that the schools retain any surplus that they accrue during the course of the school year in order to improve their programs, reimburse their faculty, or maintain the school itself. These potential surpluses could be accrued over the years. This method of financing public education balances the need of a strong publicly supported school system with the need to stimulate competition among public and private schools. It also has the benefit of making disadvantaged students attractive recruits to schools outside their own neighborhoods.

Managed school choice is a mechanism for maximizing educational freedom while ensuring educational stability. It is also a proven way to achieve racial balance within the school system. Managed school choice, however, does not imply that the state has any authority to regulate what schools teach, how they teach, or what their educational missions ought to be. Managed school choice is a method for encouraging schools to innovate by rewarding schools with educational vision and social commitment.

Creation of Model Schools

Equity is a necessary but not sufficient condition for a true educational transformation. Just as a community has a covenant to protect its children and to guarantee its children equal educational opportunity, the community has the obligation to promote individual and family liberty. Thus, if groups and individuals are able to found a school that does not violate the conditions of the social covenant discussed above, their school may be designated a "model school" and may be eligible to receive funds from children's educational trust funds. Model schools must have fifty or more students. Model schools are educational providers of services that may be public or private depending on the goals of the groups and individuals who found them. It is at this point that the virtues of the marketplace become apparent and where the power of privatization can transform education by encouraging educational innovators and families to take educational risks in the name of their children's futures. There is a possible danger that the model schools concept would be coopted by large and wealthy educational "conglomerates" which would, in effect, franchise their educational services in order to attract a very large number of consumers. It is apparent that wealthy entrepreneurs could have more market advantages than people without significant resources. There is little to preclude large educational franchises from engaging in monopolistic practices unless their market practices are, in part, regulated by state authorities. Any model school that receives public money must make the 20 percent commitment to disadvantaged children as discussed above. If founders of model schools do not violate the rule of equal access then the state should have only a small role to play in monitoring and regulating the model schools. This principle has been repeatedly supported by the U.S. Supreme Court in a number of cases, most significantly in the 1925 private school case of *Pierce v. The Society of Sisters* (Arons 1983, 18).

THE PROPOSAL

The central purposes of this voucher plan are: to promote educational experimentation, to provide equal access to educational opportunity for all

American children, and to create a world-class system of public and private schools in the United States.

The Educational Trust Fund

Who is entitled to an educational trust fund?

1. Every native born American child has a right to an educational trust fund. Each child's fund will be established one year after his or her birth.

2. Non-native-born children aged one year or older are entitled to a trust fund from the date of their first entrance into American education.

How will the trust fund be distributed?

1. Every child must receive a social security number by his or her first birthday. A child who does not have a social security number will not be eligible for an educational trust fund.

2. A computerized data base will be established for each year-old child and will be updated on an as-needed basis. This data base will include name, date of birth, home address, and notation of any handicapping conditions.

3. Each child will receive a school voucher from the State Department of Education in the state in which the child resides. State Departments of Education may lawfully appoint certain financial institutions to act as the department's agent for the distribution of trust funds.

4. The monetary worth of a voucher shall be determined by a formula that reflects the following principle: the lower the family income of a child, the greater the value of his or her voucher. Family income will be determined according to federal tax returns. If families refuse to supply these income data they may not participate in the voucher program. If parents do not file an income tax return their yearly income may be determined by alternate means.

5. At no time shall the monetary worth of a voucher exceed the annual average per pupil cost of the state in which the child resides. Every child regardless of his or her family worth, is entitled to at least a $100 voucher.

6. Vouchers will be sent to students' homes. If a student has no known address or is without a home his or her voucher will be sent to the central office of the last school district in which the student was a resident.

7. Unclaimed vouchers will be sent to the central office of the last school district in which the student was known to reside. These vouchers

will remain for three months in the school district and if unclaimed will be returned to the State Department of Education.

8. Vouchers cannot be accumulated from year to year nor are they transferable between recipients.

9. All interest accruing from educational trust funds will revert to the state and not to the child.

How will the trust funds be financed?

1. On the premise that the present method of financing public education is unconstitutional because it denies students equal protection under the law, states would revise their current method of collecting property taxes as it relates to school finance. The purpose of this revision would be to equalize the amount of money spent on education between and within school districts.

2. The revenues raised through property taxes would finance 40 percent of the voucher program. An additional 25 percent would be financed through other state forms of taxation including user taxes such as the sales tax and the import tax. Another 20 percent would be raised through public lotteries. Fifteen percent would be contributed by the federal government either through a special bond issue or by budgetary allocations. Other revenues needed to support public sector schools would be raised through property taxes, user taxes, and state-supported gambling.

3. All revenue will be kept in trust by the State Departments of Education or by their fiduciary designees.

May private and model schools charge tuition in excess of the average public school per pupil cost?

Private and model schools may determine their own tuitions and fees. However, all schools that receive public funds must reserve a minimum of 20 percent of their available places for students from families whose incomes preclude them from spending more than their voucher amount. The 20 percent policy will not be enforced if a school has not been fully enrolled within two months of the date of the school's annual opening.

Managed Choice and Model Schools

What types of schools may receive trust funds?

1. All currently operating public schools. Public schools will receive 70 percent of their revenues directly from the State Department of

Education; 30 percent of their revenues must be raised through vouchers. All public schools that receive trust funds must make a commitment to accept at least 20 percent of their students from disadvantaged backgrounds. Any monetary surplus that a public school derives from voucher income may be retained by that school for purposes of school improvement.

2. All private schools that do not espouse hatred or hostility toward others on the basis of their race, ethnicity, social class, religion, handicapping condition, or gender. All private schools which receive trust funds must make a commitment to accept at least 20 percent of their students from disadvantaged backgrounds.

3. Newly founded model schools may also receive trust funds. These model schools may be founded by a variety of public and private organizations and individuals. A model school must have a population of at least fifty students and provisions for fiduciary responsibility. Model schools may not espouse hatred or hostility toward others on the basis of their race, ethnicity, social class, religion, handicapping condition, or gender. Model schools must also meet the requirement of equal educational access. All model schools must make a commitment to accept at least 20 percent of their students from disadvantaged backgrounds.

4. Private and model schools may set the admissions criteria they wish as long as these criteria do not discriminate against students in terms of race, ethnicity, class, or gender. Schools that do not admit students with handicaps may have limits set on the amount of trust funds they may receive.

5. All public, private, and model schools will be subject to state requirements concerning health, safety, and student welfare. The state reserves the right to close a school if that school violates standards of health, safety, and student welfare.

6. The state may not mandate what schools teach, how students receive instruction, or how the schools are administratively organized.

7. All schools that are eligible to receive educational trust funds must fully disclose publicly their missions, their tables of organization, their curriculums, and such pertinent financial information that may be required by the state. This information will be made available to parents and children through published reports which will be distributed through Parent Information Centers.

8. Every private and model school must be insured and bonded to protect consumers from fraud, incompetence, and malfeasance.

Issues of Implementation

This proposal is meant to provide a conceptual framework upon which individual state plans could be developed, although the essential components could not be substantially changed without weakening the entire structure. To this author's mind there are three major areas of concern in terms of implementing this proposal: (1) the administration of the trust funds, (2) consumer information, and (3) consumer protection.

Administration of the Trust Funds

Clearly, one of the primary requirements for the transformation of American education is ending bureaucratic control over individual schools. Part of the reason that state and city educational bureaucracies have grown in the last forty-five years is that they have taken on a wide variety of functions. Some of these families are directly related to teaching and learning, but many of these functions are related to the maintenance of the bureaucracies themselves. This has proved to be an obstacle to genuine educational reform. It would make little sense to dismantle the bureaucratic regulation of schools only to substitute another bureaucracy to administer educational trust fund programs. The role of the state in the regulation of education and in the administration of educational trust funds should be minimal.

The responsibilities of the state unit that would administer educational trust funds are to be extremely circumscribed. These responsibilities would include: (a) to collect and "bank" the trust funds from the four sources of income mentioned earlier; (b) to collect the names, addresses, levels of family income and information about possible handicapping conditions of all students who have received a social security number and are state residents; (c) to determine the value of each child's voucher according to the formula determined by the state legislature, and (d) to create the vouchers and to distribute them.

In states with populations in excess of ten million many of these tasks could be divided into geographical subsections in order to mitigate the error and the delay factor that is often associated with organizations servicing a large number of clients. Before the advent of the computer the administration of educational trust funds might have been cumbersome; sophisticated computer systems, however, have made large scale data processing possible. Undoubtedly, for children who come from highly transient families or from families without homes, there would be difficulties related to administering the voucher system. Yet, using computerized data bases, children would not be lost in the system as long as each child had a social security number. If a child sought enrollment in a school district other than that in which he or she had originally enrolled, a computerized data search would reveal the size of the child's voucher. When families relocate across state lines they may apply for a new voucher. Students who transfer during the school year will have the value of their voucher determined on a pro rata basis. With the advent of computers, there are many possible efficiencies that could be built into the system. In any case, because the authority of the units administering the educational trust funds is focused and limited, it would be relatively easy to evaluate their operations by outside auditors.

Parent Information Centers

If school choice is a matter of social trust then social trust is contingent upon accessible, accurate, and universal information. In the last year I have had the opportunity to visit Parent Information Centers throughout the United States. It is evident that one of the main benefits of encouraging student and parental choice is that it compels schools to identify their missions, to examine their strengths and weaknesses, and to make this information available to parents. Research in Parent Information Centers indicates that a critical element in ensuring that parents and children use the centers to their fullest extent is an intense effort by those who manage the centers to reach every family in their district. This is done through mailings, radio announcements, television announcements, and visits to churches, nursery schools, and other locales where families are likely to gather, such as laundromats and shopping centers. Information should be available in the languages of the children living in the district. Moreover, Parent Information Centers should treat each family as unique and dignify the process by which families choose schools. Information that is collected at these centers can be used to supplement other information that the state may need in order to determine the residences of children. In essence, Parent Information Centers are community resources that bring schools and families together and act as benign brokers of educational choice. Without investments in these centers the process of school choice becomes chaotic, uninformed, and potentially destructive to children.

Consumer Protection

Advocates of free market choice sometimes fail to recognize that fraudulent marketing in education can result in children not receiving the education to which they are entitled. Moreover, it is the responsibility of the state to ensure that taxpayer dollars are not wasted through fraud or incompetence. It is extremely important that educational trust funds be used to support legitimate educational enterprises that fulfill the educational promises they make. It is important, therefore, that every school or educational provider that accepts trust funds report annually to the state its educational mission, its organizational framework, the characteristics of its faculty and students, and its financial condition. It is also important that the state reserve the right to investigate complaints by visiting schools and subpoenaing relevant records. Serious complaints of fraudulent practices could be channeled through consumer protection officers working in Parent Information Centers. These officers could turn their findings over to the local district attorney's office if it was deemed that a case warranted further investigation. Parents who wish to educate their children at home may not receive educational trust funds because there is no reasonable way to monitor whether or not these funds are used for children's education.

CONCLUDING REMARKS

The redesign of American education is absolutely essential if schools are to become productive and just learning sites. Without a redesign in the way schools are financed there is little hope that a true educational transformation can be accomplished. The just voucher is a comprehensive and feasible method of promoting greater parental and student choice, while at the same time providing equal educational access to all American children. It is suggested in this chapter that there are three essential elements for the redesign of American education: (a) establishment of educational trust funds, (b) managed school choice, and (c) the creation of model schools.

It has often been said that American education is at the crossroads. Today, this cliche is true. Do we move in the direction of innovation and equity or do we remain loyal to a system that stifles innovation and has proven to be inequitable? School choice gives voice to students and families. It is a method for balancing individual liberty with social responsibility, and it is the best way of holding schools accountable to the consumers of their services. Choice and private enterprise alone will not transform American education, but choice and private enterprise in the service of justice can create the conditions for a new era in American education.

REFERENCES

Arons, S. (1983) *Compelling Belief: The Culture of American Schooling*. New York: McGraw-Hill.

Chubb, J., and T. Moe. (1990) *Politics, Markets, and America's Schools*. Washington, D.C.: The Brookings Institution.

Cookson, P. (1989) "United States of America: Contours of Continuity and Controversy in Private Schools." In *Private Schools in Ten Countries—Policy and Practice*, edited by G. Walford. London: Routledge, pp. 57–84.

———. (1992) "Introduction," *Educational Policy*, Vol. 6, No. 2, pp. 99–104.

———. (1994) *School Choice and the Struggle for the Soul of American Education*. New Haven: Yale University Press.

Coons, J., and S. Sugarman. (1992) *Scholarships for Children*. University of California, Berkeley: Institute of Governmental Studies Press.

Friedman, M., and R. Friedman. (1980) *Free to Choose*. New York: Harcourt Brace Jovanovich.

Johanek, M. (1992) "Private Citizenship and School Choice," *Educational Policy*, Vol. 6, No. 2, pp. 139–59.

Kozol, J. (1991) *Savage Inequalities—Children in America's Schools*. New York: Crown.

National Commission on Excellence in Education. (1983) *A Nation at Risk: The Imperative for Educational Reform*. Washington, D.C.: U.S. Government Printing Office.

Ravitch, D., and C. Finn. (1988) *What Do Our Seventeen Year Olds Know*? New York: Harper and Row.

Raywid, M. (1987) "Public Choice, Yes; Vouchers, No!" *Phi Delta Kappan*, June, pp. 762–69.

United States Department of Education. (1991) *America 2000: An Education Strategy*. Washington, D.C.: Department of Education.

Walsh, M. (1992) "2 Lawsuits Seek State Vouchers for Poor Youths," *Education Week*, Vol. XI, No. 39, June 17, p. 1.

Wells, A. (1991) "Choice in Education: Examining the Evidence on Equity," *Teachers College Record*, Vol. 39, No. 1, pp. 137–55.

Wise, A., and L. Darling-Hammond. (1984) "Education by Voucher: Private Choice and the Public Interest," *Educational Theory*, Vol. 34, No. 1, pp. 29–47.

Witte, J. (1992) "Public Subsidies for Private Schools: What We Know and How to Proceed," *Educational Policy*, Vol. 6, No. 2, pp. 206–27.

8

A "GI Bill" for Educating All Children

Pierre S. duPont IV

"A great empire," Benjamin Franklin wrote, "like a great cake, is most easily diminished at the edges." No one would argue that the vast and ineffective public education empire, stretching from Washington to 15,000 school districts, with multiple layers of federal, state, and local government, union bureaucracy, and interest groups in between, is much diminished. Indeed, it continues to routinely provide most American youngsters with a twelfth-class education at a first-class cost. Something is happening at the edges.

The concept of school choice, proposed by conservative Milton Friedman in the 1950s, was in the 1980s enacted into law by liberals in the progressive bastions of Minnesota and Wisconsin and intellectually approved by the nation's premier liberal think tank, The Brookings Institution. Can it be that the hour of choice is at hand? That empowerment of tens of millions of poor and working American families to choose what is best for their children has arrived? That "civil rights" now means the right to choose a school as well as a seat on a bus, a political candidate, a house, and a job? I think so, but I am getting ahead of myself. Let us go back to the 1980s and the beginning of our nation's latest effort to improve the quality of education in our schools.

THE 1980s: REFORMS BUT NO RESULTS

"A rising tide of mediocrity," *A Nation at Risk* warned us in 1983, is engulfing our schools. Ten years later, it is still rising. You are familiar with the data: half of our high school seniors cannot locate France on a map; less than one in five can write a persuasive letter or do a math problem involving fractions. Twenty years ago the Scholastic Aptitude Test (SAT) verbal aptitude test average was 453; today it is 424. The number of students scoring above 600 on the verbal SATs, our best and brightest, has dropped 35 percent in those twenty years. Fresh data released in February shows U.S. high school students place thirteenth in the world on international math and science tests. America is losing out.

Let me bring the issue home to Delaware, where for sixteen years as a state legislator, congressman, and governor, I was very involved in education policy. Sadly, the picture is no brighter.

A decade ago, Delaware students' SAT test scores stood well above the national average, but a ten-year regression to mediocrity has left scores the lowest ever. According to *USA Today*, the 1990–1991 Delaware SAT score drop was the largest in America. SAT scores of public school seniors in Delaware are twenty-eight points lower than the national average for the same group. (By contrast, non-public school scores in Delaware exceed the national average for private schools by 40 points.) The Department of Public Instruction reports that the Class of 1993 in our high schools was 32 percent smaller than it started out in ninth grade just four years earlier—nearly a one-third dropout rate. Stanford Achievement Test scores on basic skills tests dropped in 1991 in all major subjects for three out of four grades tested. Only 17 percent of our eighth graders meet or exceed competency tests.

Unfortunately, all of this bad news comes *after* the massive and far-reaching reforms enacted in Delaware in the late 1970s and early 1980s. Educational performance is still declining—after teacher testing, after student testing, class size reduction, gifted and talented programs, special programs for learning disabled and disciplinary problem children, curriculum reform, and teacher salary increases.

In response to *A Nation at Risk*, education and political leaders in Delaware came together to map a plan for reform. The experts said to decrease class size, so we did, by 5 percent since 1982.

The experts said increase teachers' salaries, so we did. Since 1980, teachers' salaries in Delaware have risen 60 percent faster than the salaries of others; today, the average teacher's salary is $34,200, 54 percent more than the average worker's salary in our state.

The experts said increase the number of math and science courses that students must take. Delaware now requires two additional technical courses for graduation.

The experts said to begin teaching children earlier to allow them to have a longer academic career, so we did that too, through mandatory kindergarten.

The experts said to spend money—and, oh my, did we spend money. Spending on education across America, since 1980, has grown twice as fast as inflation (education expenditure per student is up 150 percent; inflation up 72 percent). In Delaware, spending per pupil has grown 120 percent since 1980, while inflation during the same time has increased 72 percent. Delaware spends nearly $6,300 each year to educate each of our students, 12 percent more than the U.S. average.

In the framework of conventional wisdom, Delaware's reforms were significant and far-reaching.

For all our time, for all our efforts, for all of this "cash register mentality," just what have we accomplished? Sadly, not very much. Education costs are rising twice as fast as inflation, while performance continues to fall (see Figure 8.1). Our good intentions have produced poor results.

What is the reaction of Delaware educators to this dismal performance? "Educators unswayed by test scores," said one *Wilmington News Journal* headline after the announcement of the most recent decline in test scores. "Officials downplay test results," said another. All of the following explanations were offered by school officials to explain the problem:

- Multiple choice questions don't accurately measure skills.
- The tests don't perfectly match Delaware's curriculum.
- Students aren't motivated since they don't get credit for taking the tests.
- Children are doing amazing things that are not reflected in the test scores.
- Hey, we're better than that.

Refuse to believe the facts, or blame the war, the students, or best of all, blame the tests—they're just not measuring the great job we know we're doing. All of us tried that one, report card in hand, on our dads. It didn't wash then; it doesn't wash now.

Delaware has recently undertaken a fresh approach to education reform, designing its own performance assessments and applying them at four different grade levels. The results are the first step in benchmarking, giving teachers and parents a sound starting point against which to measure future performance. The results are also a sobering reminder of how little our past efforts—and dollars—have achieved, and how far behind our students are. Only about 13 percent of our third, fifth, eighth, and tenth grade students meet or exceed math standards; 16 percent, reading standards, and only one student in fourteen, 7 percent, can satisfactorily meet writing standards.

OUR EDUCATIONAL STRUCTURE

Remarkably absent from all these analyses is any reference to the structure and framework which we have chosen to educate our children. Many decades ago it was decided that American youngsters could best be educated through a single, centralized school system with a common curriculum, textbooks, and classroom climate. Over the years, this well-intentioned concept has calcified

Figure 8.1
Delaware's Education: Expenses Growing Twice Inflation Rate

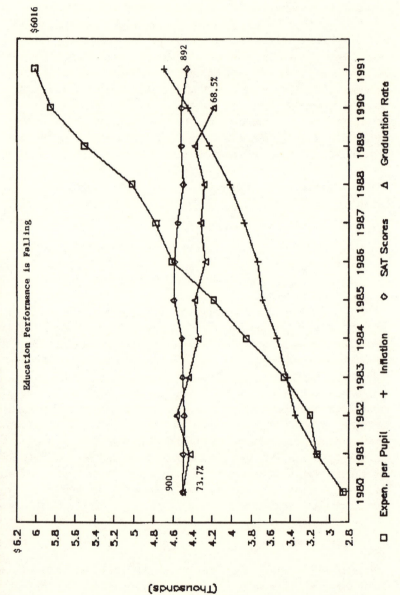

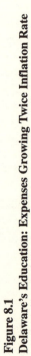

into a rigid bureaucratic regime plainly incapable of preparing students with skills for a lifetime. In spite of years of unsatisfactory results on almost every test measuring almost every kind of student and ability, educators continue to express faith in this failing monolithic structure.

Could it be that it is the system itself that is failing us? That we are pouring money and good intentions and effort into an educational structure that simply won't work for today's and tomorrow's students? I think so. The system we are using cannot work and we cannot educate young men and women with it because it is fatally flawed.

In the past two years, we have seen with our own eyes the final convolutions of deadly collectivist and centrally planned economies in Eastern Europe and the former Soviet Union. In the late 1980s, the showcase nation of central planning was shown to be a hollow shell: empty shelves in the markets, rotting food in the fields, fewer cars per capita than for blacks in South Africa, a Gross National Product (GNP) smaller than that of Turkey and still falling. For seventy years the world's largest army, most powerful and vicious secret police, and a vast pervasive bureaucracy beyond George Orwell's wildest dreams ruled a nation in which there was no private property, no free press, no political opposition, where *all* the power was concentrated in the hands of an elite bureaucracy . . . and they still couldn't make it work. The 1980s proved that central planning and the ownership of the means of production by the state is a bankrupt idea.

Yet this is the very system we use in the United States to attempt to educate our children: central planning and the ownership of the means of production by the state. Administrators in district or state bureaucracies, not teachers, or principals, or parents, decide what textbooks are to be used, tests to be taken, which curriculum and study plan will be followed. In virtually every other segment of our society we have a rolling, twenty-four-hour referendum by consumers on the products they desire. It is this ability to switch horses, to change products, to abandon the inferior and embrace the superior that gives free enterprise its fundamental superiority—both morally and practically—over centrally planned economies. Innovators in the marketplace improve products, consumers react, the quality of the product increases, and its cost declines. Individual consumers and society are both the better for it.

In education, we have but one source of supply—where the government's central planners supply the "one best product" for all students, regardless of background, ability, or motivation. There is no innovation, no reward for success, no rising tide that lifts all boats on the seas of education. Just as in the Soviet Union and Eastern Europe, our centralized bureaucracies have been unable to respond quickly enough in a rapidly changing world, so American students have continued to fall further and further behind. Our students are now thirteenth and falling in the critical math and science skills in a global economy.

America did not come to grow and prosper through two hundred years with the government providing "one best product." It is time to bring the proven American values of choice and competition into education, to replace a centrally planned education system run from Washington and state capitols with a customer-driven system in which parents choose the schools for their children and schools must compete for their students.

We should have dozens, if not hundreds, of different kinds of schools which offer choices to our children. We should have schools which specialize in mathematics; schools which specialize in English and grammar; schools which specialize in discipline; in the arts and science; schools which meet in the evenings and in the summer; where excellent teachers are paid $75,000 and all teachers can offer their services to the school in which they want to teach. Education is an industry in which a thousand flowers should bloom. They can bloom, not by the wise decisions of well-intentioned government planners, but only by thousands of free choices made by millions of free people in a free society. That, after all, is the fundamental concept that has allowed Americans to attain a quality of life unmatched in the history of the world.

THE REASONS FOR CHOICE

The first reason to have a market-based or choice system is that it is consistent with the value system of our nation. We wouldn't tolerate for a moment the idea of the government assigning us our jobs, newspapers, or colleges; neither should we tolerate government assignment of our children to elementary and secondary schools.

Some people argue that many parents are ill equipped to make the choice of a school for their children: they are too poor, too ignorant, or too uncaring to choose well. Wilmington Attorney David A. Drexler, for example, states in his rebuttal to my choice proposal in the fall edition of *The Delaware Lawyer*: "There are too many parents who are ill equipped to make intelligent choices, even for their own children. Does Governor du Pont really believe that, for example, a struggling single mother in her late teens or early twenties, who herself dropped out of school, pregnant, at age thirteen or fourteen, can really make better decisions about her children's education than a professional educator?"

Yes, he does, for that young mother knows her child, his or her personality, needs, skills, and temperament. Mr. Drexler's "professional educator" considers none of these; his school assignment is based solely upon geography, an absurdly irrelevant predictor of a child's educational needs.

Moreover, such denigration of individuals should be rejected out of hand. For centuries, cultural elitists have been arguing that the common man cannot be allowed to choose for himself, that some wiser, better educated "professional" should choose for him. Socialism and other utopian religions are based upon this belief, but America two hundred years ago rejected it. We are, in the words of the Declaration of Independence, "endowed . . . with certain inalienable rights . . . Life, Liberty, and the pursuit of Happiness." We Americans founded a nation in the belief that we are free to choose for ourselves.

Second, choice is the only viable agent of change to improve our schools. Modern school reform began thirty-five years ago following the launching of Sputnik by the former Soviet Union; it failed. Again in 1983, after *A Nation at Risk*, school reform was promised by educators; it never materialized. In spite of the ringing rhetoric of President Bush, Secretary Alexander, and armies of school board members and administrators, it is not happening now.

Reform from within is virtually impossible for any bureaucracy, as Mikhail Gorbachev demonstrated. The education bureaucracy is almost as entrenched and resistant to change as the Soviet *nomenclatura*. For example, not one of the 6,000 teachers in the Milwaukee school system had been dismissed for poor performance in the five years prior to the enhancement of a choice proposal; not one of the 1,000 new teachers hired had been denied tenure. Bureaucracies will not reform themselves, not even at the margins.

John Chubb and Terry Moe define in their brilliant analysis of American education, *Politics, Markets, and America's Schools*, the difference between bureaucratic and market-driven education systems. In the New York City public school system's central office, there are 6,600 administrators, one for every 150 students. In the consumer-driven parochial school system, there are but thirty administrators, one for every 4,000 students. One-third of all the tax dollars in the city public school system are spent to support this central bureaucracy and yet thirty years of declining performance has not persuaded the city fathers to reallocate some of them to the classroom. No, bureaucracies will not reform themselves.

It is instructive to see what happened in Milwaukee after the enactment of a very limited choice plan, one that brought choice to less than 400 students out of 97,000 in the district. Within a month of the beginning of the choice program, the public school system proposed establishing separate high schools for young black males to give them an education curriculum focused upon their special needs. It had never done that before. The public school system hired a parent liaison staff to go into homes of parents, and say, "What do you want in your school?" It had never done that before. Suddenly a policy to notify parents when their children don't show up for school was proposed. That had never been done before. Two months later, in November 1990, it was announced that the Woodruff Art School, stressing values and moral education and religion, was going to come to Milwaukee. The superintendent there, Mr. Peterkin, said, "Milwaukee public schools will be the first in the nation to have this program." Choice can be a powerful agent for change and improvement.

Eighteen months ago I debated Keith Geiger, the president of the National Education Association, the teachers' union. Mr. Geiger said, "School choice by itself does nothing to improve schools." That is a true statement. But its converse is also true, that without choice schools have not and are unlikely to improve. Choice is not a panacea, but it is a prerequisite to improved education.

The third important reason for a choice system is that it gives people a sense of shared ownership in what they have chosen. This means more interest, concern, and participation by the owners, leading to consumer-driven improvements in education. It is virtually impossible today for a school to innovate, to fit an education to the needs of an individual student; indeed, to change anything at all within a classroom. The myriad of federal, state and local government and school board rules, union contracts, and procedural manuals see to that. Only demand side pressure from consumers of education services, who choose or threaten not to choose a particular school is likely to force changes in the school supply.

Choice means fairness, too, giving all families access to the best schools now within the economic grasp of only the few. Some 20 percent of our school-aged population already exercise choice—the most affluent 20 percent. In Chicago, for example, nearly half the *public* school teachers send their children to private school. They can afford to. In North Carolina, children of legislators are by statute exempt from state and local pupil assignment regulations. They have the power to choose the best for themselves. It is the powerless, the poor- and middle-class working families whose children are most often trapped in inferior schools; it is time they were given the power to do better for their children.

Finally, choice means power—the power of every parent to choose the school best suited to each child—the power to choose our child's education as we choose our jobs, our houses, our churches, and our leaders.

In some states, Connecticut and Delaware, for example, parents are falsifying street addresses to get their children into better schools. The response of school districts has been to hire private detectives, stake out bus stops and houses, and even institute door-to-door bed checks to be sure no student emigrates out of the district to which he or she has been assigned. It would be comic if it weren't tragic: using the police power of the state to ensure no one gets a better education than they are supposed to have. Choice would end this sorry spectacle and return to parents the inalienable right to do what is best for their children.

Each of us should have the power to do what is best for our children. I do not know your children; neither does the central planner who assigns them to their school. He or she has never met them, or you, and doesn't know a thing about your family. You know best what your children need. Mr. Drexler believes that distant wise men, yellow highlighters in hand, can draw a school district map that will better serve your children than you can. To argue it is to refute it. You know it cannot be true.

My wife, Elise, and I have four children. They're all different, and they all had different educational needs. One is very bright and needed a challenging academic environment. Another is dyslexic and needed a very special school.

Another is scientifically inclined, the other more artistic; they needed schools that would suit them. Fortunately, we could choose the school best suited to each of our children. I believe all parents should have that opportunity.

Mr. Geiger, in that same debate in Washington, argued that he did not want his children taught in classrooms where teachers are not professionally trained. Neither do I want his children in classrooms with which he is uncomfortable. I want him to have the ability to choose the classrooms best suited for his children, and I the best for mine.

Finally, let us add to the list of underpinnings of a choice system a less theoretical and very practical argument: choice is a proven concept. We know educational choice works, for eighteen million Americans have successfully used it for nearly half a century. I refer, of course, to the GI Bill. From World War II to Desert Storm, millions of young men and women have used GI Bill scholarships to get a college education. Some have chosen state universities, some private colleges, some graduate schools, some vocational training. They have studied to be engineers, artists, professors, and priests, all without any of the arguments against choice being raised against them. Simply put, choice works.

ARGUMENTS AGAINST CHOICE

Of course, choice has many powerful enemies. That should not be surprising, for when any effort is made to alter the status quo, it is bitterly resisted. Others will argue the case against choice more forcefully than I, but as I have debated the issue in countless forums, let me summarize the arguments against.

There seem to be three: the constitutional argument, the practical argument, and the statist argument.

The constitutional argument rests on the separation of church and state doctrine of the First Amendment. It is undermined by the fact that educational scholarships are issued to people—children—not to schools. There is no constitutional ban to individuals using pensions, Pell grants, day care vouchers, or disability checks as we wish. The same would be true of a scholarship. Of course, the issue will ultimately be decided by the U.S. Supreme Court, but both the case law and the facts suggest prospects for approval are bright.

The scholarships of the GI Bill were used to study for the Catholic priesthood and Jewish rabbinical studies, without constitutional disapproval. The recent day care bill enacted by Congress in 1990 specifically permits day care vouchers to be used in church-operated day care centers. The use of tax dollars in religiously operated institutions can hardly be constitutional for infants and college students and somehow unconstitutional in between, for children from five to eighteen years of age.

The practical arguments are the arguments advanced by any bureaucracy threatened with change: how will the i's be dotted and the t's crossed? What about transportation, lunch, salary scales, rules, and regulations? These are valid questions, but they are largely mechanical; we have worked them out before; we will again. We should no more let school bus contractors determine education policy than NASA maintenance workers dictate whether we can put a man on the moon. When President John F. Kennedy vowed we would put a man on the moon in a decade, few argued the maintenance workers' employment contract must be decided first.

Finally come the statist arguments, the crux of the opposition. The people who run our education system, from school board members to teachers, with layers of bureaucrats in between, really do believe they can do a better job without the messy complications of the marketplace. They believe education is "special," best left to carefully trained professionals, for they can make better decisions for children than parents can. That is a time-honored philosophy, fervently endorsed by intellectuals and politicians—by Marx, Sartre, the British Labor Party, and the American Democratic Party. In the words of British Labor MP Roy Hattersley, "Competitive education which allows the few to leap further and further ahead, ensures that the less fortunate fall further and further behind. That is why the pursuit of equality of opportunity has to be replaced by the pursuit of equality itself." Inconveniently, this philosophy has just been proven wrong in the Soviet Union. A seventy-year demonstration project, built on the thesis that the elite few can choose better than the rest of us, failed so badly it even destroyed the nation in which it was tried.

The architects of our present system, most of whom are long departed, simply believed people needed educational decisions made for them. The current caretakers of our system still passionately believe it. Listen to NEA President Keith Geiger reacting to the Milwaukee choice program's 320 low-income students who chose scholarships to attend other schools.

"Ernie Boyer says that probably 15 to 20 percent of the schools in the United States are so bad we ought to go in and bomb them, and blow them up and build new schools."

"I think if a school is that bad, we ought not to allow fifteen children to escape, and the rest of the poor children will have to survive there."

Escape? An odd word to use to describe a student with a scholarship to another school. It is exactly reflective of the statist argument: we must not allow people to escape our control.

CHOICE PLANS

Choice plans in higher education have always existed: families choose their children's colleges or universities. States frequently subsidize that choice. North Carolina, for example, offers every resident $1,500 in credit towards tuition at any North Carolina college. One state, Vermont, has had high school scholarships, valid at any school anywhere in America, for over one hundred years.

In the past decade, many new choice plans empowering parents to choose the elementary or secondary school best suited for each of their children have come into existence.

The Milwaukee plan championed through the state legislature by Representative Polly Williams is for low-income city parents. Approximately 1,000 of the city's lowest income families are eligible for a $2,500 scholarship to send their children to any private, nonsectarian school in the city. In March, this plan was held constitutional by the Wisconsin Supreme Court.

The Indiana plan would provide all parents, regardless of income, a scholarship certificate worth the total amount of state and local funding allocated for each student in a school district. The scholarship could be used at any school, public or private. If school tuition were less than the value of the scholarship, the difference would be held in a lifetime account for the student, to be used for any educational purpose, including tuition at colleges, universities, or vocational education programs. This latter point is both interesting and important, for it provides the economic incentive for parents to demand the lowest possible school costs. Without it, private school tuitions would simply rise to the level of the scholarship, helping no one but school administrators.

A variety of public school choice plans also exist, and provided they contain a supply-side mechanism to permit new public schools to be easily created, they also will improve the quality of education in all schools.

The Harlem plan, now some fifteen years old, allowing choice among twenty-two junior high schools in a school district 40 percent black, 40 percent Hispanic, and 20 percent white, with 90 percent of all mothers on welfare, is raising student comprehension and test scores markedly. The Harlem district, once last in test scores in New York City, has climbed halfway to the top. Parents and students show pride, enthusiasm, and involvement in their schools.

A newly enacted plan in Minnesota complements the existing statewide public school choice program with "charter schools." Groups of licensed teachers may, with the approval of the State Board of Education, create new schools in a community. Here is power to teachers to form and lead your own schools, to offer your services to the school which wants you, and thus pays you, the most. The charter schools would be free of most existing regulations; they may specialize in students of a certain age, in certain subjects, or in a particular learning method; but they cannot discriminate or select students based upon intelligence, achievement, or athletic ability. Although still a demonstration project, increasing the supply of schools remains one of the most important goals of improved education, so the charter school project may prove a useful model.

There are many models, many ways to choose. Choice is critically important for it is the one missing ingredient in a third-of-a-century effort to reverse dwindling educational achievement.

THE DELAWARE PLAN

In September of 1990 I proposed a school choice plan for Delaware in the belief that our state, too, must offer better opportunities to our young people. It is based upon three principles: First, that the citizens of each school district should be able to choose whether they wish a choice plan; second, that any choice plan would be phased in slowly to provide time to work out the inevitable practical problems; and, third, that the plan be revenue neutral to the state government.

How might such a choice plan work? First, the state legislature would enact enabling legislation to provide each school district the option of adopting an "Education Scholarship Program," either by majority vote of the school board or by the voters in a referendum. No district would be required to participate in the plan. Thus, if the residents of a district are content with its educational opportunities, they can continue the current education system of assignment by school administrators of children to specific schools.

Once the choice concept has been approved by the school board or by the voters of a particular district, the plan would give parents three choices:

- allow the school district administrator to assign their child to a school, as it does now, where the child can attend as a matter of right;
- choose to send their child to any other public school in their home school district, or to any public school in another district which would accept the student,
- or, in the alternative, parents could accept a $2,150* state-funded scholarship for their child to attend any accredited private school within or outside Delaware. (*For religious schools the scholarship will be $1,935 [90 percent] to avoid the constitutional problems of paying for the religious part of the curriculum of sectarian schools with tax dollars.)

What would this mean, as a practical matter, to parents? Today in Delaware there are seventy-five public and thirty-five private elementary schools serving first through fourth grade, or some combination thereof. Some, of course, are far distant from a family's residence, but in the Wilmington metropolitan area (for example, if one lived in Stanton, Delaware), it is fair to say that within a ten-mile radius of one's residence there might be as many as twenty or more elementary schools. Under the Delaware choice plan, then, a family's choices of schools immediately leaps from one to twenty.

Further, if $2,150 scholarships are available, the marketplace will quickly respond and new private schools will be established. After all, there are in the Wilmington metropolitan area today some twenty schools offering elementary education for less than $2,150; the marketplace could easily create twenty more. Skeptics will deny it, but the market does work; supply will increase to meet demand, and choices for parents will increase further.

The amount of the scholarship is open to discussion; there is no magic to $2,150. In 1990 that amount does cover first grade private school tuition at thirty-one of the thirty-nine private schools in Delaware, and two-thirds of tuition at all but four. The point is not to enable parents to match school tuition dollar-for-dollar, but to expand opportunities available to students. Under this choice plan parents would have the choice of three dozen first grade private education programs, in addition to the public school options. That is an opportunity—not only to choose among schools, but to enroll each child in a school program tailored to his or her particular needs.

As for the public schools, they will quickly begin to tailor programs to attract first-graders—perhaps special reading programs, improved community inter-action programs, or programs that specialize in teaching Hispanic children to learn English. Each of the schools will try to offer something better with the result that all schools will improve. Today, there are real barriers to innova-tion—a sluggish bureaucracy, state and local rules that retard change, and no reason to try to attract new students, for it is nearly impossible under current law to send a child to a school not in the district in which he or she resides. All these barriers will fall and education in every first grade classroom will begin to improve.

What of the school districts themselves? Well, they win too. Today in Delaware, the 1990 total cost of educating a child for a year is about $6,650. If there are, say, thirty first graders in a classroom at an existing government school, and assuming ten of them leave to go to another school, approximately $26,000 of the $66,500 stays behind. Those funds include local property taxes, debt service, and federal funds. Thus, the amount available to educate the remaining first graders is increased by $26,000, so the state can spend $7,950 on each student's education, a 20 percent increase in education spending per student. This 20 percent can be used for books, lab equipment, school trips, teachers salaries, or whatever the district chooses.

Now comes the second school district safeguard: the choice program would phase in over twelve years, one grade at a time. Thus, next year only the 11,500 youngsters attending first grade would be eligible. The following year, first and second graders would be eligible, and so forth. This will allow the education system ample time to adjust to new demands placed upon it.

Finally, as to the state itself, the cost of educating a child in the current system, $6,650, is so much higher than the cost in private schools, $2,100, that the state can give a $2,150 scholarship to a child, leave $2,600 in the school which a child left to improve education for those remaining, and still break even. There is no net cost to Delaware.

CONCLUSION

Some people argue that most parents are satisfied with their current schools and that, as educators say, "We're doing a great job." That is clearly not the view of employers, many parents, and all but the most obstinate educators.

Former Secretary of Education William Bennett was once asked by a student how one could tell if the United States or the former Soviet Union was really the better country. "Apply the gate theory," Bennett replied, "open the gates and see which way the people flow."

If the gate theory were applied to public schools, there is no question the exodus would be dramatic. When choice was offered to parents among the Cambridge, Massachusetts, public schools, more than two-thirds of the parents chose a public school other than the one to which their child was assigned by school administrators. When the Golden Rule Insurance Company in Indianapolis offered a 50–50 matching scholarship (up to a maximum of $800) to any low-income child wishing to move from public to private schools, 1,200 students immediately applied. When a Community Foundation in Milwaukee offered a similar program, all 4,500 application forms were picked up in a single day, and 2,100 low-income students are receiving scholarships to attend the school of their choice.

All of us know we must do better, that America is losing out, that our current education system is failing us. Teachers know it. Education professionals know it. Parents know it. So do you and I. What we have is not good enough. As Gordon MacRea, former editor of *The Economist*, so eloquently wrote, one of the first rules of government is when you know you are doing something stupid, stop doing it. The something stupid in this case is continuing to operate a school system that is failing so many students. We need something more intelligent, a dramatic change for the better.

Fortunately, we have some benchmarks to guide us in designing a better way to educate our children: we know what doesn't work, and we know what does.

Education as it is currently structured doesn't work very well. Our high schools graduate 700,000 functional illiterates every spring (not counting the 20 to 50 percent of the students who have dropped out along the way). U.S. students are thirteenth best in the world in math and science, and with test scores flat or falling, our students continue to lose ground internationally.

Reform from within doesn't work either. Education reform was promised after Sputnik in 1957; it didn't happen. It was promised again after *A Nation at Risk* in 1983; it didn't happen. In spite of all the ringing rhetoric, it's not happening now. If we want change, we need a new system.

We also know what does work: markets, private schools, American higher education, and the GI Bill.

America is the envy of the world because of its dynamic market economy. Markets work for schools, too—in East Harlem, Milwaukee, Minnesota. They could work everywhere.

The American college and university system is acknowledged as the best in the world and it is a choice system involving public, private, and religious schools.

City parochial schools, as examples of the private education system, have better discipline, higher graduation rates and college admissions, lower dropout rates, and higher student achievement. James Coleman found that students of comparable socioeconomic background gain one full grade level in just two years in city parochial compared with city public schools.

Finally, we know the GI Bill works—brilliantly. From World War II to Desert Storm, 18 million American men and women have gone to college or post-secondary schooling using its benefits. They have attended public, private, and religious institutions—without constitutional controversy.

Why not a GI Bill for children? Such a scholarship plan would be based upon proven concepts: market choices, schools that offer a choice of discipline and academic excellence, a world-class higher education system, and the largest and most successful scholarship program in history with 18 million graduates.

Let there be no mistake about the need to fundamentally restructure education in America. Change we must, for we are losing out. We must bring choice to parents, competition into our system, and opportunity into our classrooms. Now is the time to end the government stranglehold on the education of our children, to bring excellence, opportunity, and a world-class education into every class-room, and place the power of choice on the kitchen table of every American family. America's future—and the future of the next generation of Americans—depends upon it.

9

Blending the Neighborhood School Tradition with "Choice within Schools"

Ernest L. Boyer

School choice can no longer be dismissed as arcane textbook theory. In recent years, it has emerged as an aggressively promoted centerpiece of education reform. Thirteen states and scores of districts have adopted some form of choice. Successes have been noted, yet our examination of the choice "landscape"—from Milwaukee, Wisconsin, to East Harlem, New York, and from Minnesota to Massachusetts—leads us to conclude that this strategy is not the key to widespread school improvement.

Choice, at its best, empowers parents, stimulates teachers to be more creative and, most important, gives students a new sense of attachment to their schools and to learning. We saw such achievements in school districts across the country—programs where choice has truly made a difference. On the other hand, the negative impact of selected statewide choice programs on impoverished urban districts such as Brockton and Gloucester, Massachusetts, as well as tiny rural ones like Motley, Minnesota, and Exira, Iowa, cannot be ignored. Neither can we forget that, in Milwaukee, the promise of private-school choice has, to date, outdistanced the performance.

Clearly, a myth has grown up around choice. The assumption is that the competition of the marketplace will strengthen good schools while forcing weak ones either to shape up or be closed down. The reality, though, is that parents pick schools for a variety of reasons. It is difficult, therefore, to see how moving students from one school to another will in and of itself renew public education. Other factors surely are involved, and it's a diversion to present choice as a panacea—some grand design that can sweep away all difficulties that impede schools and restrict learning.

Prof. Nathan Glazer, in a thoughtful review of the constructive changes in East Harlem, correctly acknowledges that choice was crucial but that there was something deeper. "Choice," writes Glazer (1992), "was the term selected to describe the character of the revolution in East Harlem, but parental choice was only part of the story. Indeed, the story begins with educational innovations rather than choice, which was entailed only because the innovations had to find students on which to try their ideas. A key characteristic of the innovations was that they came from the teachers, not from top administrators."

The time has come to move beyond the school-choice rhetoric and begin to shape a more comprehensive approach to school renewal—to search for common ground. It is time for educators on both sides of the debate to focus not so much on school *location* but on student *learning*. The first step is to diagnose the problem. Just why are so many schools unable to deliver on their promise? Why do so many students fail to learn?

The evidence is overwhelming that the crises in education relate not just to school governance but to pathologies that surround the schools. The harsh truth is that, in many communities, the family is a far more imperiled institution than the school, and teachers are being asked to do what parents have not been able to accomplish. Today, the nation's public schools are called upon to stop drugs, reduce teenage pregnancy, feed students, improve health, and eliminate gang violence, while still meeting academic standards. If they fail anywhere along the line we condemn them for not meeting our highminded expectations.

Consider, once again, District 4. In this poverty-ridden section of New York City, more than half the children come from homes headed by single parents. Almost 80 percent are eligible for the free lunch program. Years ago, school choice brought a new sense of energy and creativity to this district. Yet, even today, far too many students are academically deficient, and District 4 schools still struggle against almost overwhelming odds. Even with the positive influence of school choice, is it realistic to expect an island of academic excellence in a sea of social crises?

Simply stated, educational excellence relates not just to schools but to communities as well. Writing in *The Wall Street Journal*, Robert Carr (1991) declares: "The problems of America's schools stem in large part from causes deep in the national experience: urban blight, drugs, the erosion of the family, and long-standing failure to direct sufficient resources to the schools. In the face of these pressures, the schools have been called upon to take over roles formerly played by the family, churches, and other agencies, ranging from sex education to housing and feeding children from dawn to dusk, well beyond school hours."

Consider also that many problems adversely affecting the education of children begin very early, even before birth itself. Last year, in a Carnegie Foundation survey, kindergarten teachers reported that one-third of their students come to school not well prepared to learn because of poor health, inadequate nurturing, and language deprivation. A more recent survey identified lack of parental support, child abuse, poor nutrition, violence, and drug problems as serious detriments to learning (*Education Daily*, 1992). How tragic it would be if the school choice debate shifted our attention away from these pathologies that harm children and weaken schools.

If we are truly serious about better education, the time has come to launch a national effort on behalf of children. It's time to acknowledge the interrelatedness of the home, health clinics, preschools, the workplace—all of the institutions and social forces that influence children's lives. What we need is inspired leadership, a sense of urgency, and, above all, a will to create a better life for children so that all will come to school well prepared to learn.

It's also time to reaffirm public education and commit ourselves to having a school of quality within the reach of every child. Many schools are struggling, and some are failing, but others are dramatically successful. Further, thousands of teachers are performing successfully, against the odds, every single day, and it's unfair to ignore these heroic efforts. Instead of bashing schools, let's celebrate success and build on the good practices now in place.

For years, the U.S. Department of Education has identified Blue Ribbon Schools from coast to coast. Literally hundreds of public schools have received national recognition. In our own travels, we found many places where the spirit of renewal is pervasive.

Jackson-Keller Elementary School in San Antonio, Texas, serves an ethnically diverse, poor, highly mobile student population. In 1985 the school was forced to shut down due to declining enrollment. It reopened three years later with an innovative "integrated curriculum." By developing a strong partnership with parents, Jackson-Keller has achieved a new sense of community mission, steadily improving test scores and attaining an amazing 97 percent daily attendance rate. "The secret of renewal," summarizes principal Alicia Thomas, "is not vouchers or choice. It's devising your own agenda. It's about a school community reaching down within itself to find its mission, and then working to achieve it."

The setting could hardly be more different at the Orchard School, which serves 220 children in the upscale suburb of Ridgewood, New Jersey. This school might easily have rested complacently on its laurels with standardized test scores in the upper 90th percentile. Instead, a committee of teachers, parents, and the principal spent summer months and hundreds of weeknight hours devising the "Orchard 2000 Plan," which has led the school community into a dramatic re-evaluation of philosophy, curriculum, teaching, and student grading. The aim is to go well beyond traditional elementary skills and have every child leave Orchard as a self-directed problem-solver and adept communicator.

The spirit of school reform also might have bypassed New Suncook, an elementary school in Lovell, Maine. Despite the rural setting, principal Gary MacDonald has made sure that his school is anything but isolated. In 1988 and

1989, he and several teachers flew to Seattle, at their own expense, to meet school reformers and attend education conventions. Today, New Suncook has dramatically restructured itself, grouping kindergartners through second graders in five independent units within the school. The school also disbanded separate special education classes and integrated all disabled children into its regular school classes.

The above schools are but a few of the literally hundreds of public schools where the spirit of renewal has arisen not from the threat of competition but from the school's own commitment to improve. Achieving genuine national reform remains, of course, a work in progress. Still, we are convinced that neighborhood schools like New Suncook, Orchard, Jackson-Keller, and thousands of others offer daily proof that revitalization can, in the end, come from the simple act of parents and professionals working together toward common goals.

We do not suggest that all is well in public education. Some schools are failing. Some children are shockingly ill-served, and it would be foolish, indeed wholly irresponsible, to insist that what we have today should go unchallenged. Excellence in education for all students remains the key to America's civic and economic future, and indeed, it is this goal that brings advocates and adversaries of choice together. The conflict appears to be not over ends but over means, and the time has come for all educators, regardless of their position on school choice, to join in common cause.

What we propose is a national strategy for renewal that affirms the neighborhood school tradition, while also expanding opportunities for mobility and enrichment. This approach surely would include a commitment to early education, with small classes and a focus on basic skills. It would include breaking up large schools into smaller units, and making all schools places where there is active, not passive, learning. It would involve parents as partners in the process and would include high academic standards and accountability for every school.

Above all, this new strategy must assure that teachers are empowered, which is at the very heart of the school choice debate. The issue isn't whether students are free to move from school to school, but whether decision making can be shifted to the local level. School choice advocates are absolutely right in reminding us that too many schools are caught in a web of regulations, and that teachers are often held responsible for the bureaucratic rather than the educational aspects of their work.

Some districts have successfully used "choice" as a way to empower teachers and revitalize local schools. Other places have decentralized decision making within the traditional neighborhood school arrangement. Kentucky, for example, has actually mandated local school control. Under a recent school reform law, every school must establish, by 1996, a school-based decision-making council consisting of two parents, three teachers, and the principal. Each council will have specific authority over the budget, instructional materials, school management, curriculum, and other school affairs. Already, 600 of the state's 1,300 public schools have such councils.

Change is also beginning in individual districts. St. Paul, Minnesota; Cherry Valley Schools outside Denver, Colorado; and Lansing, Michigan, are among a growing number of districts working to give local schools more control. One of the boldest initiatives is in Moses Lake, Washington. For the past four years, that district's thirteen schools have been given nearly total control over supply and contract money, special-education funds, Chapter 1 aid, and certain state funds. The philosophy of the district is to turn the organizational chart upside down, putting the district's 5,600 students at the top, and the superintendent and school board at the bottom, in a support role. Until local schools have a meaningful level of autonomy, we simply will not have a real test of what is possible in education.

High academic standards and accountability are essential. Indeed, holding local schools responsible for the quality of their programs is perhaps the most important and most neglected part of public education today. What is needed, we believe, is a report card on every school, one that includes a wide range of measures related to school goals and procedures as well as progress.

Every school should be asked to demonstrate, at regular intervals, the educational effectiveness of its program, providing information on students' academic progress, attendance, graduation rates, school climate, parent participation, and curriculum standards. If a school fails to provide evidence that it is offering a quality education, an external School Evaluation Team should intervene. This review team might conclude that a school had poor leadership and recommend that a new principal be brought in. It might assign a resident advisor to the school to clarify goals and renew the program. As a last resort, the school might be closed and reopened with better leadership and a new education plan. The team might conclude that a failing school was underfunded and recommend emergency state aid.

We conclude that in this new school reform strategy districtwide choice has a place. It can, under the right circumstances, help to revitalize schools, empower teachers and principals, and assist parents in selecting the programs that are best for their children. Before choice is introduced, however, every school in the district must be a school worth choosing. It's simply not fair to have a few attractive "magnets" or "charter schools" which serve a handful of students while neglecting the rest. School choice must be viewed as a way to *supplement*, not *supplant*, the network of local schools.

Further, for a "choice" program to be effective, parents must be actively engaged. Indeed, parents might well be asked whether they want the program in the first place. They also must be fully informed about the alternatives available to them, and special efforts must be made to reach the least advantaged parents. Finally, transportation must be provided to students who might not otherwise be able to get to their preferred school. Choice has no meaning if the desired school is beyond reach.

A program such as the one we've just described may fit nicely into a community where schools are concentrated and where students can move conveniently from one place to another. What struck us so forcefully during our study is that choice is a wholly unrealistic proposal for literally millions of families. For many, there is simply no other school within easy reach, or if there is, the alternative school may be no better than the one close by. The solution is to focus choice not on a *building* but on *quality education*. Instead of providing choice only among schools, why not create choices *within* schools? If the true goal of "choice" is to discover the best fit between the educational process and the student, then we regard choice within a school as distilling this central aim and injecting it into every single institution.

Few places better illustrate the idea of "choice within schools" than South Mountain, a neighborhood high school in Phoenix, Arizona. In 1988, South Mountain was just another struggling school in that city's toughest section, known mainly for violence and a dropout rate approaching 25 percent. With the help of desegregation funds, the 3,300 student institution divided itself into five specialty schools: visual arts, performing arts, aerospace, law, and mass communications. The resulting "South Mountain Plan," now in its fifth year, also completely restructured the school day so that teachers spend half their time tutoring, making home visits, and calling parents.

South Mountain sees itself as a full-range community and social service center, operating a drug-prevention and social-work program right on campus. Academic standards have also been toughened: all freshmen, for example, are now required to take algebra. All of this has paid off handsomely: the dropout rate has been cut by more than half, to 10.9 percent, violence is rare, and the school is gaining some 300 students a year. As a result, South Mountain has been cited by the state as one of the top five high schools in Arizona. "Our school sees itself as a hub of activity for the parents and the community," says principal Art Lebowitz. "It's almost a city within a city."

What we propose in the school choice debate, then, is a search for common ground—a plan of school renewal on which all educators might agree. The stakes are far too high for policymakers and school leaders to divide into warring camps, driven more by ideology than by ideas. It is possible to break the bureaucratic gridlock and to extend the educational options for parents and students while still affirming the neighborhood school tradition and making every school a school worth choosing.

REFERENCES

Carr, Robert W. (1991) "Markets Can't Fix Schools' Problems," *The Wall Street Journal*, May 2, p. 17.

Education Daily. (1992) "Students Still Coming to School Unready to Learn, Teachers Say," Vol. 25, No. 178, September 15; citing The Metropolitan Life Survey of the American Teacher 1992.

Glazer, Nathan. (1992) "No Excuse for Failure: Urban Schools in Transition," *The City Journal* (City University of New York), Vol. 2, No. 4, August, p. 27.

10

Privatizing Higher Education

Kevin C. Sontheimer

This chapter focuses on higher education in the United States, but the issues considered are relevant to almost all countries since in virtually all countries the provision of education at the post-secondary level is dominated by the public sector. The United States is different from most countries in this regard in that the public sector presence in higher education has become dominant only more recently (but having its origin with the Morrill Act of 1862), in fact being a post–World War II phenomenon. The United States is also different in that even at this date there still is a substantial private sector component to higher education, and many of the reputedly best institutions of higher learning in the United States are private. Thus the possibility of privatizing the public sector institutions might seem more feasible in the United States than in other countries.

The richness and extent of the public sector in supporting and providing higher education services in the United States is well exemplified by the arrangement in Pennsylvania. The Pennsylvania situation also exemplifies the potential that remains for private sector provision of higher education services (and research services). The situation in Pennsylvania is given in Table 10.1.[1] The data show that private colleges and universities in Pennsylvania still remain the largest provider of services to full-time (FT) students among the categories distinguished. To provide a clearer picture of the Pennsylvania situation, it should be noted that only one of the four state-related universities (The Pennsylvania State University) receives most of its education funds from the public sector as a direct subsidy. Three of the four state-related universities receive less than half of their education funds as a direct public sector subsidy.

Thus the extent of the private portion of higher education in Pennsylvania is larger than the categories of Table 10.1 might indicate.

The fact that private sector provided education is still robust and viable in terms of market share makes it a clear, practical, and reasonable alternative institutional form as a provider of education services. Indeed, the fact that some of the very best providers of higher education in terms of quality are private institutions makes the case for private education even stronger. A typical ranking of universities and four-year colleges according to perceived quality usually has the top twenty positions dominated by private institutions. So empirically, whether assessed in terms of relative quality or financial sustainability, the private sector is a highly viable alternative to public sector provided higher education.

What are the arguments in favor of or against public sector provided higher education? First, there are no strong philosophical or economic arguments for the public sector to be the provider of higher education services. The public good argument for higher education is weak at best. While there are productivity gains from the education received at the post-secondary level, there is no evidence that the productivity improvements are not properly compensated via the market (i.e., there are no significant external economies). The public good argument via the political requirements of the democratic process also is strained when it comes to post-secondary education. The affordability or access argument based on distributional considerations (whether argued as another version of a public good case, or simply based on interpersonal, distributional considerations without any reference to externalities or social stability as a public good) also is weak, since private provision of the services with public finance to those individuals meeting subsidization criteria is a feasible option. There are, in fact, no strong philosophical or economic arguments in favor of publicly provided higher education.

Table 10.1

Institutional Categories and Enrollments in PA Higher Education (Fall Term, 1991)

		Enrollments		Percentages	
	No.	FT	PT	FT	PT
State Universities	14	76,670	20,180	20.4	9.9
State-Related Universities	4	103,311	38,627	27.5	18.9
Community Colleges	13	38,196	74,322	10.2	36.4
Private State-Aided Institutions	11	35,294	12,297	9.4	6.0
Private Colleges & Universities	76	112,939	54,774	30.1	26.8
Theological Seminaries	17	1,611	1,389	0.4	0.7
Private Junior Colleges	9	3,873	2,560	1.0	1.3
State School of Technology	1	510	---	0.1	---
Total	**145**	**375,404**	**204,149**	**100.0**	**100.0**

The fact that there are no compelling philosophical or economic arguments in favor of public sector provision of higher education services does not make a case against publicly provided higher education.

What are the arguments against publicly provided higher education? First, there are the inefficiencies that derive from tying subsidies to specific providers. If subsidies are provided to individuals there are well known utility gains thereby captured by allowing the individual to assign the subsidy to the provider of choice rather than requiring the individual to have to restrict his/her choice to a particular subset of institutions in order to gain the subsidy.

Second, there is the catalogue of problems typically associated with institutions that are part of the public sector—for example, intertemporally soft budget constraints that derive from the incremental budget process even if the political unit providing the funding has a balanced budget requirement. In the instances in which there are no balanced budget requirements, then the deficit potential of the public unit translates into a soft budget potential for the subsidiary educational unit even within a budget period. In fact, the existence of a balanced budget requirement for the political unit providing funding does not guarantee that there cannot be a soft budget constraint for a subsidiary unit, such as an educational institution; it only provides some pressure to enforce budget constraints on subsidiary units.

Indeed, the catalogue of problems that applied to state enterprises in the former socialized economies of Central and Eastern Europe apply to public institutions of higher education in the United States (though there is a significant difference of degree due to a competing private sector, a rivalrous political process, and a relatively aggressive and unconstrained press in the United States). Pennsylvania provides a good example of the intertemporal softness of budget constraints that the incremental budget process yields. Using student full-time equivalent (FTE) data as a rough measure of productivity, the data of Table 10.2 demonstrate how the real resource cost of higher education has increased far in excess of the FTE measure of output. The fact that the faculty growth was below the administrative and professional support services, further suggests that the main growth was for wasteful uses of resources.[2]

THE PRIVATIZATION EXPERIENCE

The main lesson of all the efforts to execute large scale privatization of industry is that it is not easy. It is not easy even when there is wide-spread popular support and strong political will behind the privatization effort at its outset.[3] It is definitely not easy when there is ambivalence among the political authorities and/or among the population as Russia now demonstrates.

The second lesson is that unless the transition process is well designed so as to make the costs of transition low, both the popular support and the political will for privatization will weaken as the process proceeds, and the privatization

Table 10.2
PA Growth in FTE Students versus Administration and Other Personnel
(Percentage Change from 1980–1981 to 1989–1990)

	Percent Growth	
Characteristic	State Universities	State-Related Universities
No. of FTE Students	22.9%	10.2%
No. of Instructional Faculty	3.5%	3.6%
No. of Executives, Administration and Managerial Personnel	56.6%	42.3%
No. of Other Professional	94.5%	28.9%
No. of Non-professional	10.5%	20.3%

program might not be completed, as was the case in Great Britain. The case of Great Britain is especially instructive of the difficulties of large scale privatization. Despite the advantages of the parliamentary system, a popular government with a substantial majority in Parliament, sophisticated capital markets thoroughly integrated into international markets, a world-class banking system, and so on, approximately only twenty or so firms were privatized over a period of approximately twelve years. Privatizing large scale enterprises is not easy!

The latter lesson includes the subordinate lesson that having a well-defined goal or goals for privatization is not enough to sustain support through a transition process. Goals will be abandoned if the realized costs during the transition are too high or endure too long. A program of privatization must have well-defined goals and the process of transition must not be too traumatic in that the costs associated with dislocations must not be too high, too concentrated, and endure too long. An indefinitely long path of moderate annual costs due to inefficiencies can rationally be chosen by consumers to be superior to a path with an up-front period of high costs followed by a sustained period of low costs. The intertemporal preferences of the public matter.

THE TRANSITION PROCESS: BENEFITS AND COSTS

The benefits of privatizing higher education would be broadly distributed in that the untying of public subsidies from specific institutions will allow large numbers of students to capture the utility gains to be had from larger choice sets. To the extent that the privatization of higher education would break the connection between soft budget constraints and increasing tax burdens, the general population would experience lower tax loads. The latter gains are not inconsiderable since higher education in the United States shares features in common with medical care, and they are that both have been experiencing price increases well above those of other final product and service categories and that both absorb a large portion of public expenditures (though medical costs clearly dominate higher education expenses as a proportion of gross national product).[4] So the benefits of privatization would be widely but not universally shared.

On the other hand the costs of privatization would be distributed much more narrowly. As is typical of privatization efforts, the principle costs are the employment/income losses and relocation costs that would have to be absorbed by employees in inefficient enterprises. A secondary loss is the value of the employment stability that is characteristic of public enterprise that would be sacrificed in converting to a private enterprise without tied public subsidies. Because the losses would be large to the individuals involved, and concentrated geographically (large urban public universities, the colleges of college towns), the lesson of Public Choice Theory is that the political efforts of the potential losers in opposing privatization can readily dominate the efforts of the potential gainers.

Negotiating the transition process of privatization is an exercise in the application of Public Choice Theory. It is necessary to structure the distribution of costs and benefits of privatization intertemporally and across the electorate so as to sustain political support.[5] This fact greatly influences the transition process proposed here for privatizing higher education in the United States. The feasibility of a privatization process hinges at least as much on political as economic considerations.

The specific problems with the privatization of higher education have to do with employment maintenance, regional incomes considerations, the salability of capital assets, and the fact that higher education services are highly subsidized by the private sector as well as the public sector. Since the private sector subsidies provided to public institutions are tied to the institutions via endowment funds and capital assets, all of the subsidies cannot be made portable. Also, the newly privatized institutions would have to compete with heavily subsidized sales by pre-existing private institutions. The primary component of the mechanism proposed for achieving a privatized higher education sector is a phased-in voucher system. A second component of the mechanism is a sale process for capital assets that provides for a preferential Employee Stock Ownership Plan (ESOP) bid. The privatization process is described and the likely transition experience developed in the following sections.

Employment Maintenance

Much of the efficiency gains of privatizing education would be lost if employment guarantees were given to those presently employed in the public universities, colleges, and other post-secondary educational institutions. Providing for the privatization of the institutions and untying the public subsidies to students from the institutions to allow students to vote with their feet, while guaranteeing employment in place for faculty and staff, would impose a heavy cost burden offsetting the utility gains of the students. Therefore such employment guarantees cannot be a part of a meaningful or serious privatization plan. Thus a problem is: how to put forward a program that is both serious and does not provide the foundation for its own defeat by not forestalling the opposition that a clear and present danger of unemployment would induce?

Regional Income

Resistance to privatization proposals does not just come from those for whom the threat of unemployment might be clear and present, or those in their immediate families. The notion of income and employment multipliers are well known and accepted parts of the common economic and political conceptual frameworks. Any threat of employment or income loss to a well specified subset of a community is seen to be a threat to the community as a whole, and sometimes in a distorted and exaggerated way. The resistance factor that a privatization program would induce has a multiplier associated with it.

The resistance multiplier is larger than the actual income or employment multipliers since the anticipation of who will bear the burden of the multiple employment or income losses is a matter of probability. If the employment multiplier is two, and the anticipated direct employment loss might be 5 percent of the work force so that the full loss would be 10 percent, it is quite possible that 25 percent of the work force could feel significantly threatened, for example. That is, for every additional job to be lost due to the direct effect there could be, for example, as many as five employed persons who feel that there is a reasonable probability that their position could be the one lost via the multiplier effect. A one in five chance of becoming unemployed is likely to raise the political concerns of anyone.

The regional multiplier concerns that might stem from the threat of unemployment and income losses as a result of privatization thus make the importance of dealing with the employment maintenance problem all that much greater. The regional multiplier of resistance is undoubtedly understated in the preceding paragraph since it neglects what might be called the sympathy factor.

Just as the multiplier effects result in the magnification of the resistance to privatization, so too they can magnify the reduction in resistance to privatization as the perceived threats are reduced. There is both a positive side and a negative side to multiplier effects.

Salability of Capital Assets

A second major feature of any privatization scheme is the way it deals with the disposition of the capital assets of the to-be-privatized enterprises. The privatization can allow for the piecemeal disposing of some or all of the assets, or it can keep them intact in a bundle. If some assets can be disposed of piecemeal, then the privatization plan provides for the downsizing or restructuring of enterprises up-front in the privatization process. If the scheme allows for the piecemeal disposing of all the assets, then the scheme is basically treating the enterprise as a bankrupt organization. This is not part of what is normally understood to be the focus of privatization and so will be ruled out here. It will be ruled out not because of any objection in principle, but for the pragmatic reason of trying to minimize the opposition to privatization.

The piecemeal disposing of some of the capital assets of the enterprise up-front in the process tends to raise the insecurity level of the employees and community because of the increased probability of transitional employment dislocations. Thus such a feature of a privatization program is a negative feature to be avoided, *ceteris paribus*. The piecemeal disposing of some capital assets up-front also will reduce the viability of the remnant enterprise after privatization, reinforcing the opposition to privatization. The privatization scheme to be proposed will provide that public institutions of higher learning to be privatized be privatized intact (i.e., all the capital assets kept in one bundle). After privatization, however, *qualified* piecemeal disposition of assets will be provided for.

One of the typical problems of privatization schemes in formerly socialist economies is determining the value of the capital assets of the state enterprises. The book values of the capital assets typically are meaningless, the revenue and cost data of the enterprises are almost meaningless if not meaningless, and the same is true for all capital assets in any specific region within any of the formerly socialist economies. Not only are the specific capital asset values subject to huge uncertainties, but also site values are subject to huge uncertainties.

The problem of capital asset value determination in the formerly socialist economies has a reflection in the public institutions of higher education in the United States. The problem is that most state or community owned institutions do not keep capital accounts. Thus there is more difficulty in accurately assessing the values of the capital assets than is typically the case for commercial assets. However, because the institutions are embedded in functioning market economies and site values therefore are determinable with much greater accuracy, the problem of capital asset valuation is not so severe as in formerly socialist economies. Still the estimated values of the capital assets of institutions of higher learning would have greater standard deviations associated with them than is typical of commercial firms in a well-functioning market economy. This would be especially true for the case of institutions which constitute a significant portion of the economic base of the local community, as, for example, the public college of a college town.

Because of the risk associated with the purchase of the capital assets via the pricing problem, the sale of such assets is somewhat problematic. The risk factor would induce a discounting of the sale value of the assets.

Private Sector Subsidies

Special feature of the market for higher educational services is the ubiquity of subsidies to the buyers of the services. Most private colleges and universities, not just public institutions, sell their services below cost. The subsidies come from the use of endowment income to pay for portions of overhead and operating costs and to further reduce the price imposed on the consumer via scholarships and student aid packages. Other subsidies are effectively provided by donors funding the construction or renovation of capital assets. Higher education is further subsidized by special tax treatment for private institutions.

The existence of subsidization of the sale of educational services by the already private institutions poses a problem for a to-be-privatized public institution. If the buyers of the formerly public institution have to pay the approximate market value of the capital assets, their resulting cost base will put them in a competitively disadvantageous position. The need to pay for all of their capital assets will give the newly private institutions a higher cost structure than their older rival private institutions (on average). Only if the capital assets do not have any good alternative use will capital markets discount the assets sufficiently to put the newly private institutions on a par with the cost structures of their rival and prior private institutions.

For those cases where the capital assets of public institutions have good alternative commercial uses (whether kept intact or decomposed after privatization), the subsidized pricing of rival colleges and universities will help to ensure that the capital assets would move into their alternative uses. That is, in such cases the capital assets would be withdrawn from higher education. This would mean transitional dislocations in employment and income losses up-front in the privatization process.

It might well be that there are excess physical plant and other capital assets in higher education. A process that threatens the abrupt withdrawal of the excess capacity is a process that also threatens quick and severe dislocations in terms of employment and incomes. The dislocations also would be highly concentrated geographically and politically. The process of privatization then should be designed to allow for a smoother withdrawal of excess capital assets (if any).

There is a footnote to be added on the issue of private subsidies to higher education. The vast proportion of subsidies available through public institutions comes from public funds raised via annual tax collections. However, many public institutions now have endowment funds provided by private persons or private sector institutions, and the funds are growing due to significant fund-raising efforts by the public institutions. These funds would be non-transferable in the privatization process: they would remain with the institution. (The subsidies yielded by public sector endowments would provide a trivial amelioration of the problem presented by the extensive subsidies available via the extant private institutions.)

THE PRIVATIZATION PROGRAM

A feasible process for privatizing higher education in the United States must first pass the test of political feasibility. Given that higher education in the United States is primarily a state concern and not a national (federal) concern, the political test is a stern one. The test has fifty parts.

The political test means that significant or severe up-front dislocations in employment and income are not acceptable. Other, somewhat less politically potent dislocations to students and prospective students who are attached or hope to become attached to particular institutions that would be threatened by prompt closure or severe downsizing must be accounted for as well. The process must constrain such dislocations in order to be politically feasible.

Employment subsidies to newly privatized institutions would not be an economically or politically appealing mechanism to mitigate significant up-front dislocations. The process should avoid such features. A privatization process that provides a stake for the main interest group that might otherwise oppose the privatization, but that avoids direct employment subsidies, is a more viable process. A mechanism that fits this prescription is well known, and that is to provide for significant employee ownership of the newly privatized institution.

The essential features of the privatization process would be as follows:

1. As a means of coping with the capital asset valuation problem, the privatization program should include a public bid process. The bidding should be for the intact institution, including all assets, any and all bonded or other debt, credits, and contracts of the institution.[6] The bid process should provide for a special ESOP bid to convert the public institution into either a for-profit or non-profit institution of higher learning. The request for bids should provide a certified estimate (as an attempt to provide information of value to all potential buyers) of the worth of capital assets and net worth of the institution. The bidding should require that bids cover at least 40 percent of the estimated net worth of the institution, except that an ESOP bid need cover only 20 percent of the net worth or 50 percent of the best non-ESOP bid, whichever is greater. If an ESOP bid meets the criteria, then the ESOP bid wins. If only an ESOP bids, the ESOP wins.

2. The revenues obtained from the sale of the institutions of higher learning would be deposited in a tuition fund, the earnings of which would be used to pay for the tuition vouchers to be granted to students.

3. The annual subsidies provided by government funding to the institutions, less the earnings to be obtained from the tuition fund, would be converted into per capita subsidies to students in the form of vouchers usable at any institution of higher learning within the state. The interstate redeemability of the vouchers would have to be negotiated between the various states.

4. The ESOP would not be allowed to be converted into a public corporation or otherwise sold for at least ten years. Any revenues obtained by the sale of any capital assets during the first ten years would have to be added to the endowment of the institution or invested in other capital assets.

5. Any unfunded pension liabilities would remain the liability of the public sector and would not accrue to the to-be private institutions.

Feature one serves several purposes. First, if no bids would be made for any particular institution that met the stipulated thresholds, it would be a clear demonstration to the general public that the institution in question was producing educational services of dubious value relative to the cost to taxpayers. It would stimulate consideration of closure as a means of promoting a more efficient allocation of resources if there were no buyers as opposed to the likely perpetuation of the institution under the current public funding system. A second purpose is to convert faculty and staff who are stakeholders in the institution by virtue of their employment and possibly emotional attachment into potential shareholders as well as stakeholders. The incomes and employment of the faculty and staff would not be so directly threatened because of the better terms offered to the ESOP, and in fact the faculty and staff would be offered something which they might well value and accept as some compensation for the risk that privatization as an ESOP might entail. This is to promote the feasibility of privatization (alternatively, to reduce the opposition by lowering the perceived costs). Third, by removing the assets of the institutions from the public property lists, the process promotes the possibility that the future costs to the public sector can go down since maintenance and other costs would have been shifted to the private sector. Fourth, the conversion to an ESOP and removing the institutional budget from the state budgeting process also creates an incentive for faculty, staff, and administration to slow the growth of costs and to seek out internal efficiency improvements. Finally, the potential ESOP holds out the prospect of real faculty governance at the privatized institutions. Since faculty governance is often a rallying cry on campuses, this might be another compensation for the risk that the privatization otherwise brings relative to continued public status.

The first feature also deals with the problem of the ubiquity of private subsidies in the private sector of higher education. By reducing the capital cost of the to-be-private institutions, the institutions can compete on a comparable cost basis with the extant private institutions. Thus the survival of the institutions is more a matter of their future cost control and quality of service than their historical development and legacies.

The second feature allows for a reduction in the current tax load carried by taxpayers. This spreads the benefits of privatization to a larger category than just the students who might benefit from the larger choice set of institutions to attend. This benefit is spread thinly, but it is a clear benefit nonetheless.

The third feature allows students to redistribute themselves as dictated by their preferences, rather than as dictated by the tying of subsidies to a particular subset of institutions, and thereby to achieve utility gains without any increased cost to taxpayers. Also, since direct tuition subsidies are not subject to the usual incremental budgeting process as are the budgets of public institutions, some future budgetary savings can be realized. To the extent that the direct subsidy growth can be held below the incremental rate of growth of the public sector institutional and payroll funding, the shifting of the assets reduces the rate of growth of public sector spending and therefore taxes.

The fourth feature is to prevent the faculty and staff, as members of the potential ESOP, from realizing quick capital gains from the transfer of assets. This forestalls public opposition to the privatization that would arise if the faculty and staff could quickly realize gains by immediately selling off the assets transferred from the state. Also, the fourth feature provides the faculty and staff with an incentive to promote the success of the ESOP in addition to the incentive of retaining their employment and salaries. The additional incentive is the prospect of capital gains that might come at the end of ten years if they can make a success of operating their institution in the private sector. The potential for capital gains also holds some potential as a moderating influence on wage and salary growth since the employee-owners can anticipate a trade-off between wage or salary income and capital gains.

Feature five is an important feature to promote the financial viability of the new private institutions. This feature recognizes that the liability at present does not accrue to the (public) institutions, but to the relevant government units (state or local government). It also recognizes that the unfunded liabilities are for benefits based on past service as public employees, and that the liabilities therefore properly should remain with the public sector. Leaving the liability in the public sector does not result in any new liability or future tax burden for the general public.

There is nothing in the five features of the program that prevents the failure of some of the privatized institutions, or their downsizing. To the extent that over time there is a redistribution of students across institutions, those institutions that lose students will have to downsize and/or fail, and those that gain students will grow. Faculty over time will be reallocated as will capital investments. The allocation of inputs over time will become increasingly rational but with a lag relative to the self-allocation of students.

THE TRANSITION

The point of privatizing the public institutions of higher education is not to close them, to eliminate faculty and staff positions, or to cause other and larger regional dislocations. Rather the point is to promote utility gains for present and future students and to reduce the tax burden on taxpayers. Accomplishing the latter will probably entail some employment and income losses, and in some locations failing (closing). In the event that achieving the efficiency gains will entail some significant and localized dislocations, the task then is to not allow the prospect of the dislocations to prevent the realization of any net gains.

The program proposed above is designed to minimize the resistance to changes that will realize the efficiency gains by reducing the up-front costs as much as possible and by giving the prospective losers as great an opportunity as reasonable to protect and advance their situations. Part of this strategy is to avoid rapid and precipitous change. The idea is to allow time for new market positions to be explored and developed.

The use of ESOPs is a critical factor in the transitional strategy. ESOPs are calculated to act more deliberately, if more slowly, in eliminating positions. For this reason a larger role for ESOPs than for non-employee-owned institutions is calculated to reduce the resistance to privatization.

Similarly, the deep discounting of the capital assets of the public institutions is calculated to reduce the opposition to privatization by the employee groups and community support for their opposition. The lump sum subsidy that the discounting represents will be seen as some insurance that the privatized institutions will not fail and maybe not even have to engage in significant downsizing. Indeed, the deep discounting will allow the newly privatized institutions an opportunity to engage in effective competition with the extant private institutions. At the least, it should put off the need for significant downsizing or closing for a substantial period and thereby mitigate the opposition to doing any privatization.[7]

The actual transition from public institutions to a stable arrangement of older private and recently privatized institutions will take some time. Part of the strategy should be to ensure that the transition takes some years as a way of ensuring that the costs of the transition are not bunched up at the beginning of the process. The capital asset subsidies help in that regard. But another step should be taken. The transition should not include a rapid voting-with-the-feet of the current crop of students. A prospect of a rapid and large reallocation of students between institutions should be avoided since it creates a clear prospect of institutional failures. To that end a brake should be placed on the voting-with-their-feet phenomenon.

Feature three of the privatization program provides for the calculation of an annual subsidy per student. Since the total amount available for payment of subsidies will be held constant in the privatization, and the number of eligible students will increase, the average subsidy received will fall. Nonetheless, some students enrolled at the time of privatization will opt to move with the smaller subsidy, and some students will opt to remain where they are and suffer the reduction in subsidy. The latter group would tend to oppose the privatization, so a specifically transitional provision should be added to the program, to wit:

6. Any students enrolled in a public institution at the time of privatization should have the option of remaining at their original but privatized institution with the same effective subsidy they enjoyed before privatization. Any students enrolled at the time of privatization who switch to a different institution must accept the new and lower subsidy. Students enrolled in private institutions at the time of privatization will be eligible for the voucher subsidy wherever they choose to enroll after privatization.

This feature of a privatization program will have two effects. First, it will restrain the voting-with-their-feet by students who are enrolled at the time of privatization, but have no effect on the voting-with-their-feet by future enrollees. It thereby stretches out the period of reallocation of students over a four-year period. Second, it will eliminate the opposition to the privatization program that would be induced by reducing the subsidies received by students who would choose to remain attached to their old institutions after privatization. Both features enhance the feasibility of privatization. However, the second effect also entails a higher cost to the taxpayers than an immediate adjustment to the lower average subsidy would entail. This is considered to be an acceptable effect because the higher tax cost would be diffused over a large number of taxpayers, and per taxpayer would be a small and temporary increase, while the benefits associated with the second effect would be concentrated and significant to the affected persons.

Adding feature six to the privatization program would ensure a transition to privatization that would last at least five years and probably more. Features one through six together constitute a program with a transition that keeps the up-front costs low but provides a flow of benefits that begins immediately (though feature six restrains the immediate flow of benefits somewhat). The privatization program also provides an opportunity for those most potentially involved on the cost side to participate and influence their fates via the ESOP arrangement. It also provides them with effective support (the capital asset discounts) for preserving their jobs and incomes within a framework that long-term does not increase the cost of subsidizing higher education and even allows the prospect of reducing the cost.

While the prolonged transition period will delay the failure of some institutions, it will not prevent the failures. Those institutions that cannot compete effectively under the new subsidy arrangement will ultimately fail. The capital asset discount and the initial restraint on voting-with-the-feet only can delay the ultimate rationalization of investments in institutions of higher learning.

CONCLUSION

The present arrangement of tying subsidies to institutions induces efficiency losses by constraining choice. An equally costly program of subsidies that allows individuals to assign the subsidies is possible and achieves utility gains. The program also promises further gains by taking higher education institutions out of the incremental budget processes of the public sector and thereby putting hard budget constraints in the place of soft budget constraints. The privatization program also would reduce current and future tax burdens by moving the maintenance of capital assets off the public budget. Both the number of potential beneficiaries and the potential total benefit are large.

The proposed program stretches out the costs of transition so as to minimize the political opposition to privatization. The program also increases the role and participatory share of the faculty and staff in their institutions, making the transition period less threatening. Clearly some faculty and staff groups will benefit from the self-determined reallocation of students across institutions. The ESOP arrangement allows each faculty and staff group to work out internal arrangements to give them a voice in the management of their institution. It also gives them a greater incentive, along with the hard budget constraints, to restrain cost growth and to eliminate wasteful expenditures.[8] Thus the failures and downsizing of institutions, along with their income and employment losses, are pushed further into the future and the resistance to the privatization is reduced.

The greatest impediment to large scale privatization programs in other countries is the resistance to prospective income and employment losses that come early and strongly in the process. The program proposed here for higher education avoids this problem by stretching out the period of such loss absorption and providing benefits up-front and throughout the transition process.

NOTES

1. The source for the data is *Colleges and Universities: Fall Enrollment 1991* published by the Division of Data Services, Pennsylvania Department of Education.

2. The source for the data is *Selected Output, Input and Efficiency Measures for Major Institutions and Programs of the Pennsylvania Department of Education.*

3. Chile and Great Britain are two cases where there was strong political will and, at least in the case of Great Britain, strong popular support as well. Both Chile and Great Britain had other strong advantages such as well developed capital and other markets (Bogetic and Conte 1992, 2–3)

4. For example, tuition charges for the 1980–1986 period increased by 10.6 percent annually while the Consumer Price Index increases averaged 4.8 percent (Iosue 1992, 7).

5. It should be noted that even when the burdens and fragility of democratic government do not have to be borne, large-scale privatization proves to be a long and difficult task. The large scale privatization in Chile extended over approximately twenty years and only about 200 enterprises were privatized and another approximately 350 firms were restituted to their prior owners (Bogetic and Conte 1992, 2–3).

6. Estimating the value of the capital and other assets of a firm is not an easy task. The estimates determined in takeover efforts emerge from a process which has been well documented in many cases, and the documentation clearly demonstrates the subjectivity of judgments and approximations of the procedures used. The valuations are well summarized in the following lines: "Whether raider or target, buyer or seller, the question is, what is the right price? No one knows. . . . Pricing is therefore a matter of conjecture or speculation." (A. Fleischer, Jr., G. C. Hazard, and M. Z. Klipper 1988, 135–136.)

7. The fact that some privatized institutions might grow is ignored because such prospects improve the feasibility of the privatization effort, and the focus here is on how to cope with the potential resistance to privatization.

8. For example, if colleges and universities were ESOP's, it is not at all clear that most of the present large athletic programs would endure.

REFERENCES

Bogetic, Z., and Conte, M. (1992) "Privatizing Eastern European Economies: A Critical Review and Proposal," *Mimeograph*, October.

Fleischer, Jr., A., G. C. Hazard, and M. Z. Klipper. (1988) *Board Games: The Changing Shape of Corporate Power*. Boston: Little, Brown and Company.

General Assembly of Pennsylvania, Joint State Government Commission. (1992) *Selected Output, Input and Efficiency Measures for Major Institutions and Programs of the Pennsylvania Department of Education 1980–81 and 1990–91*, Staff Memorandum, August.

Iosue, R. V. (1992) "Higher Education: Are We Getting Our Money's Worth?" In *Leading Pennsylvania into the 21st Century: Policy Strategies for the Future*, edited by D. E. Eberly. Harrisburg: The Commonwealth Foundation.

Pennsylvania Department of Education, Division of Data Services. (1991) *Colleges and Universities: Fall Enrollments*. Harrisburg: Author.

III

EXPERIENCES

11

The Evaluation of the New Hampshire Plan: An Early Voucher System

John Menge

In 1973 the education voucher was a hot topic in education, perhaps as much as, if not more than, today. Milton Friedman (1955, 1962, 1973) on the right and Christopher Jencks (1970) and J. Areen (1971) on the left were both strong and provocative proponents of vouchers, along with a considerable number of other academics and education critics who were attracted to the voucher concept as a means of reforming education and ameliorating such social inequities as segregation and unequal employment opportunities (Brozen and Weil 1971; Clark 1969; Fantini 1971; Ginzberg 1971; Havighurst 1970; Hentoff 1971; Lekachman 1971; McCann 1972; Olsen 1971; Overlan 1972; Sizer 1969).

FIRST LIGHT

In the early 1970s Richard Nixon, a strong education voucher advocate, was president of the United States. Arch conservative Meldrim Thomson, another strong voucher advocate, was governor of New Hampshire—his only prior political experience was chairing the school board in a community of less than 1,000. The governor believed that "[t]his free choice by the taxpayer—the kind of competitive education they might want for their children—is the very essence of American freedom" (Thomson 1974, 2). Conservative Republicans dominated both houses of the New Hampshire State Legislature. The chairman of the New Hampshire State Board of Education, a retired businessman, believed that the free market attributes of vouchers were the Sword of Damocles with which to cut the Gordian Knot of the education bureaucracy (Bittenbender 1973). The National Institute of Education (NIE), a section of the Department of Health, Education and Welfare (HEW), was staffed with a group of young Turks who were convinced that the time was ripe for educational reform—and in 1973 they had significant unobligated research funds available to further that objective through the implementation of a New Hampshire free market education voucher test project.

In a sense, the origin of this NIE New Hampshire voucher project dated to the year 1970, when the U.S. Office of Economic Opportunity (OEO) sent letters to superintendents of major school districts throughout the country proposing a test of the voucher idea as defined by Christopher Jencks and the Cambridge Center for the Study of Public Policy (CCSP) in Cambridge, Massachusetts (Center for the Study of Public Policy 1970). It was hoped that a field test of education vouchers would result in a resolution of many of the controversial issues associated with the concept so that the way would be opened for widespread implementation of vouchers—or that the idea would be buried once and for all (OEO Pamphlet 3400–1, January 1971). Six school districts studied the Jencks "regulated compensatory" voucher proposal in some depth, but five of them declined to proceed with the experiment in the face of strong opposition from teachers' groups, community racial tensions, and uncertainties about legal issues. In the end, only one, the Alum Rock Union Elementary School District of San Jose, California, decided to give the Jencks "transitional" quasi-voucher a try—and then mainly on the district's own terms. One of several school districts within the city of San Jose, California, Alum Rock served some 15,000 pupils in a poor, predominantly Hispanic section of the city. The district superintendent, William Jefferds, had long sought to upgrade the schools by encouraging parent participation on the one hand, and giving greater autonomy to individual principals on the other. He saw the proposed OEO "voucher" test program as a way of continuing this trend, while at the same time bringing new federal moneys into the district (Spitzberg 1974, 3).

Jefferds soon found that he faced enormous problems in implementing a field test. To begin with, the whole idea of alternatives was new and threatening to administrators, teachers, and parents. These disparate groups worried about the social, professional, and economic effects that student transfers and the mechanisms employed would have on them and on their schools. Would children still be permitted to attend their neighborhood schools? Would teachers continue to be secure in their jobs? Would principals lose authority to parents? What role would outside experts and the proposed Education Voucher Advisory Authority—composed of equal numbers of parents and school staff members—play? In addition, OEO initially contemplated the inclusion of parochial and private schools in the test, but there were no independent private schools within ten miles of Alum Rock and the Catholic schools feared outside control of curriculum and admissions. To make matters even more difficult, the California legislature temporized on passing special legislation which would have permitted nonpublic schools to participate in the project.

What eventually emerged was something far less than the definitive test that education voucher advocates had been seeking (*National Review*, October 13 1972). OEO and Alum Rock worked out a compromise "transition voucher model" which would only include public schools, and a very restricted number of public schools at that (just six out of the twenty-six elementary schools in the Alum Rock district). Parents thus lost the option of sending their children to the other twenty Alum Rock public elementary schools, to other San Jose public schools outside the Alum Rock district, to public schools outside the city of San Jose, to parochial schools, and to non-sectarian private schools. To simulate choice the resulting severely limited the number of six participating public schools were each required to develop at least two alternative educational programs, called "mini schools." Parents would receive a "voucher" valued at the average cost of educating a child in the Alum Rock district. In addition, poor parents would be given a bonus, or "compensatory" voucher, over and above the base voucher. Upon enrolling their children in the "mini school" and program of their choice, parents would submit their "vouchers" as payment. The total received by each "mini school" would—in theory—determine its budget. In this manner, it was hoped the Alum Rock model could be interpreted as at least approximating the educational marketplace envisaged by voucher proponents.

Even the limited and contrived Alum Rock initial version of the education "market" concept did not survive the planning and implementation stage (NIE, December 1973). To allay the fears of teachers, principals, and administrative personnel, the OEO and local voucher advocates were forced into concessions which made it virtually impossible for schools to react to the economic forces of supply and demand. For example, all district employees received guarantees of full job security. The participating schools also found that they had no new or added local resources at their command for experimentation and innovation. The only such funds available at the "mini school" level were those supplied by the federal government.

A more serious concession struck at the heart of the voucher concept. One of the crucial claims of education voucher advocates is that a voucher system will put more power over education into the hands of individual parents. Different children require different kinds of schooling (so the argument goes), and parents, as consumers, are the best judges of the appropriate education program for their own children. Consistent with this philosophy, the Alum Rock model provided for an autonomous staff which would counsel parents about their options and encourage their active participation in making educational choices. Because these staff members would be independent of the participating local schools, they would not try to "protect" school administrators from parental involvement in, and concern for, the educational process. Early on, however, the six principals involved raised objections to this aspect of the plan, and they emerged from the ensuing power struggle with considerable administrative and policy control over the various parent counseling activities.

In the end, the Alum Rock quasi-voucher experiment did promote autonomy—but at, or within, the individual school rather than at the parent level (Spitzberg 1974, 7; NIE 1973). It was the principals and teachers who wound up with greater choice and greater programmatic autonomy and overall authority within the system. The parents, however, gained only very constrained choice (the range of which was determined by the teachers and the administrators)—and consequently almost no market power. From this perspective, the demonstration project merely accelerated the trend toward "alternative education" which was already underway in Alum Rock even before the project began. Not surprisingly, most children continued to attend their neighborhood schools—and parents, not surprisingly, approved of the increase in curricular enrichment and diversity in their neighborhood school engendered by increased federal funding.[1]

Severely circumscribed as it turned out to be, the Alum Rock test could neither lend credence to the dire warnings of voucher critics nor legitimatize the optimistic expectations of voucher advocates. Ultimately both sides of the debate attributed this failing to the inadequacies of the experiment; for while Alum Rock attempted to use the voucher form, it abandoned the voucher content.

ANOTHER CHANCE—ON TO NEW HAMPSHIRE

After a disappointing start in California, the new education voucher battle cry was to become, in essence, "New Hampshire Here We Come (Right Back Where We Started From)." In a sense, this was true. New Hampshire, for more than seventy years, utilized significant voucher-like programs in certain smaller school districts that chose not to operate elementary and/or high schools. These particular local districts had, and still have, school boards that allocate funds, raised mostly through local taxes, to primary and secondary education. Such funds are not allocated to purchasing paper, pencils, and chalk; to hiring teachers, janitors, and coaches; or to heating and lighting buildings. Instead, they are used to give local parents the choice of any public elementary or secondary school anywhere in the state or in another state, as long as such schools are approved by the New Hampshire State Board of Education.

The value of an elementary school "voucher" in these instances is limited to the New Hampshire state average cost per pupil of current expenses of all New Hampshire public elementary schools, or the current expense of the particular receiving school plus a 2 percent rental charge for the capital investment of said district, whichever is less. If a parent chooses a school that charges more than the value of the voucher, the parent pays the difference. The secondary school "voucher" is more generous.[2] The sending district must pay full tuition at whatever public New Hampshire or other approved public high school the parents choose, even when it exceeds the state average, subject to the statutory provision that no receiving high school may charge more than the school's per pupil current variable costs plus a 2 percent rental fee. In some instances, such as in Hanover, the site of Dartmouth College, the local public high school tuition rate is higher than that charged by all but a few of the most prestigious private schools in the East. The value of this type of New Hampshire education "voucher" is obviously significant.

Based upon the rather high probability of a warm welcome from the governor and the chairman of the State Board of Education; upon the existence of a tradition of choice in local school districts; and upon the strong support of academicians at Dartmouth and Harvard, HEW and NIE (as the successor to OEO in sponsoring voucher test programs) turned their attention to the Granite State. Here one might at last plant the voucher flag and battle for a real test of "pure" free market education vouchers. By the fall of 1973 NIE, the New Hampshire State Board of Education, the New Hampshire Education Department, and consultants from several universities and public policy institutes put together a New Hampshire free market education voucher program which presumably would test all the assumptions left untested in Alum Rock (New Hampshire State Board of Education 1973; Adams 1973).

GOLD OR GRANITE—THE NEW HAMPSHIRE VOUCHER

It was envisioned that the New Hampshire voucher test would be implemented according to a three-part schedule (New Hampshire State Board of Education 1973). First, there was Phase I, the transition year, when the New Hampshire State Board of Education would select the particular school districts which would participate in the voucher plan. Considerable emphasis was placed on distributing information to local school boards and to the respective communities to obtain the "informed consent" of the school districts to elect (to vote) to participate in the test project. Phase II consisted of the initiation, in the chosen school districts, of the test program utilizing vouchers in public schools only—on the condition that the legality of cashing vouchers in out-of-state public schools be first established. One year after Phase II had been implemented, Phase III would become operative, and non-sectarian private schools would begin to participate in the program. At the end of five years from the start of Phase III all federal subsidies to the districts for taking part in the project (administration, testing, etc.) were to be eliminated.

It should have been easy! In the fall of 1973 the New Hampshire State Board of Education signed the final contract with NIE to conduct the test of the free market education voucher. It was contemplated that, within the next few months, most if not all 200-plus New Hampshire school districts (which for the most part are coterminous with township boundaries) would be given information about the voucher to fully inform them about the details of the test program. By the time annual school district meetings took place in March and April of 1974, a significant number of these districts would presumably have voted to apply to participate in the voucher project—from which applicant pool the state board would select one or more districts as test sites. Ideally the district, or contiguous districts, chosen would have a primary and secondary school student population of 8,000 to 12,000 individuals. After the site selection in the spring of 1974, the chosen districts would work with the New Hampshire State Department of Education and with consultants representing NIE and the New Hampshire State Board of Education to initiate the five year free market education voucher test in September of 1974. Conceptually, the test was relatively simple:

1. An Education Voucher Authority would be established by the NIE and the New Hampshire State Board of Education to administer the test.

2. After the test had been approved by the selected local districts, the State Board of Education, and NIE, it would be fully operational for five years with an additional two years for phasing out federal funding of any test functions and activities.

3. A local Voucher Review Committee would recommend to the local district school board the voucher values for consideration at the annual school district meeting—the exception being that in the first year of the test the value would be the district's current budgeted cost per pupil. In succeeding years the voucher value could be whatever the community wished to spend, provided that this amount was at least equal to the local cost per pupil (if the district operated schools) or was of sufficient value to purchase an education at a state approved alternative educational site if the district decided not to operate schools.

4. A voucher, representing the sum of money approved at the school district meeting, would be provided every district-resident parent/legal guardian for each eligible child.

5. The parent/legal guardian would be able to cash the voucher at any public or private school in the continental United States (approved by the New Hampshire State Board of Education or its counterpart in other states) that was willing to accept the voucher as full or partial payment for education services.

6. Any school accepting vouchers would have to certify that it was legally qualified to accept public moneys for the educational services it rendered.

7. No-fee transportation would be provided (within the provisions of existing state statutes) for all participating children attending any approved school within school districts contiguous to the participating district.

8. Local districts would be expected to maintain the existing level of financial effort to support education in the district. Additional costs *due to the implementation of the test* would be borne by the NIE as part of its commitment to the test.

9. A one-time-only monetary grant, equal to 30 percent of the district's total appropriation for the school budget of the year immediately preceding implementation of the test, would be given to each local district as an incentive to participate.

10. Parents could transfer their children from one alternative education site to another at any time during the test period.

11. Public schools would operate with the moneys received from the vouchers of pupils attending those schools plus any additional amount voted by the school district at the annual meeting.

12. A local school board could operate several schools at the same grade level with different programs, but these would qualify as only one option for parental choice. There would have to be another separate, politically autonomous, educational entity available to provide parents with a choice of, at a minimum, one alternative school program (New Hampshire State Board of Education 1973).

As an example of how these guidelines were to operate, suppose that the Lyme School District had applied for inclusion in the voucher test in the spring of 1974 and had been selected to participate. In the fall of 1974 the parents of *all* its students (whether currently enrolled in public or private schools)—approximately 260 or more in grades K–12—would be given vouchers at (a) the elementary school level or (b) the secondary school level. The values of these two vouchers would be equal to the respective elementary and secondary per pupil expenditures approved at the school district meeting in the previous April of that year 1974. Parents of elementary school students could cash the voucher at the Lyme elementary school, where it would cover the entire tuition for the year. On the other hand, a parent could send a child to Hanover, New Hampshire, where the tuition charge exceeded the Lyme voucher value. In this case, the parents would have to make up the difference. If the child were sent to Orford, New Hampshire, however, where the tuition charge was less than the Lyme voucher value, the Lyme school district would have more current funds to spend on pupils remaining in the Lyme school, or would be able to add to the surplus shown in its year end budget.[3]

In the second voucher test year, at the school district meeting in the spring of 1975, the district would set a value for the voucher for the new 1975–1976 academic year and would include this item in the proposed budget. The voters of the Lyme school district would have before them a recommendation from the local Voucher Review Committee (VRC) for an appropriate level of voucher funding.[4] This recommendation would either endorse a higher valuation than, or the same valuation as, the last year's voucher value—and would be accompanied by a listing of the reasons for such a recommendation. These reasons would focus on providing a comprehensive array of desirable educational characteristics that could be found in various elementary and secondary schools where Lyme's vouchers could be cashed—and the costs associated therewith. The VRC would be expected to recommend a voucher amount that would enable parents ultimately to choose among a fairly wide array of such desirable options. Just how wide this choice might be in practice would be determined by the school budget appropriations approved by the Lyme voters. The only restriction was that the district could not reduce its existing level of support for education.

An additional responsibility of the VRC, related to its task of recommending a possible voucher value, would be to provide as much pertinent information as possible to Lyme parents about the various educational institutions at which their district approved vouchers could be cashed in full or partial payment of the annual tuition fee. Data pertaining to types of curricular programs offered, class sizes, achievement test scores, extra-curricular activities, facilities, counseling programs, transportation costs, etc., at the education providers eligible to accept the Lyme voucher, would be gathered and made widely available to Lyme School District parents. Parents wishing to choose a more expensive alternative, either because of a tuition fee higher than the approved Lyme voucher amount or because of increased transportation costs to a remote non-contiguous geographical location, could supplement their Lyme voucher as necessary from their own financial resources.

Over the five-year test period Lyme parents would exercise their right to choose based upon widely available current information as to the competitive characteristics of all probable educational providers. Students would be expected to gravitate toward those institutions best serving the parents' preferences, with the State of New Hampshire, through the State Board of Education, assuring that society's basic educational requirements were met through mandated minimum standards. Students might end up in private non-sectarian schools, in the local Lyme district public school, or in public schools in other districts. The supply of educational options available to Lyme students would ebb and flow, and would change in response to the entrepreneurial and administrative capabilities of those in charge of all the various voucher eligible schools. Schools, both private and public, might be newly created, might expand or contract, or might go out of business. The educational arena would become a vibrant free market constantly changing and adapting to the forces of demand and supply—and thereby optimizing the educational consumers' (the Lyme parents') satisfaction through the choices they made among education options.[5]

EXTINGUISHING THE LIGHT—THE REASONS

There was only one catch in this process—it was never tried. The New Hampshire Free Market Education Voucher taxied a very long way, but it never was able to get off the ground. Ultimately it stalled, for good, at the end of the runway. Although the project lingered on until 1976 in the form of "planning grants" to several smaller communities, by June of 1974 voters in sixteen critical targeted school districts decided not to buy the voucher test proposal. It was indeed a crushing defeat—the New Hampshire Education Association labeled it "The Annihilation" (New Hampshire Education Association 1974, 1). Apparently most parents didn't care much one way or the other—few turned out, in many instances less than 1 percent of the eligible voters. Those few who were motivated to cast their ballots wanted no part of a New Hampshire free market voucher test program. The reasons for this singular lack of free market voucher aerodynamic capacity have important implications and provide relevant lessons for continuing attempts to utilize vouchers to "improve" the education of the students currently enrolled in America's elementary and secondary schools.

Lack of Demand

The first, and perhaps most significant, lesson is that there must be a demand for the exercise of "parental demand" for choice in education, (i.e., for vouchers). Theoretically, education vouchers can have an impact on the possibility for increased parental choice, but practically parents may have little, if any, interest in increasing their current range of educational options. This appeared to be the case in New Hampshire in the early 1970s. In a 1973 survey for the New Hampshire State Board of Education of parents in eight representative large New Hampshire school districts, in *none* of the districts was the quality of public schools perceived to be below average (Cambridge Survey Research 1973). Interestingly, many of the parents who were surveyed indicated that they knew little, if anything, about the quality of their local public schools—but few parents rated their local district public schools below average. In the town of Salem, for instance, 44 percent of the parents indicated that they didn't know what the quality of education was in the district's high schools, but only 5 percent of the parents who had an opinion on the subject considered the schools to be below average. When it came to elementary schools the number of uninformed parents dropped dramatically. Salem again had the most in the "don't know" category 19 percent, but an overwhelming 85 percent of those who did know thought that the quality of education in the local Salem elementary schools was average or above. Parents apparently had even less information about the quality of alternatives—that is, private and parochial schools. In the city of Rochester, where 26 percent of the student population was enrolled in parochial schools, 73 percent of the parents "didn't know" about the quality of the local parochial high school and 51 percent had a similar lack of familiarity with the local parochial elementary school offerings. The "unknown" factor was even higher for private non-sectarian schools, ranging all the way up to 95–100 percent in the city of Berlin.

In general, the survey results indicated that local school district parents did not perceive the quality of public school education to be particularly lacking— and even if they had, they were overwhelmingly ignorant of the quality of possible parochial and private non-sectarian school alternatives. As a consequence, there was minimal latent grass roots support for vouchers, or a voucher test program, at the local public school district level. Nowhere was this lack of concern more apparent than at information meetings with parents held in school districts where the local school boards had evinced some interest in at least exploring the voucher concept. In Claremont, an economically depressed city of approximately 14,000, with a public high school increasingly under fire by accrediting agencies as to acceptable minimum standards, only fifty-three people attended a highly publicized education voucher information session (*Claremont Daily Eagle* 1974). The session had been designed to provide the Claremont voters with the knowledge they would need to make an informed decision on the voucher article (question) in the school district warrant to be voted on at the forthcoming annual district meeting. This demonstrated lack of public interest in Claremont was, without exception, typical of such information sessions in all the school districts where intensive efforts were made to interest voters in participating in the proposed test of education vouchers.

The New Hampshire voucher experience would seem to indicate that at the local school district level voters most likely will not endorse (demand) an education voucher program. A sizable majority of parents is not dissatisfied with the local public school program and, furthermore, is not aware of any acceptable alternative in the form of private non-sectarian or parochial schools. The chairman of the New Hampshire State Board of Education admitted as much after the rather conclusive rejection of the voucher test proposal in the sixteen key local districts in the spring of 1974. At the time he stated, "I am disappointed in the results, but not surprised. Several recent studies of public opinion have shown that there is a great deal of satisfaction on [sic] what's going on in schools. Between 90 and 95 percent of parents are satisfied. This says something to me" (New Hampshire Education Association 1974, 1).

Even though a small minority of parents might welcome wider choice among education options, at the local school district meetings the majority rules. The majority, which by and large approves of and validates the existing local district education program, perceives that it has little, if anything, to gain educationally as the result of being offered more school options to choose from. Further, there is a very real probability of an added burden financially if such education choice options were to be made available. Under these circumstances the majority of parents and non-parents alike cannot reasonably be expected to welcome a locally based school district voucher program.

The very essence of an effective education voucher program is that *all* parents will be offered a real choice among a number of different education options. However, the very essence of an effective and salable education program at the local school district level is to offer the *majority* of the parents in the district the singular educational program, or choice, the majority wants. A successful voucher program should empower *both* the minority and the majority. The difficult political problem for voucher advocates is to convince the majority of the school district's voters to opt for a more costly program which that very majority perceives to result in little that would be of significant educational benefit for itself. Increasing the range of choice in *any* economic marketplace is seldom without cost, but where it is successful, the perceived benefits outweigh the costs. For this reason alone, regardless of what its hypothetical educational merits might have been, the New Hampshire voucher test program was doomed from the start. The demand for education vouchers, or for a test of education vouchers, must come, if at all, from a constituency other than the voters in a local school district: it must come from legislation enacted by state legislatures or from mandates issued by state boards of education and be based upon a broader view of the benefits which might derive from choice.

Lack of Supply

A second lesson to be learned from the New Hampshire experience is that supply is no less important than demand in the marketplace—education or otherwise. It is all very well to offer choice, the ability to exercise parental demand among options—if there are options. In New Hampshire, as in all probability is true in the other forty-nine states, parochial schools, for constitutional reasons, were not a factor on the supply side. Even if they had been, most New Hampshire parents knew little about parochial school educational programs (Cambridge Survey Research 1973). In addition, private non-sectarian schools were few and far between—and with extremely limited excess capacity. They could do little to enlarge the range of choice available to most parents who wished to cash their vouchers at an option other than that of their local public school. Public schools in other school districts were potential sources of increased supply, but once again the number of open slots for student transfers was limited, and parents were even less informed about neighboring public school districts than they were about their own (Cambridge Survey Research 1973). The possibility of new schools, private or public, springing up to take

advantage of the limited market of students comprising a local school district—
or to compete for the 12,000 (or less) students in a New Hampshire education
voucher test program lasting five years—was, and is, remote. Even if the
majority of a district's voters desires to opt for choice, such choice would most
probably be "the substance of things hoped for, the evidence of things unseen."
The size of the investment required and the market risk to be run relative to the
size of the potential market are simply too great to guarantee that an increase
in supply would respond to an increase in demand.[6]

No Lack of Bureaucracy

The third lesson is that even the most simple and most basic of market
concepts is quite apt to be transformed by the education establishment, or
any established bureaucracy, into an administrative nightmare. The essence
of education vouchers is their simplicity. It should be easy to make choices,
not difficult. The more difficult choice becomes, the fewer choices that can,
and will, be made. The New Hampshire Free Market Education Voucher was
initially designed to be simple—easy to understand and easy to use. The
architects of the New Hampshire test program were well aware of the
indignities Christopher Jenck's Center for the Study of Public Policy, in the
name of choice, had inflicted on the exercise of choice (New Hampshire
State Board of Education 1973). The provision of information on education
options by a school district's Education Voucher Authority in the CSPP
voucher model (as opposed to the New Hampshire model) necessitated a
description overflowing twenty-five pages of fine print. The prologue to this
more detailed description of the structure for the task of providing information to parents is informative:

VII. The Structure of the Information Agency
The Information Agency (IA) we have proposed could probably be cut
back considerably at [the] end of the demonstration's first year. Initially,
however, the agency would have three major "divisions," each of which
would have smaller units called "sections" and even smaller units called
"components." Each Division could be administered by an "Assistant
Director." The three Assistant Directors would then report to the IA
director, who, in turn, would report to the Director of the EVA (Center for
the Study of Public Policy, March 1970, VII–9).

Yet even the best intentions of the authors of the New Hampshire program
to design and test a plain and uncomplicated market voucher were ultimately
thwarted. By January of 1976, 228 printed pages were necessary to describe
the "simple" free market voucher which the State Department of Education was
trying to sell to local districts (New Hampshire State Board of Education 1976).

Tempting as it might be to present the entire 228 pages of the report, the table of contents alone should suffice to indicate how complicated simple things can really be—if one tries hard enough (see Figure 11.1).

By January of 1976, the date of this report, the original architects of a free market test of vouchers no longer publicly or privately supported what was left of the New Hampshire free market education voucher concept. There was little reason for voucher tears to be shed when the 1976 cobbled-up bureaucratic version of New Hampshire education vouchers evoked no interest and found no takers among the state's 200-odd public school districts.

No Lack of Ideology

A fourth and final lesson pertains to ideology. Ideologues, both on the right and on the left, tend to oversell the education voucher, raising expectations that can't be fulfilled. The extreme free marketers in New Hampshire already knew before the inauguration of any test program how vouchers would work. Vouchers would give all parents more education options; they would improve the quality of education; they would lower the cost of providing education services, and they would demonstrate the bankruptcy of the current public school education paradigm. Furthermore, the governor already knew that "[t]his free choice by the tax payer—the kind of competitive education they might want for their children—is the very essence of American freedom" (Thomson 1974). On the other hand, to social planners on the left, all, or some of, the virtues extolled by their counterparts on the right might well transpire, but regardless of such outcomes, they also knew beforehand that vouchers would increase parental participation in school affairs; would improve educational achievement; would result in less social and ethnic segregation, and would refocus debate away from the politics of educational content and toward how education should be financed. Further, the structuring of educational programs would be left to the professionals with educational expertise who would strive to meet the revealed educational demand of parents cashing their vouchers.

The problem with an ideological approach to vouchers is that it tends to scare off the vast majority of parents and voters who are in the middle. These are the individuals who might be persuaded to try the education voucher concept to determine whether a better education in terms of certain objective measurements—for example achievement test scores, dropout rates, employment statistics, evidence on integration and data on costs—might result from adopting an education voucher program, were it not for their concern that the concept was being used and abused to attain something other than widely accepted and legitimate educational objectives.

Figure 11.1
Table of Contents for New Hampshire Free Market Voucher System Requirements

APPENDICES

GLOWING EMBERS—THE FUTURE

Since voters, or parents, do not appear eager to support radical change in education, a politically feasible first step in the continuing saga of education vouchers might be quasi-voucher programs limited to initiating and improving statewide choice among schools and education programs in different public school districts. Even here it should be recognized that a program of change must always be subject to change.[7] Education vouchers and choice are not the stuff of revolution, but they can be a means of continuing evolution toward a goal of providing all parents (the majority and the minority) with the education program they would have liked to be able to vote for. New Hampshire's aborted free market education voucher test was one of the first flickering lights in that evolutionary education voucher chain. With a lot of political luck, that light may not entirely fail.

NOTES

1. The local Alum Rock American Federation of Teachers president indicated to a New Hampshire observer in May of 1973 that the local program wasn't really a voucher plan at all, it was an open enrollment plan. He ridiculed the whole idea of "people in the front office shuffling those little green cards," maintaining that there is no voucher, only a bookkeeping process. He believed that the so-called "voucher" plan brought the district only one thing it really needed—money.

2. Lyme, New Hampshire, is an example of a community which has always used some form of choice, or vouchering, for its secondary school students. Lyme is a town of approximately 1300 located just north of Hanover on the Connecticut River, which forms the boundary between New Hampshire and Vermont. The town has never felt that it had either adequate resources or a sufficient number of students to have its own local high school. As a consequence, the district annually budgets an expense for high school tuition based upon a poll of the graduating eighth grade class as to individual parents' public high school preferences. In 1986–1987 the eighty-nine high school students (grades 9–12) attended:

School Students Attending	Community	# Lyme
Hanover High School	Hanover, New Hampshire	58
Orford High School	Orford, New Hampshire	19
Hartford High School	Hartford, Vermont	7
Thetford Academy (semi-private)	Thetford, Vermont	3
Oxbow High School	Bradford, Vermont	1
Lebanon High School	Lebanon, New Hampshire	1

In 1991–1992 a much smaller student population of fifty-nine students (principally due to the "Baby Bust") chose:

School	# Lyme
Students Attending	
Hanover High	40
Orford High	12
Thetford Academy	4
Hartford High	3

The fact that these parents are actually making meaningful choices is especially significant considering that *no* transportation is provided by the Lyme School District for senior high school pupils. Also, contrary to conventional wisdom in many educational circles, not everyone rushes to the high priced school with his or her voucher to get one's "money's worth" (Town of Lyme 1985, 1991).

3. If, over time, the Lyme elementary school were progressively to lose increasing numbers of students to other schools not a part of the local school district, the district might well decide to close the local school and pay outside educational providers for educating all Lyme students at the elementary level, just as it was currently doing at the secondary school level.

4. The local school board could constitute itself as a Voucher Review Committee or it could delegate the task to an appointed committee consisting of local citizens, one or more of whom might be school board members.

5. It was assumed that a district such as Lyme would be part of a much larger test group of contiguous school districts. Lyme's approximately 260 students would have been part of the larger targeted student test population of 8,000–12,000 pupils.

6. Recognizing this supply side limitation, the New Hampshire voucher program guidelines were, late in the game, unfortunately and in desperation amended to allow a single public school to divide itself schizophrenically into two different entities: "An 'Alternative Program' is one that can be provided *in the same public school* within the district, another public school or private school within the district, or in public schools or private schools outside the school district" (New Hampshire State Board of Education 1976) [emphasis added].

7. Eight states now allow choice among all public schools in the state—Arkansas, Idaho, Iowa, Minnesota, Nebraska, Ohio, Utah, and Washington. Even in these jurisdictions, choice is currently limited and often socially suspect. See, for instance, "Des Moines Acts to Halt White Flight After State Allows Choice of Schools," (*The New York Times*, December 16 1992).

REFERENCES

Adams, T. (1973) "The New Hampshire Voucher Project," *The Massachusetts Teacher*, December.

Areen, J., and C. Jencks. (1971) "Education Vouchers: A Proposal for Diversity and Choice," *Teachers College Record*, February.

Bickford, D. (1974) "Will New Hampshire Vouch for Free-Choice Education?" *New Englander*, March.

Bittenbender, W., and B. Morrison. (1973) "New Hampshire Vouchers: Free Market Test," *The Common*, October.

Brozen, Y., and R. Weil. (1971) "The Voucher System," *The American Conservative Union*, Washington, D.C.

Cambridge Survey Research. (1973) "A Preliminary Report on the Attitudes toward the Voucher Program in the State of New Hampshire," *CSR* #247, July.

Center for the Study of Public Policy. (1970) "Education Vouchers: A Preliminary Report on Financing Education by Payments to Parents," March.
———. (1970) "Education Vouchers: A Report on Financing Elementary Education by Grants to Parents," December.
Claremont [New Hampshire] *Daily Eagle*. (1974) "A Voucher Plan?" March.
Clark, K. (1969) "Alternative Public School Systems," *Harvard Educational Review* (Winter). Reprinted in Equal Educational Opportunity. Cambridge: Harvard University Press.
Fantini, M. (1971) "Options for Students, Parents, and Teachers," *Phi Delta Kappan*, May.
Friedman, M. (1955) "The Role of Government in Education," In *Economics and the Public Interest*, edited by R. Solo. Rutgers, N.J.: Rutgers University Press. Revised in M. Friedman (1962), *Capitalism and Freedom*. Chicago: University of Chicago Press.
———. (1973) "The Voucher Idea," *The New York Times Magazine*, September 23.
Ginzberg, E. (1971) "The Economics of the Voucher System," *Teachers College Record*, February.
Havighurst, R. (1970) "The Unknown Good: Education Vouchers," *Phi Delta Kappan*, September.
Hentoff, N. (1971) "Vouchers: Educational Choice," *Civil Liberties*, February.
Jencks, C. (1970) "Giving Parents Money to Pay for Schooling: Education Vouchers" *The New Republic*, July 4. Reprinted in *Michigan Journal of Secondary Education*, Fall 1971. Reprinted as "Giving Parents Money for Schooling" in *Compact*, February 1971. Revised version printed as "Giving Parents Money for Schooling: Education Vouchers" in *Phi Delta Kappan*, September 1970.
Lekachman, R. (1971) "Vouchers and Public Education," *The New Leader*, July.
Lyme, Town of. (1987) "Annual Report of the Town of Lyme, New Hampshire." For the year ending December 31, 1986.
———. (1992) "Annual Report of the Town of Lyme, New Hampshire." For the year ending December 31, 1991.
McCann, W. (1972) "The Politics and Ironies of Educational Change: The Case of Vouchers," *Yale Review of Law and Social Action*, Summer.
National Institute of Education. (1973) "Education Vouchers: The Experience at Alum Rock," December.
National Review. (1972) "Two Cheers for Alum Rock," October 13.
New Hampshire Education Association. (1974) *Educator*, Vol. LIV, No. 6, June.
New Hampshire State Board of Education. (1973) "New Hampshire Educational Voucher Project: Revised Feasibility Study." November 14.
———. (1974) *The Voucher*, Vol. 1, No. 1, April.
———. (1976) "Education Vouchers Study and Planning Project, Phase II Report," January.
The New York Times. (1992) "Des Moines Acts to Halt White Flight After State Allows Choice of Schools," December 16.
Office of Economic Opportunity. (1971) "A Proposed Experiment in Education Vouchers," *OEO Pamphlet* 3400–1, January.
Olsen, E. (1971) "Some Theories of Efficient Transfers," *Journal of Political Economy*, January-February.
Overlan, S. F. (1972) "Do Vouchers Deserve at Least a Sporting Chance?" *American School Board Review*, November. Condensed in *The Education Digest*, March 1973.
Sizer, T. (1969) "The Case for a Free Market," *Saturday Review*, January 11.
Spitzberg, I. (1974) "Vouchers at Alum Rock: Promise but Not Panacea." New York: Institute of Current World Affairs, January.
Thomson, M., Jr. (1974) "Preface," *The Voucher*, Vol. 1, No. 1, April.

12

The Milwaukee Choice Program

Thomas Hetland

There is a dense fog surrounding elementary and secondary education in this country. Teachers and students alike try to chart a course through it, but many lose their way. In 1990 a beacon began to burn in Wisconsin to help lead the way for a few. It was a small beacon, but its light continues to penetrate the fog far beyond Wisconsin's borders. The beacon is the Milwaukee Educational Choice bill, enacted by the legislature thanks to an exceptional coalition led by State Representative Polly Williams, a liberal black Democrat. Key to the success of the coalition was the significant support she received from Governor Tommy Thompson, a conservative white Republican.

A BRIEF BACKGROUND

The Milwaukee Public School System (MPS) is the home-away-from-home for 100,000 children, 70 percent black, who invest a dozen years of youth in pursuit of a rewarding adulthood. However, given the city's staggering 50 percent dropout rate, only 50,000 of these are expected ultimately to graduate from high school.

Milwaukee's teachers have long recognized the hollow promise. "A 1987 University of Wisconsin survey found that 62 percent of Milwaukee teachers wouldn't want their children to attend the school at which they teach. It's no wonder then that nearly half of the children of Milwaukee's public school teachers attend private schools, double the average for all school-age children. Few send their children to non-magnet public schools" (Fund 1990).

Milwaukee's is a system in which student achievement hovers around a D+ average (1.62 grade point average). Despite that miserable performance, in the five-year period just preceding the adoption of the choice program not one teacher in 6,000 had been fired for poor teaching and not one of the 1,000 new teachers hired in that period had been denied tenure (Fund 1990).

The Milwaukee School Choice Plan extended an opportunity limited to just 1 percent of the city's public school population. Up to 1,000 students from financially disadvantaged backgrounds (family income no more than 1.75 times the national poverty line) would be permitted to choose from among participating non-sectarian private schools in Milwaukee.

By promoting such a program Polly Williams placed herself at odds with many of her liberal Democratic colleagues. Plain-spoken as ever, she challenged the ideology of her own party: "If liberals in the party are so good for blacks, why are we in such bad shape? . . . Basically, I see the Democratic Party as being a leech that lives off of black folks" (Ragan 1991).

In September 1990, 341 students enrolled in seven participating private schools. Dr. John Witte of the University of Wisconsin-Madison reports that test scores and survey questions indicate that these students were not succeeding in the public schools and that they probably had higher-than-average behavioral problems. Fifty-nine percent of participating families were receiving public assistance, and 76 percent of those participating were single—parent families (Witte 1991).

Who would fight to deny these children an alternative opportunity? Who would feel threatened by a pilot program involving less than one-half of 1 percent of MPS students? Who would begrudge approximately $2,500 in state tax funds to these students, when that amount is less than half the $6,000 that MPS spends on average, and when MPS was permitted to retain the $3,500 difference even though the student was not enrolled?

Many would. So many, in fact, that it became a David and Goliath story whose final performance was given on the stage of the Wisconsin Supreme Court. The lawsuit names one "Lonzetta Davis, acting on her own behalf and on behalf of her daughter, Sabreena Davis," along with a dozen other children and parents. Weighing in against this small but intent troupe, determined to make sure that Sabreena and others like her would spend all their days and keep all their tax dollars in the Milwaukee public schools, was Herbert Grover, the State Superintendent of Education. He was officially joined in the suit by The Wisconsin Association of School District Administrators, the Wisconsin Education Association Council, the Association of Wisconsin School Administrators, the Milwaukee Teachers Education Association, the Wisconsin Congress of Parents and Teachers, the Milwaukee Administrators and Supervisors Council, the Wisconsin Federation of Teachers, and the Milwaukee Branch of the National Association for the Advancement of Colored People. Together they made a formidable Goliath, but one no more victorious than the Bible's original when the court rendered its final decision in March 1992.

EVALUATION OF PROGRAM

In September 1990, pursuant to its statutory responsibility the state Department of Public Instruction appointed Professor John Witte of the University of Wisconsin at Madison as the independent evaluator of the Milwaukee Parental Choice Program. Witte's research would extend beyond the schools of choice to include some comparative analysis with respect to Milwaukee Public Schools.

Methodology

Witte's evaluation program employed several methodological approaches:

- Surveys at the beginning of the school year and again at the end to all parents whose children were accepted to choice schools
- Surveys of a random sample of more than 5,000 MPS parents
- Detailed case studies of four of the schools of choice including class-room visitations, faculty/administration interviews, and student questionnaires
- Analysis of achievement test scores, attendance rates, and attrition from the program

Student Achievement

Throughout his report Professor Witte emphasizes the preliminary nature of his findings, due to the relatively small number of students and a single year of operation on which to base the report. He writes, "Preliminary outcomes after the first year of the Choice program were mixed. Achievement test scores did not register dramatic gains and the Choice students remained approximately equal to low-income students in MPS (higher on reading, slightly lower on math)" (Witte 1991, iv). He emphasizes repeatedly that it is not only too soon to make any definite judgments about achievement, but that making any judgment at all would be difficult. According to the report, "Almost all of the students in the program are elementary or middle school students. It is extremely difficult to measure outcomes or achievement for children at those ages" (Witte 1991, iv).

Parental Satisfaction

Witte investigated many factors other than academic achievement. Of particular note are his findings on parental satisfaction with schools of choice: "Parental attitudes toward their schools and education of their children were much more positive than their evaluations of their prior public schools. This shift occurred in every category (teachers, principals, instruction, discipline, etc.)" (Witte 1991, v). When asked to assess the importance of various factors affecting their decision to participate in the choice program, parents identified the following factors as "very important" or "important":

Educational Quality in Chosen School	97%
Discipline in Chosen School	98%
General Atmosphere in Chosen School	97%
Financial Considerations	94%
Frustration with Public Schools	83%
Special Programs in Chosen Schools	89%
Location of Chosen School	80%
Other Children in Chosen School	66%

Although between 70 and 80 percent of the parents indicated they were satisfied with information available on the program and on particular schools, barely 60 percent were satisfied with the assistance they received from the Department of Public Instruction in the state capital of Madison.

Student Satisfaction

Student attitudes also were surveyed, and Witte reports:

The results are generally positive, with some striking findings. Over 80 percent of the students at both grade levels believe their school gave students a good education. Students generally approved of teachers and teaching practices. . . . Nearly all students reported that principals had visited their classrooms. . . . The environment in the school was also quite positive. Students reported they felt safe everywhere in the school, and almost no one reported drug or alcohol problems. . . . Students confirmed what other evidence has indicated, that expectations by both parents and teachers were very high (Witte 1991, 15–16).

On the negative side Witte does note that nearly 40 percent of the students reported that "fighting" was a problem and that more students disagreed than agreed with the statement, "I trust most of the people in my school."

Parental Involvement

Witte's survey allowed important comparisons to be made between the choice schools and their MPS counterparts. Parental involvement, for example, clearly was higher in the choice schools:

	Choice	MPS
Attend Parent/Teacher Conference	98%	84%
Belong to Parent/Teacher Org. (PTO)	20%	21%
Attend Meetings of PTO	74%	64%
Take Part in Activities of PTO	63%	35%
Belong to Other School Organizations	24%	16%

Witte explains that the rather low percentage belonging to PTO in the choice schools "may be because formal membership in PTO-type organizations is not stressed and what it means to be a member is often unclear" (Witte 1991, 16).

Student Attrition

Witte was alarmed by what appears to be a high attrition rate in the program. Of the 341 students who began in September 1990 only 249 were still participating in June 1991. However, most of this attrition was due to the mid-year closing of Juanita Virgil Academy, which is explained in more detail below.

Witte uncovered, however, a more puzzling attrition statistic. Of those 249 students participating in June, only 155 continued to participate in the program the following September. "We know that of the ninety-four students who were in the program in June but who did not return in September, eight graduated from Choice schools. Excluding these students, there still is an attrition of 35 percent over the summer" (Witte 1991, 17). Witte intends to study this more thoroughly in future analyses, but for now speculates that some of this defection could be due to the uncertainty that the program would survive the lawsuits pending against it at the time. He also reports a 33 percent mobility rate for all students in MPS, and he notes that students in the choice program reflect that high rate as well.

Parental Satisfaction as Reported in the Press

Besides the Witte report there are many indications of parental satisfaction with the Milwaukee School Choice Plan.

"Why poor parents like the program's options" ran in *The Milwaukee Journal*. Among the stories was that of Diamond Williams, five, who entered Lakeshore Montessori School at age three. Her mother says "I like it because she likes it. . . . It's a more educational environment than public school. She's learning a lot of things you wouldn't expect them to be learning at that age" (Ahlgren 1991). Diamond's education almost was delayed a year because public school officials told her mother that she was too young to enter four-year-old kindergarten. Mrs. Williams sought out Lakeshore, saying "I knew what she needed and ignored what they said" (Ahlgren 1991).

The Philadelphia Inquirer carried "Parents love 'choice' as Milwaukee does it," in which it reported "Test scores for the . . . students haven't improved, but families involved in the plan love it." The article specifically cites the positive feelings of Gwenn Eggson, aunt and guardian to thirteen-year-old Casey Washington. She says, "In public school, Casey was doing terrible. Since he's been at Guadelupe, he's improved almost a whole grade level. It's just what he needs, and I couldn't afford it without choice" (Barrientos 1991).

In an article on Polly Williams, *Insight* magazine reports the high parental satisfaction at Urban Day School with a reference of its own to John Witte: "More than 90 percent of the parents who enrolled their children in Urban Day want their children to return next year, [Witte] says. This year the school has received 600 applications under the voucher program for a few more than 100 spaces" (Ragan 1991).

Doris Pinkney is a Milwaukee parent who had the opportunity to tell the story of her daughter, Tinika, in *The New York Times* in a special series on school choice.

When Tinika was in first grade in the Milwaukee public schools, she had a terrific principal who didn't put up with any foolishness. . . . The teachers taught and the kids learned. But then she left, and a new principal came, and that's when everything started to fall apart. The new principal let the kids do whatever they wanted, and Tinika started to get bad grades (Pinkney 1992).

The school said that the plummeting grades were Tinika's problem. Mrs. Pinkney disagreed, and decided to transfer Tinika because "the Milwaukee Public Schools just lost interest in her" (Pinkney 1992). With the help of the Milwaukee School Choice Plan she was able to place Tinika in the fourth grade class at Harambee School, "where she's having the best educational experience of her life. She loves school, is learning a lot, and is on the honor roll. Moving her to private school may be the best decision we ever made" (Pinkney 1992).

In February 1992, an editorial of *The Wall Street Journal* reported:

The Wisconsin Policy Research Institute decided to see how the debate on school choice has affected public attitudes. A Gordon Black poll of Wisconsin residents found that support for a voucher system that included private schools is now at 59 percent, up from 44 percent in 1988. Support among blacks, who have the majority of the children in Milwaukee's choice program, is an astounding 83 percent.

THE JUANITA VIRGIL STORY

Perhaps the most repeated criticism of the Milwaukee Choice Plan concerns the closing, after just one semester of participation, of Juanita Virgil Academy. Most of its sixty-three choice students returned to the public schools. Critics say that these students lost precious time and fell behind their classmates, that Juanita Virgil was obviously a fly-by-night school, and that the choice program is without merit because something like this can happen.

In an article for *Conservation International*, Mike Rose tells the story of Juanita Virgil: "Don't tell Phyllis Purdy that using public money to send kids to private schools is the 'magic bullet' that will make education reform a reality. The first time Purdy tried it for her kids, the magic bullet bombed" (Rose 1991). Purdy said she was happy when her children entered Juanita Virgil. She had heard it was a good school, and the brochures were promising, but the experience was a disaster, and she felt her children definitely were behind when they re-entered the public schools.

Another Virgil parent, Leah Wallace, said "For what the school was getting [the students] had nothing to show for it. It was nothing more than a baby-sitting service" (Rose 1991). Author Mike Rose, however, was still able to report: "Although neither Purdy nor Wallace has given up on private schools as an option for this and coming school years, the disappointment of both parents with their first foray into the private arena is clear" (Rose 1991).

Although Juanita Virgil Academy has become a lightning rod for criticism of the Milwaukee Choice Plan, this author cannot find the same depth of disappointment in the story. In fact, I see it as just the opposite—evidence of the success of the program.

The parents themselves would have come, eventually, to the conclusion that Virgil was not meeting their children's needs. One-by-one the students would have transferred to other schools. Virgil Academy admitted after only four months that it could no longer fulfill the promise it had made to the students and their parents. It may be distressing, but certainly not disastrous. To be a few months behind is not as bad as being a few years behind or a full twelve years behind. Virgil Academy did these families a favor by folding quickly. Some schools have been failing children for years, never needing to admit it, and continually enjoying their share of a captive market along with all the tax dollars attached to that share.

Neither is Polly Williams willing to consider the Virgil story evidence of her plan's failure. She concentrates instead on those schools of choice that are fulfilling parental expectations: "For every person that moves out of poverty and these dismal schools, there is one less social scientist and incompetent teacher needed to lead them. These socialcrats have built their lives around taking care of us. Now they're running scared that they'll lose their jobs. When we no longer need them to take care of us, what are they going to do?" (Ragan 1991).

THE MAYOR RESPONDS

Certainly a headline like "Mayor sees end of urban schools" would grab attention in any big city, and the citizens of Milwaukee were thus confronted on January 2 1992 in the *Milwaukee Sentinel*.

Public schools should ultimately be eliminated in favor of a voucher or choice system of education, Mayor John O. Norquist said. "I doubt whether the current system of urban education can be reformed. I think it should ultimately be scrapped and replaced with a new system—essentially a voucher or choice system. We should give city parents the purchasing power they need to enroll their children in any public or private, non-sectarian school that complies with essential standards (Lampke 1992).

Four months later Norquist decided to expand his prescriptions beyond the non-sectarian schools. Another *Milwaukee Sentinel* headline proclaimed, "Norquist says parochial schools will soon get public money."

"Milwaukee would be a much poorer place if the Catholic schools were not here. Not only are the Catholic schools good for Catholics, but they are good for any neighborhood they are in [Mayor John Norquist said]". . . . Financing religious schools "is more practical in Milwaukee than it is in any place in the United States right now. It's more practical because we already won the battle for non-religious schools. We're ready for the next step."

Norquist said that Canada and Holland provided public money for parochial schools without posing a threat to religious freedom. Providing parents with vouchers for their children would not be different from allowing a veteran to use the GI bill to attend a Catholic college or university, he added. "I don't think it would harm our [public] schools," Norquist said. "In fact, it would rescue them" (Rohde 1992).

THE PUBLIC SCHOOLS RESPOND

At the end of the first year of the choice program, the MPS found itself with a new superintendent of schools, Howard Fuller. In "Strategy for Change," his eight-page memo to members of the School Board, he embraces the concept of choice and is brutally frank about the shortcomings of the status quo. He writes:

The public knows we are failing. A 1990 MPS survey of Milwaukee parents and taxpayers showed that 72 percent believe their children would get a better education elsewhere.

For too long we have lived with unacceptable results.

[A] continuation of classroom conditions where children cannot learn and teachers cannot teach [is unacceptable].

Parents will be more involved in their children's education if they choose the school their children attend and if those schools are accessible.

We have an organization without consequence for failure . . . where everyone is protected except the children.

Fuller makes several recommendations, among them:

Increase parental participation in existing choice programs within the public schools.

Inform parents of their opportunity to select a private school of choice.

Build schools where children live.

Allow dollars to follow the student (Fuller 1991).

THE BEACON AND THE FOG

The beacon of school choice is burning in Milwaukee. Surely it could burn more brightly, but were it not for the Wisconsin Supreme Court it could easily not be burning at all.

Polly Williams burned a small hole through the dense fog surrounding American Education. About 500 kids saw a new path and stepped through. The court said the beacon can continue to burn. Some more kids can come through. The court didn't say Milwaukee had to limit the number who came through the hole, nor did they forbid a larger hole. It's time to begin the expansion of the program in a steady progression that ultimately will admit the participation of all students. A brighter beacon will burn when more than 1 percent of the students are allowed to participate.

Similarly the program must expand to include religious-affiliated schools. Many students are routinely denied this option because their parents cannot afford a parochial school tuition. To limit tax-supported choices exclusively to public and non-sectarian private schools is a violation of the free exercise clause of the First Amendment, frequently dwarfed in the shadow of the establishment clause.

Students, of course, would be the major beneficiaries of the expansion of educational choice opportunities, as well they should be. Whether public schools are helped or hurt by this expansion of freedom is entirely up to the public school systems themselves. The response of MPS Superintendent Howard Fuller is a good indication that public schools can and will change from the inside when given the ultimate incentive. If not, their facilities will soon be taken over by new management that will offer the students what they want, presumably with many of the same staff members, but free of stifling regulation and able to respond quickly to students' needs.

The debate over school choice causes people to raise many questions. Will it destroy public schools? Will it violate church/state separation? Will it cost too much? Will it leave the poor behind? The list goes on.

When the beacon of choice finally burns most brightly, and the fog has lifted, perhaps we will realize that all these questions are relatively minor when considered in a larger perspective. Perhaps then we will ask only how we could have missed the point that should have loomed largest of all. John Coons says it in a five-word title to an article: "School Choice as Simple Justice."

[W]hat many people still fail to appreciate is that the case for choice in education goes much deeper than market efficiency and the hope to overtake Japan. Shifting educational authority from a government to parents is a policy that rests upon basic beliefs about the dignity of the person, the rights of children, and the sanctity of the family; it is a shift that also promises a harvest of social trust as the experience of responsibility is extended to all income classes (Coons 1992).

REFERENCES

Ahlgren, Priscilla. (1991) "Private School Choice: Empty Promises?" *The Milwaukee Journal*, November 24.

Barrientos, Tanya. (1991) "Parents Love 'Choice' as Milwaukee Does It," *The Philadelphia Inquirer*, Nobember 25.

Coons, John. (1992) "School Choice as Simple Justice," *First Things*, April.

Fuller, Howard. (1991) "Strategy for Change" (A memo to members of the Milwaukee School Board), August 6. All quotes and references are from this memo, on file with the author.

Fund, John. (1990) "Milwaukee's Schools Open—to Competition," *The Wall Street Journal*, September 4.

Lampke, Kenneth R. (1992) "Mayor Sees End of Urban Schools," *The Milwaukee Sentinel*, January 2, p 1.

Pinkney, Doris. (1992) "Tinika's Story," *The New York Times*, February 2, placed by the Educational Excellence Network, made possible by a grant from the Olin Foundation.

Ragan, Mark Lawrence. (1991) "An Enigma Fights for School Choice," *Insight*, August 26, pp. 32–35.

Rohde, Marie. (1992) "Norquist Says Parochial Schools Will Soon Get Public Money," *The Milwaukee Sentinel*, April 28, p. 1.

Rose, Mike. (1991) "Private School Choice: Empty Promises?" *Conservation International*, November.

The Wall Street Journal. (1992) Editorial, "Choice Facts," February 6.

Witte, John. (1991) "First Year Report—Milwaukee Parental Choice Program," Madison: University of Wisconsin-Madison, November, p. iii.

13

A Public-Private Partnership: South Pointe Elementary School of Dade County, Florida

Thomas H. Peeler and Patricia A. Parham

A UNIQUE PARTNERSHIP

When South Pointe Public Elementary School opened its doors for the first time in September 1991, it became the first public-private educational partnership of its kind in the nation. Education Alternatives, Inc. (EAI), a private, for-profit educational company, and the Miami Dade County Florida Public Schools signed a five-year contract which stipulated that EAI would manage the classroom activities at the school. This meant that the staff at South Pointe would implement EAI's Tesseract Way educational programs. ("Tesseract" comes from the famous children's book, *A Wrinkle in Time*, by Madeleine L'Engle, in which she writes about children who take a fantasy trip through a tesseract, a fifth-dimensional corridor for traveling to exciting new worlds.) Tesseract is the trademark for all EAI schools.

Dade County Public Schools pay EAI the same amount they would spend to start and run any other new school in the district. In addition, EAI solicits grants and raises money from private and other sources to fund the additional materials, equipment, technology, and the additional certified and associate teachers at South Pointe Elementary School.

South Pointe Elementary School has received a great deal of media attention. The school has been featured twice on "Good Morning America"; it has been featured on the nightly news of all three major television networks; major magazines like *Time* and *Newsweek* have written about the school, and leading newspapers from *The New York Times* to *The Los Angeles Times* have written articles about South Pointe.

The school has received this extensive publicity for two reasons. First, it is the nation's first public-private partnership venture in education, and perhaps more important, the teaching/learning process as practiced at South Pointe is dramatically different from what is practiced in most schools in the country. This chapter is an attempt to paint a picture with words that describes the world of South Pointe Elementary School and the unique public-private management organization between the Dade County Public Schools and Education Alternatives, Inc. In addition, we will describe the refinements that EAI has made with the Baltimore Public Schools by adding Johnson Controls and Peat Marwick to assist them in their operation of nine schools in that city.

Demographic Information on South Pointe

South Pointe Elementary School, which serves approximately 800 students, has a pre-school program for four-year-old children and kindergarten through sixth grade classes. Sixty-six percent of the students are Hispanic, 11 percent are black, and the remaining 26 percent are white and/or from other ethnic groups. All of the four-year-old children are on the federal free and reduced lunch program as well as 80 percent of the children in kindergarten through grade six.

The school has a pupil-teacher ratio of fifteen to one. This is accomplished by Educational Alternatives, Inc. (EAI) reallocating funds and hiring one associate teacher from the graduate program of the University of Miami for each class of thirty pupils.

Restructuring Domains of Educational Alternatives, Inc.

EAI has attempted to bridge the gap between "school improvement" efforts of the past three decades and the "restructuring" efforts being proposed by leading educational reformers.

To differentiate "school improvement" from "educational restructuring," theorists describe school improvement initiatives as efforts to improve teaching and learning within the existing or conventional paradigms of school organization and practice. By contrast, the goal of educational restructuring is to introduce new models of pedagogy and practice and to replace existing models of school structure and management with ones that support the new models of pedagogy and practice. Leading educational reformers focus on three main dimensions of restructuring: (1) changes in the core technology of the teaching and learning process, including the roles of teachers and students; (2) changes in the occupational situation of educators, including school structure, conditions of work, and decision making about rules, policies, and customs; and (3) changes in the distribution of power between schools and their clients and in the institution's responsiveness in empowering parents along with teachers to develop Personal Education Plans (PEP) for students.

The major sections of this chapter will focus on these three main dimensions of restructuring and how EAI's Tesseract Way program is addressing them. Each section will contain educational principles drawn from research by the leading educational reformers, and each principle will be compared to the programs being implemented at EAI's schools.

EAI's public/private ventures have been in operation for less than two years in Miami with the Baltimore operation starting in September 1992.

Over the past several years a growing body of knowledge has emerged from cognitive psychologists, critical pedagogists, and philosophers that calls for radical changes in the teaching learning process—a new definition of learning. There is broad consensus among these leading educators that indicates tomorrow's adults must be prepared for a lifetime of inquiry, analysis, collaborative learning, problem solving, and decision making in a context of uncertainty, innovation, and change. These areas will be the "basic skills" of the future.

The new definition of learning requires that the teacher's role will become more like a coach, facilitator, listener, model, guide, and mediator. The student's role will become more of a self-regulated learner who can think strategically, solve problems, work in cooperative learning groups, and be a critical thinker.

This section addresses cognitive principles of learning and relates these principles to their practical applications to learning at South Pointe Elementary School.

1. Successful learning is internal to the individual and not controlled by persons outside the learner (Walton 1991; Bonstingl 1992; Brandt 1990; Sizer 1992).

a. South Pointe children do not receive traditional grades. You will not see smiling faces drawn or pasted on papers and you will rarely hear active praising or criticizing.

b. Instead, children are gradually getting the idea that the work they are doing should please them, not necessarily the teacher—which is what most students think all the way through graduate school.

c. I have observed scores of South Pointe students sitting beside teachers and going over their work. Rarely do you hear outward praise of the work, rather, you hear the teacher and the child or cooperative group reviewing the work with the child explaining the strong areas in the paper or report and the teacher assisting the student in areas that need strengthening. You get the feeling that the teacher's role is more to assist the child in developing good self-evaluation skills and building the idea of what quality work is all about.

d. The Tesseract philosophy is based on the principle that the only real evaluation is self evaluation and the teacher's role is to develop good self-evaluators.

e. You often see a child sitting alone, puzzling over a math manipulative or carefully observing material in a science center.

f. It is evident after visiting a few classes that writing of all kinds is a priority at South Pointe; from essays, expository pieces, reports, and daily entrees in their journals to rearranging the ending of a story on the computer.

2. The main role of the teacher should be that of coach, facilitator, listener, and guide. The active learner, not the teacher, is on center stage. (Brandt 1990; Fullan 1991; Kagan 1992; Wiggins 1993; Sizer 1992).

a. At South Pointe Elementary School you rarely see a teacher conducting a directed lesson for all students in the class. The closest thing you might see to a directed lesson is a story being read by a student, volunteer, or teacher.

b. You often see children working cooperatively at one of the three computers in each class.

c. You see teachers working with math manipulatives with a small group of students; teachers working with a cooperative student work group on a science, social studies, or other group assignment.

d. You see children working in cooperative groups with no direct supervision or students working alone or in pairs on math, reading, or other content area assignments.

e. You often see a first grader being assisted by his fourth grade reading buddy.

f. You see the teacher and a group of students at the Discourse Computer lab working on complex questions with each child responding on his or her "studycom" or interactive keyboard.

3. Cooperative learning is a powerful learning tool that develops positive interdependence and personal responsibility, increases student achievement, and improves social and affective development among all students (Kagan 1992; Slavin 1983; Fullan 1991; Reich 1992).

a. You see children using cooperative learning in critiquing each other's writing assignments.

b. You see children working cooperatively on science or social studies long-term projects. Children determine what areas of the project they will work on and how they are going to present the final project to the teacher.

c. You see children working cooperatively on computer software problem-solving programs such as "Wagon Train" where cooperative learning groups can dialogue with each other in order to reach consensus on a problem-solving activity.

d. You see teachers stepping in and out of cooperative groups providing help as needed or requested.

e. You see children working cooperatively in solving math problems or assisting each other in various drill and practice activities.

4. Cognitive perspectives on learning focus on higher order thinking, including strategic thinking, self-regulated learning and recognition of both teacher and student learning modalities (Resnick 1987, Reich 1992; Schlechty 1990; Brandt 1990; Gardner 1983; Glasser 1990).

a. At South Pointe when you ask a student where he or she can get help on assignments, they have ready answers such as: from one of my peers or friends, from my sixth grade tutor, from the computer, from the library, from one of my teachers, or from a volunteer. It is evident when talking to children that they are beginning to understand they have lots of resources at their command to help them learn and gain power over their learning environment ranging from peers to the computer.

b. When you visit classrooms at South Pointe you see many activities in which students are engaged in helping each other solve problems or complete tasks.

c. You often see two children working on a computer story, discussing how the characters can be rearranged, and then discussing how the story could be changed with the movement of the story characters.

d. You get the feeling from the students that they value their peers, not only for their social support but also for their power to learn from each other. Observing students discussing assignments is the rule at this school rather than the exception.

e. Teachers often model their own thought processes for students, particularly in their process writing assignments. (This idea appears to be a very powerful way for students to understand better what strategic thinking is all about.)

f. Each child in the school is administered the Swassing/Barbe Learning Modality Inventory. Teachers indicate they use the results most often when a student is having a learning problem, and they also recognize that their own learning modality may not be the most appropriate for other learners.

g. Teachers have indicated to me they know how students will begin a project or assignment based on their learning modality. The auditory learners want to talk about it among themselves prior to beginning: the visual learners get right down to work by doing additional reading or starting on the assignment; the kinesthetic learners may get right down to work but need varying activities to keep them at their task. (The point seems to be that teachers allow students to complete work based on what best works for them. As a result you see many different settings as you walk through the rooms ranging from students talking to each other, to students working alone on assignments, to teachers working with individuals or small groups.)

h. It is evident when talking to students that they feel good about themselves and feel empowered to work on assignments on their own or with others. Students tell me that they never feel embarrassed to ask teachers for help in any area.

i. One of the big surprises you get when visiting the school is to see children, beginning in second grade, plan their own math lessons for the next week. Students not only plan their own lessons, they have to be prepared to meet with the teacher to discuss the next steps in their learning process.

5. Meaningful learning is associated with authentic testing and tasks built on real experiences with meaningful interaction with others (Wiggins 1992; Langford 1991; Glasser 1990).

a. It is evident when you walk into classes that you are in South Florida. You will see learning centers focused on the sea, you will see children working in cooperative groups studying the environment of the Everglades, and more recently you see students working together analyzing the problems brought about by Hurricane Andrew.

b. It is not unusual to see a math lesson or other content area being conducted outside, using the school grounds and surrounding areas as a laboratory for learning.

c. Each student has his/her own portfolio of work that includes group and individual assignments. Students have a great deal to say what goes into the portfolio. It is evident that they take great pride in their portfolios and will gladly discuss some of their work.

d. Teachers have indicated to me they use the portfolios in several ways. First, portfolios let the children know they can evaluate their own work over time. Second, at parent conferences, parents and students can review the items they contain. Lastly, teachers indicate that portfolios provide an excellent tool for them to judge the progress students have made over time and to fill in gaps in their learning.

During the past decade a reform movement has been building in both the public and private sectors to make organizations more democratic and less authoritative in their approach to decision making. Goodlad espouses the idea that the individual school must become largely self-directing with control over budgets, curriculum, and staffing.

Just as major corporations are trying to involve employees at all levels in the decision-making process, many school districts are piloting shared decision-making techniques to decentralize these mechanisms to the school site level. In its broadest sense, shared decision-making shifts the major decision-making processes from a central or area office to the school level, specifically to principals, teachers, and parents. Shared decision-making in schools can also be defined as a comprehensive strategy to professionalize teaching and education.

The major principles governing this area are listed below:

1. If educators are given autonomy and held ultimately accountable for the work of their students . . . they will perform to the best of their imaginative ability. Equally important, the career of teacher will become more attractive than it is now. Talented people seek jobs that entrust them with important things (Sizer 1984; Boyer 1991; Elmore 1990; Peeler 1991; Goodlad 1984; Walton 1986; Deming 1990; Reich 1992).

a. The personnel at South Pointe Elementary School have a shared decision-making council made up of teachers, members from EAI school administration, parents, and students. This council makes the major decisions on all budget matters, hiring of personnel, and curriculum concerns. Decisions are made by consensus with the principal having the final decision in case consensus can't be reached. After a year and a half of operation all decisions made by the councils were made by consensus.

b. Many of the rules, policies, traditions, and customs that govern traditional schools are not found at South Pointe. Indeed, you might say a paradigm shift has occurred. The Dade County School Board has waived the grading rules and policies for the school. Teachers at South Pointe have the authority to substitute the long-held tradition of students' grades with a more authentic portfolio/project approach to assessment. In addition, the teachers' union and the board have waived policies and contract language to allow teachers at South Pointe to start school three weeks earlier in order to conduct parent conferences prior to the opening of school. Both the board and union waived policy and language to allow teachers and students to work a longer day. In addition, teachers' after-school inservice activities are extensive and sometimes require Saturday work. Board policy was waived to allow the teachers and administration total power over the new hires at the school, in addition to allowing the staff to convert administrative personnel units to other types of units in order to improve the instructional delivery system for students.

d. South Pointe Elementary School's mission is: Every child has a gift and a talent. We accept the challenge to find and nurture these qualities in each child. We have met with many of the teachers at South Pointe both individually and in small team settings, and it is evident that the professional autonomy granted to them has been extended to their interactions with students. We have never heard a derogatory remark about a child. If a child is having a problem it's the teacher or teaching team's problem to solve—in other words they are taking the responsibility to help children reach their potential, and not placing the blame on the child's background or environment.

e. Teachers take great pride in the philosophy and beliefs found in the Tesseract Way as indicated by the results of the annual teacher survey.

f. Teachers are treated as true professionals at the school. Each teaching team of two teachers has its own office, equipped with a telephone and computer. In addition, teachers have their own business cards.

Changes in the Distribution of Power between Schools and Their Clients

Research has shown that parental involvement is a prime determinant in children's learning and success in school. Children live in families; families live in communities. The environment of family and community life affects the life of a child in school. Therefore the school is obligated to do all it can to help children and empower the family and community at large to become involved in the educational programs at the school.

This section addresses the principle of empowerment and relates this principle to the parental/community activities practiced in EAI schools.

1. The principle of empowerment is based on the notion that people working together tend to empower each other. Power shared is usually power multiplied. Empowerment encourages people to work together for common causes (Giroux 1989; Sergiovanni 1991; Peeler 1991; Goodlad, Soder, and Sirotnik 1990; Fullan 1991; Reich 1992; Lewis 1989; Deming 1990).

a. The teachers hold four parent conferences a year, with the first conference held prior to the opening of school and devoted to developing goals for the child. During this conference the parent, teacher, and child jointly set the year's social and academic goals. Subsequent conferences devote considerable time to discussing the progress the student has made towards accomplishing these goals and then setting new goals. With the exception of special education students, parents in most public schools are rarely given the opportunity of assisting in the development of educational goals for their children.

b. Even though the school has a high number of minority and poor students, well over 90 percent of the parents attend these conferences and large numbers of parents attend regularly scheduled parent workshops on areas such as discipline, health related topics, and tips for helping students work at home. In addition, a parent satisfaction survey was conducted at South Pointe last year and the parents overwhelmingly rated the school outstanding and were especially pleased that they had a say in their child's education.

Relationship with the Baltimore Public Schools and EAI

The above remarks pertain primarily to EAI's first public/private venture at South Pointe Elementary School in Miami. In September 1992, Educational Alternatives, Inc. signed a five-year contract with the Baltimore Public Schools which called for nine schools to be operated under this public/private arrangement. As in the Dade County, Florida, contract, EAI will receive the same amount of money per child ($5300) that other schools in the district are receiving. The professional staff was trained to follow the same educational principles as outlined for the South Pointe staff. In addition, several board and union policies were waived in order to sign the agreement with EAI.

EAI has also been joined by Johnson Controls World Services, Inc., and KPMG Peat Marwick in their Baltimore venture. Johnson Controls designs and implements programs to provide high-quality, noninstructional services to the schools, and Peat Marwick reengineers the business practices. EAI is responsible for fulfilling the educational mission of dramatically improving learner results and, as such, is in charge of overall project management.

Officials from EAI see the relationship with the two companies as a step forward in operating schools. For instance, Johnson Controls cross-trains custodians so they can perform many maintenance functions (plumbing, electric, painting, etc.) that in traditional school districts call for someone from the central office to come and fix a leak or make some other minor repair.

CONCLUSION

We can state unequivocally that the teaching/learning process as practiced at South Pointe is different from any public school I have seen or supervised. They appear to be practicing the best principles of learning that are available today, implementing sound governance techniques to include extensive shared decision-making mechanisms, and empowering parents to be a part of their children's education.

However, the jury is still out on whether this unique arrangement of a private for-profit company running public schools will be successful. Considering the breadth of changes being implemented at these schools it will probably take several years to evaluate the effects EAI's programs have on student achievement, and the related governance, maintenance, fiscal, and parent empowerment areas.

REFERENCES

Barker, J. (1992) *Future Edge.* New York: William Morrow and Company, Inc.

Bennis, W., and B. Nanus. (1985) *Leaders: The Strategies for Taking Charge.* New York: Harper and Row.

Bonstingl, John J. (1992) "The Quality Revolution in Education," *Educational Leadership,* November, Vol. 50, pp. 4–9.

Boyer, E. (1991) *High School.* New York: Harper and Row.

Brandt, R. (1990) "Conversation with Lauren Resnick," *Educational Leadership,* December, January, Vol. 46, pp. 12–16.

Covey, S. (1989) *The Seven Habits of Highly Effective People.* New York: Simon & Schuster.

Deming, W. E. (1990) *The Revolution in American Industry.* PBS Video Tape.

Elmore, R. (1990) *Restructuring Schools—The Next Generation of Educational Reform.* San Francisco: Jossey-Bass Publishers.

Fullan, M. (1991) *The New Meaning of Educational Change.* New York: Teachers College Press.

Gardner, H. (1983) *Frames of Mind.* New York: Basic Books, Inc.

Giroux, H., and R. Simon. (1989) *Popular Culture, Schooling and Everyday Life*. Westport, Conn.: Bergin & Garvey.

Glasser, W. (1986) *Control Theory in the Classroom*. New York: Harper and Row.

————. (1990) *Quality Schools—Managing Students without Coercion*. New York: Harper and Row.

Goodlad, J. (1984) *A Place Called Schools*. New York: McGraw-Hill.

Goodlad, J., R. Soder, and K. Sirotnik. (1990) *The Moral Dimensions of Teaching*. San Francisco: Jossey-Bass Publishers.

Joyce, B. (1990) *Changing School Culture through Staff Development*. Alexandria, Va.: Association for Supervision and Curriculum Development.

Hilliard, Asa. (1991) "Do We Have the Will to Educate All Children?" *Educational Leadership*. Vol. 49, September.

Kagan, S. (1992) *Cooperative Learning*. San Juan Capistrano: Resources for Teachers, Inc.

Langford, D. (1991) *Quest for Quality*. Arlington, Va.: AASA Audio Workshop.

Lewis A. (1989) *Restructuring America's Schools*. Arlington, Va.: American Association of School Administrators.

Oakes, J. (1985) *Keeping Track—How Schools Structure Inequity*. New Haven: Yale University Press.

Peeler, T. (1991) "Principals: Learning to Share," *Thrust for Educational Leadership*, Vol. 20, No. 6.

————. (1992) *South Pointe Elementary School Assessment Project*. Tallahassee: Florida Department of Education.

Peters, T. (1992) *Liberation Management*. New York: Alfred A. Knopf.

Reich, R. (1992) *The Work of Nations*. New York: Vintage Press.

Resnick, L. (1985) *Education and Learning to Think*. A Special Report Prepared for the Commission on Behavioral and Social Sciences and Education, National Research Council.

————. (1987) "Learning in School and Out," *Educational Research*, 16(9), pp. 13–40.

Restructuring to Promote Learning in America's Schools. (1990) Elmhurst, Ill.: North Central Regional Educational Laboratory.

Schlechty, P. C. (1990) *Schools for the 21st Century*. San Francisco: Jossey-Bass.

Sergiovanni, T. (1991) *The Principalship: A Relective Practice Perspective. Needham Heights*, Mass.: Allyn and Bacon.

Senge, P. (1990) *The Fifth Discipline*. New York: Doubleday.

Sizer, T. R. (1984) *Horace's Compromise*. Boston: Houghton Mifflin.

————. (1992) *Horace's School*. New York: Houghton Mifflin.

Slavin, R. (1983) *Cooperative Learning*. New York: Longman Press.

Sleeter, C. (1991) *Empowerment Through Multicultural Education*. Binghamton: State University of New York Press.

Towards the Thinking Curriculum: Current Cognitive Research. Alexandria: The 1989 ASCD Yearbook.

Walton, M. (1986) *The Deming Management Method*. New York: Putnam Publishing Company.

————. (1991) *Deming Management at Work*. New York: Putnam Publishing Company.

Wiggins, G. (1992) "Creating Tests Worth Taking." *Educational Leadership*, May, Vol. 4.

————. (1993) *Assessing School Performance*. San Francisco: Jossey-Bass.

14

Making Choice an Option for Parents: East Harlem, New York

William E. Ubinas

The issue of choice has permeated the educational reform debate since the early 1980s when the concept of vouchers was introduced.[1] One can conceptualize the various movements in terms of waves. In 1983, with the publication of *A Nation at Risk*, it was argued that the public schools were not meeting the needs of the American agenda, particularly in regard to the business sector. The first wave of school reform basically prescribed much of the same: four years of English, mathematics, foreign languages, and standardized testing. Mostly driven by state reform, the existing structure of American schools simply expanded. The actual conditions of teaching and learning remained unchanged. *A Nation Prepared* looked at the need to change the teaching profession by establishing career ladders, raising teachers' salaries, and developing the profession. The decade of prescriptive reports argued that funds spent on education did not obtain the expected outcomes.[2]

Other reports emanating from the 1980s included School-Based Management Programs; The Coalitions of Essential Schools Program, spearheaded by Ted Sizer; The Family Collaborative Model, developed by James Comer; Slavin's research on Cooperative Learning Techniques, and the Accelerated Program developed by Henry Levin at Stamford. All are examples of the second wave of reform.[3]

A key aspect of American education is the idea of local control of schools. From the early years of school organization in Massachusetts, schooling was relegated to local citizens. In the mid-1850s, in his state board reports, Horace Mann eloquently articulated the concept of the historical nature of localism in American education. The first superintendent, William Maxwell, was nothing but a bureaucratic response to the burgeoning problem of controlling the schools.[4]

The historical and dialectical underpinning of the tension between decentralization and centralization continues in the contemporary debate of reform. School choice is really another example of this same tension played out one more time in one of the nation's oldest democratic institutions, the public school.

This paradigm of school reform is frequently referred to as the second wave and led to the call for the restructuring of public schools. Looking at the individual school, classroom, and teacher/student relationship, as well as the development of an interdisciplinary curriculum, supported by alternative assessment strategies and a reshaping of the teaching profession, led to a renewal of the decade-long debate on school change.

Choice has become the third wave of school reform, furthering the debate on who will decide the fate of public schools. However, this time the focus is on the consumer and the school's ability to compete in a free market economy. This chapter will analyze the current debate on choice as it affects one urban school district. A case study on successful programs and business partnerships will be presented as an alternative for families caught in the cycle of dependency, despondency, and poverty. The question of schools as part of the marketplace and the role of parents as education consumers trying to make rational decisions about the kinds of schools they want for their children are the ethos of choice.

A current review of the literature on choice can be categorized into three areas, according to the latest Carnegie Report.[5] Statewide choice programs attempt to look at the inequities of funding related to the tax base. After the pioneering efforts in Minnesota, approximately eighteen states have developed a variety of choice options. However, the debate continues to focus more on funding and the inability of districts to compete based on their economic development and the effects of educational parity.

On the other hand, private schools have been moving toward the idea of choice for a long time. The proponents favoring a voucher system, which would enable students and their families to choose a private, public, or sectarian school, have been gaining acceptance in the last few years.

This chapter will focus on the third type of choice-reform: district-wide programs within the public school sector. Whether one looks at the controlled choice plan of Cambridge, Massachusetts, the suburban Montclair, New Jersey model, or New York City's District 4 model, the issues of educational achievement, desegregation, transportation, parental involvement, funding, and the role of unions must be dealt with by every superintendent and school board. The Carnegie Report cautioned, "We must not allow the debate about choice to divert us from the urgent problems that profoundly affect the lives of children and diminish the effectiveness of school."[6]

Although choice has become a centerpiece for school reform, the issues of families, coordination of services, alignment of the curriculum, recruitment, maintaining staff and adequate funding must be taken care of before true choice can be achieved.

The National Center for Restructuring Education Schools and Teaching defines restructuring as an effort "to create schools that are more centered on learners' needs for active experiential, cooperative, and culturally-connected learning opportunities supporting individual talents and learning styles."[7]

If connected to the reshaping and rethinking of the American-urban classroom, one develops a comprehensive, family collaborative, with support for lifelong learning and participation—one can then start to think about choice for the urban populace. A more concrete definition of the choice initiative, as it relates to both parents, teachers, and the community, can be found in a statement published by The Center for Educational Innovation of the Manhattan Institute: "Affording school professionals the freedom to design innovative and distinctive school programs; and giving parents the right to choose, in pursuit of those innovations, the public school that their child will attend."[8]

NEW YORK CITY

A recent position paper on choice by the New York State Association of Superintendents described the impediments to choice for parents implementation as defining regulations, bureaucracy, funding, and unions.[9]

This issue was articulated by Chubb and Moe in *Politics, Markets, and America's Schools*. In economic terms, market-driven forces foster competition among schools. This healthy competition should shake out poor performing schools, leaving those who can truly compete on their merits to survive. Schools would be legally autonomous; free to govern themselves as they want, specify their own organizations, select their own student bodies, and make their own personnel decisions.

However, the analysis is perhaps flawed when looking at the urban schools that are often located in cities beset by drug-infected neighborhoods, inadequate housing, and what John Kenneth Galbraith defines as the "political economy of contentment where the fortunate find themselves paying, through their taxes, the public cost of the functional underclass."[10]

A recent book written by Samuel G. Freedman, *Small Victories*, begins by describing the setting in a Lower East Side School. "The path that led me to an overcrowded, underfunded, dilapidated public high school in a notorious immigrant slum in New York City's Lower East Side began in a setting seemingly remote from any such social or educational ills."[11]

Most graduates of Community District One schools attend Seward Park High School which is part of the High School Division and controlled by New York City's Central Board of Education.

To understand New York City's educational policies and administrative structure is an arduous task. Twenty-two years have passed since the first decentralization law was enacted by the New York State Legislature.[12] The 1969 decentralization law divided the city into thirty-two districts, each under the auspices of a nine-member, locally elected school board. The responsibility of each board included the management and control of the elementary and intermediate schools within its jurisdiction. High schools and special education programs remained under the jurisdiction of the city's central board of education and the Office of the Chancellor. Aspects of collective bargaining, purchasing, and certification remained with Central Headquarters. A recent report entitled "Downsizing 110 Livingston Street" summarized the institution:

> The New York City Board of Education is a unique institution from nearly any perspective. It is huge, the largest school system in the nation by far with some 950,000 students and 1,000 schools. It reputedly operates the nation's sixty largest feeding operations, a security force larger than the police forces of all but five American cities, and a budget, at last count, that was larger than 36 states.[13]

It was never clear whether the New York City decentralization experiment fell under the administrative or political paradigm of decentralization. On the one hand, administrative functions were delegated to the district offices, and members of the community were elected to local boards. However, the policy-making focus of the boards in areas of personnel, budgets, and curriculum has gradually centralized. The latest debate came up in the recent mandate of the chancellor and the central board in the "Children of the Rainbow Curriculum" for first graders which advocated the teaching of alternative life-styles and suggested gay literature in the curriculum. This policy, credited to Joe Fernandez, was one of the major factors in his dismissal, and forced New York City's Board of Education, the nation's largest educational bureaucracy, to search for a new chancellor, its sixth in the last eleven years.

The overlapping and administrative duplication and monitoring has created a bureaucratic structure unparalleled in the annals of American educational history. With more than 4 thousand administrators, not including district personnel, and severe financial cutbacks in the last three years, a number of alternatives have been put forward to change the current structure: from the total elimination of the central board to the creation of borough boards (there are five boroughs in New York City) to making each of the thirty-two districts Local Education Agencies (LEA's) within the state. The administration and political lines that are currently debated do not address the fundamental issues that pertain to the local schools or to the parents. Choice in New York City began with the High School Division over twenty years ago. Although these so-called option schools, according to Moore, created a new form of segregation based on a combination of race, income, and previous success in school, most students (84 percent) got their first choice. However, few students from minority districts attend the specialized high schools. The application process is extremely cumbersome, with more than three hundred choices, and few parents or students actually make an informed choice.[14]

The overall dissatisfaction of New York City Schools was summarized by Domanico and Genn in their paper published by the Manhattan Institute:

54% of New York City School children (compared to 73% of students nationwide) graduate from high school—NYC students total SAT scores average about one hundred points less than either state or the national average. In 1991, just slightly over half of NYC Public School students read at or above grade level. 60% of all students now score at or above grade level in mathematics. In short, the schools are not providing the education parents want for their children.[15]

In light of the Board of Education's dismal statistics and directionless bureaucracy, Joe Fernandez's School Based Management/Shared Decision Making (SBM/SDM), coupled with a well-organized choice process might, in fact, hold the possibility for the creation of a successful reform effort.[16]

The variety of reform efforts in the city stemming from the effective school literature to the new SBM/SDM plans continues to be snagged by a bureaucratic structure overseeing 1,000 buildings and the necessity of dealing with thirty-five unions and a budget estimated around $7 billion.

Another problem stemmed from the SBM/SDM process which bypassed the district office creating an unfavorable response by most superintendents. The process is incredibly complex, as well as cumbersome, with a wide variety of school teams varying from Chapter I school-wide programs to straight SBM/SDM teams, all defined and spelled out in different administrative circulars. Parents, the clients of the educational system and the consumers of the process, have little say in this central type of reform.

The Community

The Lower East Side offers a distinct and unique forum for the discussion of choice and the current debate on school reform. The community, one of the premier immigration gateways, offers a rich and diverse population including European Jews, Ukrainians, Polish, Puerto Rican, Whites, African-Americans, and Asians who create an environment which is not often found in a close geographically knit community.

The school district is composed of eighteen school buildings with a variety of educational options: two K–8 schools, fourteen K–6 elementary schools, four junior high schools that comprise grades 7–9, one high school grades 7–12, and three family and childhood centers. In all, the district's 10,000 students are divided ethnically as follows: 8.1 percent Asian, 73.1 percent Hispanic, 15.5 percent African-American, and 3.3 percent other. The total minority population accounts for almost 96 percent of the total student body. Eighty-four percent of all students attending District One schools are members of low-income families as compared to New York City, in general,with 54 percent of students from low-income families. All schools in the district are eligible for Chapter I. The median family income on the Lower East Side is $10,727 a year as compared with $16,818 for the rest of New York.

Within the neighborhood there are eleven temporary housing facilities for the homeless. Drug abuse is endemic and there has been a dramatic increase in the number of AIDS cases.

The district currently ranks twenty-sixth in reading achievement and twenty-fourth in mathematics out of the City's thirty-two community school districts. However, in grade two, students rank thirty-two out of thirty-two in both reading and math. The unpreparedness of children entering the early childhood grades is one of the main problems faced by urban schools.

In 1990, after many years of educational neglect and the advent of a new administration, District One went through a major restructuring effort. The attendance rate in junior high schools was close to 80 percent and only a few elementary schools reached 90 percent. On any given day, one thousand students were not in attendance (and the number of junior high school students not returning to class after lunch was noteworthy).

One of the first agenda items of the new administration was the development of an SBM/SDM choice plan that would empower teachers and parents in order to revitalize the ailing and demoralized school district. The "Blueprint for Progress," a three-year strategic plan with a vision of collaboration among schools, families, local agencies, and strong business partnerships was the first position paper of the new superintendent, William E. Ubinas.

The debate in the choice process within the public schools is based on the notion that the schools will be challenged to innovate and reshape the educational services for the consumers.

Certain variables, however, must be taken into account if there is to be meaningful choice in the urban school districts. The first is space. In a district beset with the problem of overcrowding, choice becomes a secondary process. District One has a 65 percent utilization rate.

Second, is compactness. The district's boundaries range from Third Avenue on the west, to the FDR Drive on the east; from Fourteenth Street on the north to the Brooklyn Bridge on the south. This area comprises approximately two miles from the two most distant points. Thus, the proximity of all the schools to each other makes choice for the parents a real and viable option.

Third, is desegregation. However, in order to understand this, one must look particularly at housing patterns. Although the district is 96 percent minority, new families are moving into the northeast side of the district. In addition, Joe Fernandez's choice plan,[17] which allows parents to choose schools across district lines (if seats are available), thus doing away with the "sacred district boundary lines" of the past, opens up many unthought-of possibilities. Although this artificial choice plan promotes movement, little movement based on choice is really expected. Most good schools will already have their full complement of students, as middle class and informed parents will, no doubt, have already exercised their rights of choice. Many of the ill-informed, disenfranchised, and minority parents will be left with few alternatives and probably no choice.

The fourth is educational options. Real choice plans provide parents with many quality educational alternatives. The creation of new, innovative schools where teachers, parents, and administrators work collaboratively in developing meaningful programs and curricula provide choice.

The fifth, and most important, is the access to information. When parents, as educational consumers, do not really understand choices, that is, the philosophic or curricular differences in the various schools being sponsored by the district, they will, in most cases, simply choose the school nearest their home.

Choice for the parents of District One became a reality, after the first year of the new administration. Realistically, many choices are fashioned by economic reality, and the range of possible choice is driven by budgetary considerations. One of the main driving forces that support the creation of option schools is the Federal Magnet Grant which allows districts to develop "themes" in order to desegregate its schools. Many recent success stories involving choice programs can be directly attributed to this very special kind of desegregation grant.

District One received a Federal Magnet Grant for the years 1991 to 1993. Because of the grant, the district was able to establish eight educational option sites. In the first evaluation of the program's progress, indicators showed increases in student academic achievement, attendance, and enrollment of non-minority students. Overall, the district's white population increased by 2 percent. More significant, however, was an increase of 233 new students, above and beyond the projected 1992–1993 figures, thus ending a ten-year downward trend.

One of the most important components in the evolution of the choice process was the development of a business partnership with IBM. Working with this corporate sponsor, the district developed a strategic plan, two technology-driven schools, an effective conceptualization of SBM/SDM teams, and a Principal Leadership Institute.

Although IBM has recently experienced some economic setbacks, its newly formed educational subdivision, EduQuest, is an example of decentralization taking place in industry and which will probably become the norm in the years to come.

The development of effective school leaders and strong SBM teams is key to the establishment of any successful choice project. Only when committed administrators, teachers, and parents work together can a choice program be successful. What really drives choice in a minority community is the realization that parents have a say in their children's education.

District One has been attempting to coordinate all of the different groups necessary to create a successful program of choice. An aggressive campaign to promote smaller schools was begun. Parental programs, which ranged from basic literacy to participation on the SBM teams, were established. A joint venture with the New York City's Division of High Schools was begun, in which the district and the division established a joint-governance high school.[18]

The newly formed East Side Community High School is the third of it kind in New York City and will be run under joint governance with the High School Division. In its first year, it attracted eighty students. The school's curriculum focuses on New York's living environments. The concept, based on the successful program developed by Debbie Myers at the Central Park East High School, created smaller units and a work-internship program for the students.

The East Side Community High School's curriculum is integrated within the area of the humanities. There is a strong staff development component. Teachers are involved in curriculum planning, and children's progress is measured through authentic assessment. Students work in heterogeneous groups and, based on Ted Sizer's Coalition of Essential School's Model, the teacher's role becomes a mentor/coach and the student's role changes from a receiver of information to a learner/apprentice.

At a public hearing in District One on Schools of Choice, a parent commented about how she saw the East Side Community High School:

> What attracted me was the traditional setting, small class size, and children meeting with their advisors once a week. I liked the one to one relationships I saw between the students and teachers and the open discussions they had. I particularly like the Service Learning Program which enables the students to obtain real work experience twice a week.[19]

The cumbersome governance aspects of the school involved countless meetings with the United Federation of Teachers, the Council of Supervisors and Administrators, central and local school boards, the Division of High Schools, and a steering committee that disbanded as soon as the Memorandum of Agreement was signed. Not only are schools regulated by local, state, and federal mandates but also the power-play among the various constituencies for a school of 500 students portrays the cumbersome political and bureaucratic inexperience which make it difficult for choice to take place in urban districts.

A second restructuring effort involved The Chancellor's Model School Project. The project's basic thrust was to research and develop models which demonstrate that all students can achieve academic excellence when given the appropriate structure, support, and time.[20] The school was one of the District's first restructuring efforts at the elementary level. The school was housed in Public School 19, which was recently redesigned as a K–8 school. During its first year, the school enrolled sixty-one students; by the second year, the registration had risen to 121.

Historically, sixth grade graduating students of P.S. 19 did not attend District One junior high schools. Parents opted to send their children to private or parochial schools, with others registering in District Two schools. The Chancellor's Model School completely reversed this trend.

A collaboration of IBM, Cooper Union, and Columbia University was forged by Gil Lopez, the school's director. No selection criteria was utilized for admission to the Chancellor's Model School. Admission was open to every sixth grade student at P.S. 19. Thus, a truly representative student body, cutting across all ethnic and socioeconomic lines, became the first class of the Model School.

One of the first goals articulated for the school was for the students to achieve a level of excellence that exceeded the average of the district on standardized mathematics and reading tests. In the first year of operation, 97 percent of the students scored above the fiftieth percentile in mathematics and the seventy-fourth percentile in reading, thus accomplishing its goal of exceeding the district's average. Attendance figures for the Model School's students were exceptionally high. City-wide, junior high school attendance rates were about 89 percent; the Model School's attendance average was 96 percent. Clearly, something very special was happening at this school.

A project-oriented curriculum was infused into the core subjects in the humanities, mathematics, and science. A state-of-the-art computer laboratory was utilized to support writing, mathematics, geography, and art. A vast array of technical equipment was used in the study of science. Cable television and a wide range of video tapes that were linked to specific topics and projects were used to support the curricular innovations of the school.

It is expected that as a result of the successes demonstrated by the Chancellor's Model School that a District Research and Development Center will be created. This center will sponsor the development of projects and learning technologies, as well as provide professional development and training.

Because of its model school status, the Chancellor's Model School has been evaluated very carefully. There is no doubt as to the academic success of its students; however, it is the opinion of the director and the district superintendent that the most important variable in the success of the school was the belief that the students could achieve at a very high level if given the appropriate resources. Working closely with its parents, the Chancellor's Model School provides not only a curriculum of excellence but an alternative in which parents can make real, informed choices for their children.

The last example of choice that will be dealt with is an Early Childhood Center located at Public School 63. Known as the Neighborhood Enrichment School, it is very unlike Mr. Roger's neighborhood—for this neighborhood school is surrounded by the same problems that beset most urban schools.

Utilizing a child-centered curriculum and founded on Piaget's developmental theories, the school selected four highly motivated teachers and a director who would attract parents interested in an alternative to a traditional school.

In a recent *New York Times* article that described District One's schools of choice, one of the Neighborhood Enrichment School's teachers, Ms. Laurie Engel described learning at the school:

> The girls are learning about free exploration. They fill the various geometric shapes with water and determine which holds the most water. It's great. They are learning and they don't even know it yet. The water's green because they wanted to make lime ice cream.[21]

However, within the choice question, this school is a good example of working class White, Hispanic, Black, and Asian parents who were looking for a real alternative. The parents who chose the neighborhood school also had an opportunity to make an informed choice. Thus, provided with a quality alternative, empowered parents can make important, informed choices for the education of their children.

Whether one looks at the East Side Community High School, the Chancellor's Model School, or the Neighborhood Enrichment School, it is clear what can be accomplished when there is a combination of school-based management, business and university partnerships, decentralized decision-making, and parents making informed choices about educational programs.

The arduous and complex debate on educational policy and governance continues to be at the top of the current curricular and reform agenda. Certainly, this third wave of reform will not be the last. Probably only a tidal wave, which would sweep away many of the unnecessary regulations and constraints that characterize the bureaucratic world of education, would be a start.

In New York City and in many areas across the nation, high school dropout rates are approaching 40 to 50 percent. Industry is spending billions of dollars on in-house training of workers—when it can find them. Will empowered parents, making informed choices in their children's education, be the catalyst for change? Will school choice alter the basic structure of American education? No longer can educators hide behind the walls of the little red schoolhouse. If change and reform are not implemented now, then many of the concerns, fears, and predictions articulated in the *Nation at Risk* will certainly become reality. In the end, one must never lose sight of the reason why the education business exists in the first place: the children are our future!

In closing, one might gain some insight into the myriad of problems besetting students today. In a *Network News* article, entitled "I Just Might Transfer," a young student named James Tiew, from P.S. 137 in Manhattan, said,

The Lower East side is certainly not the best neighborhood in the world. It really smells around the playground. There are lots of fights around here. All I ever see are junkies hanging around the park. It will never be clean around here because there are so many litterbugs. There is so much graffiti it looks like a bunch of people threw paint all over the place. I hope it will get better around here or I just might transfer to another school.[22]

In the end, choice by itself will not create the necessary catalyst for change in America's schools. Unlike the market and economic theory, urban and public education continues to be highly regulated and contested in terms of funding. Education, as it is currently structured, is not the great equalizer. It would take a major effort from government to deregulate and coordinate all of the agencies that are currently serving families. It behooves the new administration and the education establishment to move away from the single agency into the comprehensive service conglomerate, one that takes the community, families, and schools and gives meaningful options to America's children.

NOTES

1. Although the concept of vouchers deals with the economic argument and the public/private debate, Mario Fantini's book, *Public Schools of Choice*, New York: Simon and Schuster, 1973, was the first upscale argument on choice.

2. National Commission on Excellence in Education, *A Nation at Risk*, Washington, D.C.: U.S. Government Printing Office, 1983; and Task Force on Teaching as a Profession, *A Nation Prepared: Trades for the 21st Century*, New York: Carnegie Forum on Education and the Economy, 1986.

3. For more information see Ted Sizer, *Horace's Compromise: The Dilemma of the American High School*, Boston: Houghton Mifflin, 1984.

4. See Lawrence A. Cremin, *The Transformation of the School: Progressivism in American Education 1876–1957*, New York: Knopf, 1961; and David Tyach, *The One Best System: A History of American Urban Education*, Cambridge: Harvard University Press, 1974.

5. The Carnegie Foundation for the Advancement of Teaching, *School Choice*, Foreword by Ernest Boyer, 1992.

6. Carnegie Foundation, *School Choice*, xviii.

7. Ann Liebermann, Linda Darling-Hammonds, and David Zucherman, "Early Lessons in Restructuring Schools," *NCRET*, August, 1991, IX.

8. Frank Ambrosie, Tim Clay, and A. Wayne Jones, *Choice in New York State Schools*, unpublished manuscript, Council of School Superintendents, Albany, New York, 1992.

9. E. John Chubb and M. Terry Moe, (1990) *Politics Markets and America's Schools*, Washington D.C.: The Brookings Institution, p. 226.

10. Kenneth John Galbraith, *The Culture of Contentment*, Boston: Houghton Mifflin, 1992 p. 44.

11. G. Samuel Freedman, *Small Victories: The Real World of a Teacher and Her Students and Their High School*, New York: HarperCollins, 1990, Introduction.

12. For analysis of the Decentralization Law, see M. Nancy Lederman, S. Jeanne Franhl, and Judith Baum, "Governing the New York City Schools' Roles and Relationships in the Decentralized System," New York: Public Education Association, February 25, 1987, p. 58.

13. The City Project, *Downsizing 110 Livingston Street: The Budget for the Central Headquarters of the New York City Board of Education*, New York: Arete Corporation, October 1992, p. 3).

14. Temporary State Commission on New York City School Government, *Governing for Results: Decentralization with Accountability*, April 1991, as quoted by Moon 1989, p. 223.

15. J. Raymond Domanico and Colman Genn, "Putting School First: Changing the Board of Ed's Priorities," *The City Journal*, Spring, 1992, p. 47.

16. There are two discussions on the relationship of Choice and SBM: Domanico and Genn, cited above, and Myron Lieberman, *Public School Choice: Current Issues Future Prospects*, Technomic, Pennsylvania, Chapter 6.

17. Chancellor's Regulation A-181 was accepted by the central board, which changed the inter-district transfer policy. In short, parents who wish to transfer their child to another district do not have to get a variance approved from both the sending and receiving superintendent. Parents are only guaranteed their choice upon space availability. Few parents are expected to take advantage of the new choice policy because transportation is not provided as part of the policy.

18. As noted earlier, the Decentralization Law established thirty-two community districts, and the central division of high schools. This new joint governance established collaboration with the district superintendent and the Manhattan superintendent of the high school division for the supervision of the principal.

19. Community School Board One, Public Meeting "Zoning For Schools Of Choice," February 3, 1993.

20. Gil López, *The Chancellor Model School Project*, unpublished manuscript, December 21, 1992.

21. Joseph Berger, "Making School Choice Real Choice," *The New York Times*, September 17, 1993, p. B1.

22. James Tiew, "I Just Might Transfer," *Network News*, College of Architecture and Urban Planning, Urbana-Champaign: University of Michigan, Vol. 3, No. 1, September, 1991, p. 4.

15

Public Choice in Minnesota

Michael C. Rubenstein and Nancy E. Adelman

In 1985, Minnesota began establishing itself as the nation's leader in passing state-level school choice legislation. As in many states, Minnesota statutes already gave school districts the option of negotiating tuition agreements among themselves that would, under certain circumstances, allow limited numbers of students to cross district lines to attend school. However, in 1985, then-Governor Rudy Perpich proposed comprehensive school choice legislation designed to place the initiative to cross district lines in the hands of parents and students rather than with school boards. One provision recommended that students should "be able to select the public school that best serves their individual needs," including schools in non-resident districts. Another provision enabled high school juniors and seniors to take classes at postsecondary institutions for either high school or college credit. In both cases, state foundation aid would follow the student to the school or institution of his or her choice. The state legislature rejected most of the package, passing only the latter provision, subsequently known as the Postsecondary Enrollment Option Program (PSEO).

In 1987, the Minnesota legislature once again took up the issue of school choice, passing two landmark pieces of legislation. Open Enrollment legislation gave parents the option of applying to enroll a student in a non-resident district. Except for the three cities with desegregation court orders (Minneapolis, St. Paul, and Duluth), districts could not bar any students from leaving their district to attend school in another district. Participating districts could reject applications only because of lack of space or, in the cases of the three cities, because of racial balance considerations under existing desegregation court orders.

Ninety-five out of 433 districts volunteered to accept non-resident students under Open Enrollment in 1987–1988, the program's first year of operation; the number grew to 153 districts in the second year. By the third year, the legislature had passed new legislation that phased in mandatory participation over two years. In 1989–1990, all districts with enrollments greater than 1,000 were required to participate in the program; full implementation involving all districts began in 1990–1991.

Under Open Enrollment, parents submit an application for each child whom they wish to enroll in a non-resident district. The non-resident district may reject the application only if the capacity of the particular school, grade, or program to which the student is applying is limited; the district may not reject applications on the basis of a student's prior or current academic achievement, athletic or extra-curricular interest, handicapping condition, proficiency in English, or disciplinary proceedings. The legislation stipulated that school boards could pass resolutions declaring their district closed to all non-resident students, but very few took this step.

The second choice program passed by the legislature in 1987 was the High School Graduation Incentives (HSGI) program (also known as the "second-chance" program). HSGI's major objective was to reduce the high school dropout rate by making alternative educational programs more accessible to potential or actual high school dropouts. To qualify for participation in this choice option, students must meet one or more of these criteria:

- Two or more grades below grade level
- One year behind in graduation credits
- Pregnant or a parent
- Drug or alcohol dependent
- A self-defined high school dropout

Under HSGI, secondary school students meeting one of the above criteria have three options. They may choose to enroll in a regular high school other than the one to which they are assigned by residence. Another option is one of the private, non-sectarian alternative programs, located primarily in the Twin Cities. The third alternative is Area Learning Centers (ALCs), which are regional alternative schools that meet certain criteria established by the state. Specifically, ALCs must operate year-round; allow students to attend full- or part-time; offer day, evening, and weekend classes; emphasize job preparation as well as fulfillment of academic requirements for high school graduation; and provide transition services to further education or employment. State foundation aid follows the student no matter which alternative he or she selects.

STUDY METHODOLOGY

This article summarizes findings from first- and second-year reports of a three-year evaluation of the Minnesota educational choice options.[1] The study originated as a joint venture between the U.S. Department of Education (ED) and the Minnesota Department of Education (MDE); it is currently sponsored solely by ED. Specifically, the studies sought information in four areas: Who used the options programs? How did they find out about the options programs? Why did they decide to attend a non-resident or alternative school? What effects did the options programs have on students and districts?

The first stage of data collection occurred during the 1989–1990 school year, the year in which Open Enrollment became mandatory for districts with enrollments above 1,000. Surveys were mailed to the homes of all 2,663 families and 1,966 secondary school (grades 7–12) students participating in Open Enrollment that year. Area Learning Centers and private alternative schools administered separate surveys to a random sample of students enrolled in these options for at-risk students. In addition, a third survey was mailed to the superintendents of all operating school districts in Minnesota.

Despite several follow-ups to non-respondents, response rates for many of the surveys did not reach optimal levels. Fifty-two percent of participating families and 33 percent of secondary school students returned usable surveys on their experiences with Open Enrollment. Seventy-eight percent of district superintendents returned surveys. At Area Learning Centers and alternative schools, a combined total of 33 percent of students returned the surveys. Forty-four percent of the students in our samples had left the ALC or alternative school by the time the surveys were fielded, reflecting the high student turnover rate reported by most of these institutions. Most non-responding students had either dropped out, transferred back to a traditional school, or graduated. When appropriate, we supplemented our analyses with complementary data collected by the Minnesota House of Representatives' Research Department (1990).

Data collection during the second year (1990–1991) of the study consisted of site visits to ALCs and alternative schools, focus group interviews with ten groups of minority parents in the Twin Cities, and informal telephone interviews with administrators in school districts experiencing relatively large enrollment gains or losses because of Open Enrollment. These research activities were undertaken to expand our understanding of educational choice issues among populations with particularly low survey response rates. Third-year data collection (currently under way) consists of two separate activities. The first compares Open Enrollment's effects on districts experiencing significant enrollment gains or losses with the impact on districts that experienced little or no change in enrollment due to Open Enrollment. The second research effort is a feasibility study on methods of determining Open Enrollment's potential effects on participating students' performance in school.

OPEN ENROLLMENT

The debate over Open Enrollment's potential or actual effect on students, schools, and parents has continued since the legislation was first introduced in 1985. Among the most pressing issues are whether Open Enrollment will encourage systemic educational reform throughout the state, whether all students would truly benefit from the opportunity to choose a school, and whether some districts would experience undue hardships as a result of losing too many students to neighboring districts. Although the relatively low survey response rate for Open Enrollment families renders our findings less than conclusive, the available data shed some light on these issues.

Participation in Open Enrollment

In Greater Minnesota, minority and low-income families were proportionately represented among Open Enrollment participants. In the Twin Cities, however, minority family participation was limited by a variety of factors, including the existence of intradistrict choice and limited access to transportation and information.

On average, the socioeconomic status (SES) of Minnesota's student population is higher than that of the nation in general. In 1990, Minnesota's student population was 90 percent white, with minorities concentrated in the Twin Cities; by contrast, less than 70 percent of the nation's school enrollment was white. The state's high school graduation rate (about 90 percent) is consistently among the highest in the country. The median household income in 1989 exceeded the national average by almost $900. By contrast, the Twin Cities have substantial minority populations. Enrollment in Minneapolis was 50 percent minority (primarily African-American) at the time of the study, and in St. Paul was 42 percent minority (primarily Southeast Asian).

This contrast between the Twin Cities and Greater Minnesota (as the rest of the state is called) prompted some speculation that Open Enrollment would primarily benefit higher-SES families in the suburbs. Critics feared that limited-English-proficient Asian and Hispanic parents would not receive information on Open Enrollment in their primary languages and that information on Open Enrollment would not reach isolated, lower-income families in the inner-city and rural areas of the state.

Survey results found that minority families were proportionately represented among families participating in Open Enrollment (except in St. Paul).[2] Lower-income families were also proportionately represented,[3] but parents of students participating in Open Enrollment have completed more years of formal schooling than have adults statewide. With respect to this latter finding, 86 percent of Minnesota adults in 1989 had graduated from high school (Kominski 1991). In contrast, 96 percent of fathers and 99 percent of mothers with children in the Open Enrollment program had graduated from high school. Similarly, 22 percent of Minnesota adults in 1989 had attended college for four or more years (Kominski 1991), while 36 percent of fathers and 32 percent of mothers with children in the Open Enrollment program had attended college for four or more years.

The exemption given to the Twin Cities by the Open Enrollment legislation meant that both cities could prevent some families from leaving the district if their departure would upset racial balance in the schools. In fact, only Minneapolis elected to take advantage of this provision to restrict movement into or out of the district depending on the race of each particular family; St. Paul allowed families to leave or enter the district regardless of their race. The implications of these two policy decisions were tremendous. In Minneapolis, where minority students make up a majority of the enrollment, white families were restricted from using the state's Open Enrollment option since their departure would, by definition, upset the racial balance. Minority students were theoretically eligible to leave. However, during 1989–1990, only 30 minority students from Minneapolis actually enrolled in suburban districts. Contrast this with St. Paul, where 58 percent of the student population was white. In 1989–1990, with no restrictions on use of the choice option, 308 students left the St. Paul school district to attend public schools elsewhere; 85 percent of these students were white. Although district officials and the local media downplayed these facts, the obvious conclusion is that Open Enrollment facilitated "white flight" from St. Paul's public schools.

The reasons for the disproportionately low number of minority families in St. Paul and Minneapolis who used the Open Enrollment option to transfer to suburban districts provide an interesting case study of the dynamics of public school choice. Two contextual factors may have played a major role in keeping minority participation in the cities to a minimum. First, public school choice has existed *within* St. Paul and Minneapolis since the 1970s. In 1991–1992, about half of St. Paul's elementary school student population attended one of twenty-two citywide magnet programs; seventeen additional specialty programs served students in grades 6–12. In Minneapolis, parents could choose from among twelve elementary-level and fourteen secondary-level magnet programs. Minority families in the cities may have been sufficiently satisfied with the quality and diversity of these schools and thus perceived no need to send their children across district lines. Race may also have been a factor. Minority families may have been uncomfortable sending their children to suburban schools where they might be the only minority student in their class, if not the school. A third factor, according to focus group interviews with minority parents in the Twin Cities, is transportation. Most parents we spoke with said they could not consider sending their students too far from home because of the time and trouble involved with getting them there. The fourth factor that may have limited minority participation in Open Enrollment was lack of familiarity with the Open Enrollment option. This issue is addressed in the following section.

Familiarity with the Open Enrollment Option

The most common methods for distributing information about Open Enrollment—school or district-based print media—are not effective strategies for reaching low-income and minority families.

To make appropriate educational decisions for their children, parents must have access to detailed and accurate information about the options available to them. Neither the state nor most school districts developed comprehensive plans for disseminating information about the options programs or individual schools within their boundaries. The original Open Enrollment statute stated that school districts "are responsible for informing students" about options programs. The state's contribution to this effort consisted of a sample flier (including a Spanish language version) that districts could use as a model in preparing materials to disseminate to families. Ninety-five percent of districts indicated that they made information on the options program available to all resident parents and students. However, the state did not monitor compliance with this requirement, so districts responded in many forms, some far less effective than others. Only 56 percent sent printed information to every household in the district. In many cases, this meant including an article on the options in a generally distributed district or school newsletter. Only 12 percent of districts actually mailed a separate flier or pamphlet to all households.

Survey data indicated, and the focus group interviews with minority parents confirmed, that these dissemination strategies failed to inform hard-to-reach parents. Whereas most districts relied on school-based print media to relay information about options programs, minority families tended to rely on networks of friends and neighbors for information about schools. Only 9 percent of participating minority parents said that their most important sources of information about Open Enrollment were principals, teachers, counselors, or school newsletters, compared with 31 percent of white parents. Similarly, 22 percent of participating minority parents said that their most important sources of information on Open Enrollment were relatives, friends, neighbors, and employers, compared with 10 percent of white parents. During a series of focus group interviews with parents from every major minority group in the Twin Cities, most (particularly recent immigrants) indicated that they obtained most of their information about the school system from their friends and neighbors. For instance, Hispanic parents were most familiar with St. Paul's only Spanish-immersion magnet school; they were not familiar with other district magnet schools or with the statewide Open Enrollment option. In a 1992 study of St.

Paul's magnet program, the League of Women Voters of St. Paul (1992) also found that "networking with others appears to provide a parent's first insight into the . . . magnet schools" (p. 17).

This lack of congruence between most districts' strategies for disseminating information to parents and minority parents' most common sources of information on schools probably contributed to the low level of minority participation in the options programs in St. Paul and Minneapolis. Many minority parents simply were not familiar with the option because they did not come into contact with the most popular methods of disseminating information about it. The League of Women Voters of St. Paul study (1992) also found that many families did not understand the student assignment system. This was especially surprising because St. Paul mails every parent a Magnet and Specialty Choice brochure with descriptions of every magnet and specialty school in the district and an explanation of the district's student assignment policy. These findings point to the need for a more aggressive community outreach program to inform all parents about their choice options.

Reasons for Using Open Enrollment

Parents select non-resident schools primarily because of their strong academic reputations, but they also give serious consideration to a school's proximity to the family's home.

While some supporters of Open Enrollment praise it because it gives parents the opportunity to find the most appropriate educational program for their children, critics contend that it allows parents to make decisions about their children's education for what the critics believe to be "wrong" (noneducational) reasons. For instance, critics have speculated that parents of good athletes will send their children to schools with strong or winning athletic programs rather than schools with strong academic programs. If parents' decisions about schooling were driven by such considerations, schools would have a stronger incentive to improve their extracurricular program than their educational program.

Our surveys found that while transfers for athletic and other "wrong" reasons do occur, they do not predominate. As a whole, parents reported that the most important factor in their decision to send their children across district lines was the academic reputation of the non-resident school. The second most important reason was the school's proximity to their home—a factor of some significance in a rural state like Minnesota, where a farm may be twenty miles from the resident school, but only two miles from a school in an adjoining district. Roughly the same pattern holds true for minority families, although they are more likely than white families to consider the availability of childcare and extracurricular activities in or near the school.

Effects of the Open Enrollment Program

Effects on districts. Open Enrollment's low participation rate has minimized its effect on district-level decision making. In theory, interdistrict choice programs might be expected to drive school improvement efforts. According to Chubb and Moe (1990), competition for students would force schools to upgrade their entire educational program. Our data fail to confirm this effect— so far. The district surveys found very little evidence that Open Enrollment was affecting district-level decision making, planning, or programs. The reason for this seems quite straightforward. The number of students using Open Enrollment at the early stage studied was not sufficient to attract the attention of most district administrators. Fewer than 1 percent of Minnesota students used Open Enrollment in 1989–1990; about 75 percent of the districts gained or lost fewer than ten students. Thus, it is not surprising that at least 75 percent of district administrators said that enrollment shifts resulting from Open Enrollment had not had *any* impact on such things as student/teacher ratios, the availability of student support services, or classroom instruction.[4]

However, among the handful of districts that lost relatively large numbers of students, the effects were sometimes devastating. A few small districts were forced to close a school or lost hundreds of thousands of dollars in operating expenses. On the other hand, a small number of districts used Open Enrollment as a pretext for becoming more entrepreneurial. These districts—generally located in remote parts of the state—have opened magnet schools in an effort to become a regional attraction.

Open Enrollment has been largely responsible for encouraging a number of school districts to consolidate. Like many midwestern states, Minnesota has a large number of very small rural districts. A report on the state's high schools by the Office of the Legislative Auditor (1988) found the quality of education in many small districts to be inferior and recommended that districts should reorganize (consolidate) so that no high school in the state would serve fewer than 100 students. In 1989–1990, 31 percent of district administrators accurately predicted that Open Enrollment would result in greater cooperation among districts. Since then, district consolidations have reduced the number of operating school districts from 432 to just under 400.

Effects on students. Parents and secondary students were uniformly pleased with their choices. Ninety-five percent of secondary school students responding to our survey were satisfied or very satisfied with their new schools. Slightly more than half (52 percent) said that they were doing better in their new school than they had in their old school.[5] Among parents, at least 50 percent said that their child had shown improvement in the following areas: academic performance, motivation, self-confidence, and sense of responsibility. Parents also said that they were more directly involved in their children's education but were less involved in the PTA and other school or district organizations.

HIGH SCHOOL GRADUATION INCENTIVES OPTION

Available survey and site visit data indicate that Minnesota's "second-chance" choice programs for eligible youth have proved fairly successful in keeping disaffected students in school and bringing back students who had already dropped out. However, while students in the urban alternative schools and the Area Learning Centers (ALCs) indicate high levels of satisfaction with these programs, the quality of the education they receive remains an unexplored issue.

Student Characteristics

Students attending urban alternative schools are more likely to be minorities than students attending ALCs. However, both groups of students have similar needs that are being met by these second-chance programs.

Urban alternative schools, because of their inner-city locations, tend to serve higher proportions of minority students than do the ALCs, which were initially located in suburban and rural areas.[6] Fifty-seven percent of urban alternative school students were minority, compared with only 8 percent of ALC students. These figures generally reflect the overall composition of student populations in the Twin Cities and Greater Minnesota. About 40 percent of students (or their families) in both types of schools had received some form of public assistance in the last five years, and at least 50 percent had dropped out of school one or more times.

During site visits to five urban alternative schools and three ALCs, we formed an impression that many, if not most, of the students at these institutions were academically capable students who, due to negative peer influences, family circumstances, teacher indifference, or inflexible school policies, fell behind. Although many of these students had struggled academically, their poor records were more likely to be caused by their social problems (e.g., chronic absence, substance abuse, or an "attitude") than by poor academic skills. In short, they were the high schools' "square pegs" who, during focus group discussions, were generally articulate and insightful.

Sources of Information

Data from both the surveys and the focus groups revealed that virtually all of the students first heard about the alternative programs from friends or relatives, not from counselors, teachers, or principals. However, the survey data showed that students who consulted counselors generally found them to be supportive.

Sixty-three percent of ALC students discussed their decisions with their counselors, and more than three-fourths of them found their counselors to be supportive. Only 33 percent of alternative school students conferred with counselors, and almost three-fourths of them found the counselors to be supportive.

Reasons for Attending Alternative Programs

According to students, ALCs and alternative schools offer a more person-alized atmosphere that gives the learner more responsibility and develops higher self-esteem than the comprehensive high schools that they had previously attended.

Seventy-seven percent of ALC students and 83 percent of alternative school students reported that they turned to the second-chance programs to help them stay in school. Slightly more than half from both groups added that they did not like their previous high schools. During focus group interviews, students expanded on their reasons for disliking their former schools. The most frequent complaints were that classes were too big and teachers did not have enough time to give them the help they needed. Typical comments from students were: "You can't talk to teachers in public schools"; "I can't get along in public schools because of the bigger classes"; "Teachers don't have time to help you"; "Teachers don't want to teach, and they certainly don't want to answer students' questions." Minority (particularly Native American) students also complained of discrimination by teachers and students in public schools (e.g., in one school, only minority students were assigned to special classes on alcoholism). Other students objected to the social cliques and unreasonable (in their view) rules and regulations at the comprehensive high schools.

Benefits and Pitfalls of Second-Chance Programs

The clearest advantage of the second-chance programs is that they keep students who would otherwise have dropped out of school on track for their high school diploma. However, many of these programs carry a stigma because they are perceived by some as not offering as challenging an academic program as the high schools.

Although the survey data are sketchy, they seem to show that these programs steer students away from dropping out and toward continuing their education at the postsecondary level. Eighty-four percent of ALC students and 69 percent of alternative school students said that they were more confident that they would finish high school than they had been before they enrolled in the programs. The reasons for this varied by program type: ALC students were most grateful for the opportunity to proceed at their own pace, while alternative school students saw the smaller class sizes as the greatest benefit. This gave them an opportunity to forge friendships with adults at the school who had the time, and made the effort, to care about them. Students also valued being treated more like adults than they had been at their previous high schools.

Despite this apparent level of success, the second-chance programs still face unresolved challenges. Their own records indicate that approximately 30 percent of their students drop out of the programs without re-enrolling in another educational institution. While 61 percent of ALC students and 78 percent of urban alternative students report that they attend school more regularly, program administrators admit that attendance rates remain unacceptably low. Finally, the instructional programs offered at these institutions are often marked by low expectations for student achievement.

One school that we visited seemed more concerned with enhancing students' appreciation of their cultural heritage than in developing their academic skills. Another graded all classes on a pass/fail basis. On students' transcripts (which came from a local high school under an agreement with the Minneapolis school district), a "Pass" grade was converted to a "C," reflecting the stigma associated with attending an alternative program. Students who expressed a desire to attend competitive four-year postsecondary institutions did not seem to understand that most of these institutions would not accept them with a "C" average. This same school offered math only up to, but not beyond, Algebra I, typically a ninth-grade course. Finally, most of the schools offered students the chance to progress at their own pace, which often meant computer- or worksheet-based units that students could complete individually. These units were largely focused on basic skills and did not expose students to interesting literature, science laboratory experiments, or other staples of the standard high school curriculum.

OVERALL ASSESSMENT OF CHOICE IN MINNESOTA

Judging whether school choice has benefitted or harmed public education in Minnesota depends on one's view of its purpose. The arguments in favor of choice in Minnesota fall into two distinct sets. One argues that the purpose of choice is to enable students to attend a school that best fits their needs and strengths. The other promotes choice as a catalyst for systemic change because it injects competition for students into an otherwise complacent bureaucracy.

From the first perspective, choice in Minnesota would have to be considered at least a qualified success. Although the state has long enjoyed one of the highest graduation rates in the country, HSGI enables the small number of students who are not well served by the traditional comprehensive high schools to succeed in viable alternatives. Claims that these programs dispense devalued high school diplomas may be valid, but so are counterclaims that these programs open new doors for likely dropouts by steering them toward technical or community colleges. Open Enrollment allows a small number of families in unique circumstances to find more appropriate educational opportunities for their children. In one well-publicized case, Open Enrollment enabled students who lived within walking distance of a non-resident school but twenty miles from their resident school to avoid the lengthy commute by attending the non-resident school.

School choice in Minnesota has not, however, served as a catalyst for systemic change throughout the state. In 1991–1992, 1 percent of all students in Minnesota participated in the Open Enrollment option. This has meant that, except in a few extreme cases, the number of Open Enrollment transfers has not been large enough to warrant drastic changes by either sending or receiving districts. While the availability of other options (magnet and specialty schools in the Twin Cities and the Postsecondary Enrollment Option) has clearly limited participation in Open Enrollment, the combined impacts of the major state choice initiatives have been relatively minor on school districts. PSEO has been widely credited with increasing the number of advanced placement courses offered by high schools in an effort to keep students (and their state foundation aid) in the school districts rather than at postsecondary institutions. Open Enrollment encouraged district consolidations and the creation of a handful of magnet schools in rural areas. Beyond that, however, superintendents report few changes in school governance and accountability structures, instructional strategies, or support services. Even most of the districts hit hardest by Open Enrollment have shown little inclination to rethink the way that they educate their students. Finally, despite the continued growth in the number of alternative schools serving potential or actual dropouts (including Minnesota's first Charter school, St. Paul's City Academy), comprehensive high schools have not shown any signs of refocusing their efforts on addressing the needs of this sub-population of students.

NOTES

The research and data collection on which this article is based were supported by the Planning and Evaluation Service, Office of Policy and Planning, U.S. Department of Education. The opinions expressed and conclusions drawn do not reflect official department policy, and no endorsement of the article's contents by the department should be inferred. Copies of the two reports on which this article is based may be obtained from the U.S. Department of Education's Office of Policy and Planning. Contact Stephanie Stullich at (202) 401–1958, or at the Office of Policy and Planning, U.S. Department of Education, Room 3127, 400 Maryland Ave. SW, Washington, D.C. 20202.

1. The Postsecondary Enrollment Option program has been examined elsewhere (Nathan & Jennings 1990; Minnesota House of Representatives Research Department 1993).

2. Data on students' race/ethnicity are for all Open Enrollment participants and were included in the House research report on Open Enrollment; other data about participating students are derived only from the surveys.

3. Lower-income families are those with incomes below the statewide median family income: $36,916 in 1989, according to the U.S. Census.

4. A 1992–1993 update of Open Enrollment's district-level effects is currently in draft.

5. The final stage of this study, currently under way, involves a feasibility study of possible methods for determining Open Enrollment's effects on students' performance in school. Data are being gathered from students' school records.

6. Since the conclusion of this study, several ALCs opened in urban areas.

REFERENCES

Adelman, N. E. (1992) *Minnesota's Educational Options for At-Risk Youth: Urban Alternative Schools and Area Learning Centers.* Washington, D.C.: U.S. Department of Education.

Chubb, J. E., and T. M. Moe. (1990) *Politics, Markets, and America's Schools.* Washington, D.C.: The Brookings Institution.

Kominski, R. (August 1991) *Educational Attainment in the United States: March 1989 and 1988.* Washington, D.C.: U.S. Department of Commerce.

League of Women Voters of St. Paul. (December 1992) *Public School Choice in St. Paul: Is It Working?* St. Paul: Author.

Minnesota House of Representatives Research Department. (February 1993) *The Postsecondary Enrollment Options Program.* St. Paul: Author.

Minnesota House of Representatives Research Department. (February 1990) *Open Enrollment Study: Student and District Participation 1989–90.* St. Paul: Author.

Minnesota Office of the Legislative Auditor. (December 1988) *High School Education.* St. Paul: Author.

Nathan, J., and W. Jennings. (December 1990) *Access to Opportunity.* Minneapolis: Center for School Change.

Rubenstein, M. C., R. Hamar, and N. E. Adelman. (1992) *Minnesota's Open Enrollment Option.* Washington, D.C.: U.S. Department of Education.

Bibliography

Areen, J., and C. Jencks. (1971) "Education Vouchers: A Proposal for Diversity and Choice," *Teachers College Record* (February).

Bolick, C. (1991) "Choice in Education: Part II Legal Perils and Legal Opportunities," The Heritage Foundation, *Backgrounder*, No. 809, February.

The Carnegie Foundation for the Advancement of Teaching. (1992) *School Choice*. Princeton, N.J.: The Carnegie Foundation for the Advancement of Teaching.

Chubb, J. E., and T. M. Moe. (1990) *Politics, Markets, and America's Schools*. Washington, D.C.: The Brookings Institution.

Clark, K. (1969) "Alternative Public School Systems," *Harvard Educational Review* (Winter). Reprinted in (1992) *School Reform and the Need for School Choice*. Washington, D.C.: The Brookings Institution.

Coleman, J. S. (1987) *Public and Private Schools*. New York: Basic Books.

———. (1990) "Do Students Learn More in Private Schools Than in Public Schools?" The James Madison Institute for Public Policy Studies, *The Madison Papers*, No. 4.

Coleman, J. S., T. Hoffer, and S. Kilgore. (1981) *Public and Private High Schools*. Washington, D.C.: National Center for Education Statistics, U.S. Department of Education.

Cookson, P. (1994) *School Choice and the Struggle for the Soul of American Education*. New Haven: Yale University Press.

Ellig, J., and J. High. (1988) "The Private Supply of Education: Some Historical Evidence." In *The Theory of Market Failure: A Critical Appraisal*, edited by Tyler Cowen. Fairfax, Va.: George Mason University Press.

Elmore, R. (1990) *Restructuring Schools—The Next Generation of Educational Reform*. San Francisco: Jossey-Bass.

Fullan, M. (1991) *The New Meaning of Educational Change*. New York: Teachers College Press.

Glenn, C. (1988) *Myth of the Common School*. Amherst: University of Massachusetts Press.

———. (1989) *Choice of Schools in Six Nations*. Washington, D.C.: U.S. Department of Education.

Hulsey, A. (1993) *School Choice Programs: What's Happening in the States*. Washington, D.C.: Heritage Foundation.

Johanek, M. (1992) "Private Citizenship and School Choice," *Educational Policy*, Vol. 6, No. 2:139–159.

Johnson, D. (1990) *Parental Choice in Education*. London: Unwin Hyman.

Lannie, V. P. (1968) *Public Money and Parochial Education*. Cleveland: Case Western Reserve University Press.

Levin, H. M. (1990) "The Theory of Choice Applied to Education." In *Choice and Control in American Education*, edited by W. H. Clune and J. F. Witte, Vol. 1. London: The Falmer Press.

Lieberman, M. (1989) *Privatization and Educational Choice*. New York: St. Martin's Press.

National Commission on Excellence in Education. (1983) *A Nation at Risk: The Imperative for Educational Reform*. Washington, D.C.: U.S. Government Printing Office.

Rasell, M. E., and R. Rothstein. (1993) *School Choice: Examining the Evidence*. Washington, D.C.: Economic Policy Institute.

Singal, D. J. (1992). "The Other Crisis in American Education," *The Atlantic Monthly*, November.

Thernstrom, A. (1990) "Is Choice a Necessity?" *The Public Interest*, 101, Fall:124–131.

United States Department of Education. (1991) *America 2000: An Education Strategy*. Washington, D.C.: U.S. Government Printing Office.

Uzzell, L. A. (1992). U.S. Department of Education, Center for Choice in Education. "Public Opinion on Choice in Education." Washington, D.C.: U.S. Government Printing Office.

Wells, A. (1991) "Choice in Education: Examining the Evidence on Equity," *Teachers College Record*, Vol. 39, No. 1:137–155.

Witte, J. F. (1991) *Public Subsidies for Private Schools*. Madison: University of Wisconsin-Madison.

Witte, J. F., A. B. Bailey, and C. A. Thorn. (1993) *Third Year Report Milwaukee Parental Choice Program*. Madison: University of Wisconsin-Madison.

Young, T. W., and E. Clinchy. (1992) *Choice in Public Education*. New York: Teachers College Press.

Index

About the Editors and Contributors

GARY W. BOWMAN, Associate Professor of Economics, has been at Temple University since 1973. His research focuses on applications of microeconomics including public and managerial decisions and policy in such areas as privatization, regulation, and antitrust. He has published approximately fifteen articles, edited two books, and headed funded research projects from the National Science Foundation and other sources.

SIMON HAKIM is Professor of Economics at Temple University. He has published more than thirty scientific articles and has edited four books as well as conducting funded research projects for governmental agencies and private companies. His work centers on analysis of criminal behavior, police operations, and privatization of justice institutions.

PAUL SEIDENSTAT is Associate Professor of Economics at Temple University. He has been principle investigator for several research projects for federal government agencies and has served local governments as finance director and financial advisor. His research has been in the area of state and local government, finance and management, and urban and environmental economics. He has published a book and several articles in these fields.

NANCY E. ADELMAN is Senior Research Associate with Policy Studies Associates, Washington, D.C. She evaluates federal and state educational programs for disadvantaged students.

DAVID BEERS is Assistant Professor of Economics at Wichita Collegiate School, Wichita, Kansas. He was formerly a policy analyst for Citizens for a Sound Economy, Washington, D.C.

ERNEST L. BOYER is President of The Carnegie Foundation for the Advancement of Teaching. He served as U.S. Commissioner of Education and Chancellor of the State University of New York.

PETER W. COOKSON, JR., is Associate Dean of the School of Education at Adelphi University, Garden City, New York, and the author of several books in the field of education and school choice.

PIERRE S. DUPONT IV, a Delaware attorney, is a former governor of the State of Delaware and U.S. Congressman. In 1988 he was a candidate for President of the United States. He is currently associated with several organizations that focus upon foreign affairs and domestic policy issues.

JERRY ELLIG is Assistant Professor of Economics and Associate Director of Center for the Study of Market Processes at George Mason University, Fairfax, Virginia.

TOM FEENEY is an attorney and a member of the Florida House of Representatives. The author of legislation on parental choice in education, he is Chairman of the Education Task Force Committee for the American Legislative Exchange Council.

THOMAS HETLAND is Executive Director of the Center for Rebuilding America's Schools and President of Driscoll Catholic High School, Addison, Illinois.

PAUL T. HILL is Director of the joint University of Washington—RAND Program on Reinventing Public Education. He is both a Senior Social Scientist for RAND and Research Professor in the Graduate School of Public Affairs at the University of Washington, Seattle, Washington.

THOMAS H. KEAN is President of Drew University, Madison, New Jersey, and former governor of New Jersey. He chaired the New American Schools Development Corporation and the National Environmental Education and Training Foundation.

JOHN MENGE is Professor of Economics and Chair of the Department of Economics at Dartmouth College in Hanover, New Hampshire. He has been a member of the New Hampshire legislature and consultant to the National Institute of Education and the New Hampshire State School Board.

PATRICIA A. PARHAM is Principal of South Pointe Elementary School, Miami, Florida. She is the recipient of the Florida Commissioner of Education's "Excellence in Leadership" award.

THOMAS H. PEELER is Associate Professor of Education at California State University, Los Angeles. He currently directs a major evaluation project on the performance of the South Pointe Elementary School program in Dade County, Florida. He was Superintendent of Schools in Santa Barbara and Clarement, California, school districts.

BELLA ROSENBERG is Assistant to the President, American Federation of Teachers, Washington, D.C. She previously served as Research Associate at the National Institute of Education.

MICHAEL C. RUBENSTEIN, Research Associate with Policy Studies Associates, Washington, D.C., evaluates federal and state educational programs for disadvantaged students.

ALBERT SHANKER is President of American Federation of Teachers, Washington, D.C.; Vice President of the AFL-CIO, and founding President of Education International, a federation of 20 million teachers from democratic countries around the world.

KEVIN C. SONTHEIMER is Director of the Economic Policy Institute of the University of Pittsburgh, Pittsburgh, Pennsylvania.

WILLIAM E. UBINAS is Superintendent of Community District One, New York City Public Schools.